Text and design copyright © 2001 André Deutsch Limited

This edition published by
André Deutsch Limited 2001
An imprint of the Carlton Publishing Group
20 Mortimer Street, London W1T 3JW

A CIP catalogue record for this book is available
from the British Library
ISBN 0 233 99988 4

Printed and bound in Dubai

Editorial Manager: **Venetia Penfold**
Art Director: **Penny Stock**
Senior Art Editor: **Barbara Zuñiga**
Project Editor: **Zia Mattocks**
Editor: **Sian Parkhouse**
Design: **DW Design, London**
Production Manager: **Garry Lewis**

The authors and the publisher have made every effort to ensure
that all the information in this book is correct and up to date at the
time of publication. Neither the authors nor the publisher can
accept responsibility for any accident, injury or damage that results
from using the ideas, information or advice offered in this book.

This book is printed on paper produced from wood from
a replenishable forest.

GREEN LIVING

ECO-FRIENDLY HOMES • NATURAL GARDENING •
ORGANIC FOOD • ENERGY SAVING • RECYCLING

SARAH CALLARD & DIANE MILLIS

ANDRE
DEUTSCH

contents

chapter 3:

Green Growing and Eating 118

green living
introdu

We would like you do something. It won't require much effort and you should benefit in many ways. What we are asking you to do is to consider the way in which you live your life and to change one aspect of it to make it more environmentally friendly. You shouldn't be hard-pressed to find a way in which to do this, since this book contains thousands of ideas – and, of course, we are hoping that if you do it once you'll manage it again and again. The point is, that for a difference to be made to the global environment, all it takes is for every citizen to make just one change.

Why bother? Well, by now you should be familiar with the fact that we are coming perilously close to environmental catastrophe. If you needed any persuading of this fact, then the increasing number of floods, ice storms, hurricanes, cyclones, droughts and severe winter storms around the world, should have done the trick. Barely a nation in the world has been spared these dramatic climatic events, with devastating effects for both humans and wildlife.

ction

The main cause of this climate change is the shift in balance between carbon dioxide (CO_2) emissions and absorption. Burning fossil fuels, such as peat, coal, oil and gas, to generate power results in the release of large amounts of CO_2. In less CO_2-heavy times these emissions were absorbed by trees and plants, but they are no longer able to keep up, especially since only one-fifth of the world's original forests remain as they were.

These emissions and others, such as methane from landfill sites and unused piles of manure, and chloro-fluorocarbons (CFCs) and (hydrochlorofluorocarbons) (HCFCs) from fridges and freezers, sit in our atmosphere, preventing the sun's radiation from escaping. The net result? The global average temperature is forecast to rise by up to 6°C (43°F) between 1990 and 2100 – a rise which has probably not been experienced in at least the last 10,000 years. Polar ice caps are melting, sea levels are rising and the natural balance of life is being altered as a result.

The loss of our planet's forests also has an impact on our climate and environment in other ways. Rainfall in tropical areas is falling as there are no trees to provide the moisture that builds up in clouds above the forest canopy; soil is exposed to the drying effects of wind and sun and, without tree roots to hold it in place, is being eroded at a massive rate, leading to landslides and drought; and many plants and animals are moving towards extinction as their habitat is destroyed. And this is all so you can have disposable nappies (diapers), garden furniture, beefburgers and envelopes!

It is not just deforestation that is having an impact on global biodiversity. Pollution is playing a huge part in the demise of plants, insects, animals and humans. Toxic chemicals are sprayed liberally over our crops, ending up in the insects and animals that dare to nibble on them, as well as in our food. Some of these pesticides will also leach into groundwater supplies, joining the other chemicals that have been dumped from households and factories into our waterways and oceans. Fish and other aquatic lifeforms are soaking up these toxins, passing them on up the food chain and dying or becoming deformed or infertile in the process.

Add to this the unknown consequences of genetic pollution from genetically modified (GM) crops – a gene from GM maize has already cropped up in supplies of organic maize in the USA – on biodiversity and our health, and you will comprehend the true scale of the threat from pollution.

But if you think that events in fields, forests and factories around the world are out of your control, think again. Simply by buying tropical hardwood furniture, a bag of apples, some bleached white cotton towels and a roll of clingfilm (saranwrap), you could unknowingly be supporting these acts of environmental vandalism and potentially damaging your health, as you absorb the chemicals in timber preservatives, pesticides, bleaching agents and plasticizers. (In fact, the amount of chemicals used in everyday household products is so great that you could be experiencing more pollution inside your home than out! So, if for no other reason than concern for your health, change is worthwhile.)

It is not just the outside world that you should seek to alter through your buying habits. The way in which you run your home has as much impact on the environment, since households are a major source of waste. Look at how you use the basics – gas, electricity and water. By using less energy and investigating alternative sources of power you will reduce the demand for fossil fuels and the amount of CO_2 saturating our atmosphere. Using less water will save this dwindling resource and reduce demand on sewage systems.

Think, too, about how much you throw away. Landfills are becoming ever more clogged with non-biodegradable products or waste that pollutes both land and water as it breaks down. How much do you contribute to this?

We are hoping that by reading further, you will be left in no doubt as to just how important your household is in the environmental equation and how much you stand to gain by making some changes. But the key word here is 'some'. We don't want to make you so depressed about your current activities and their impact on the environment that you are unable to do anything about them. The point of this book is not to overwhelm you with guilt and fear, but to give you the confidence and knowledge to make informed choices in your daily life – be it in the do-it-yourself store, supermarket, clothes shop or electrical-goods store. Every step you take will contribute in many ways – from making manufacturers realize they can no longer get away with using petrochemicals in their products to raising awareness among your friends and family that alternatives exist. If you only have the time and energy to swap a single item on your shopping list with an eco-friendly option then it is worth doing.

As a rough guide, however, if you manage to make the following five changes in the next five years, you'll be doing well:

● **Decrease your reliance on fossil fuels:**
Save energy in the home, choose plant-based
materials for decorating your interior, and avoid
all petrochemicals in cleaning products, bodycare
items and cosmetics.

● **Reject all toxic pesticides:** Buy organic food
and practice organic gardening.

● **Stop buying plastic:** Most of it won't biodegrade,
its manufacture is highly polluting and it can
leach toxic chemicals into your food

● **Recycle as much as possible:** Recycle as many
items as you can, reject disposable products
and use a composting system.

● **Buy from sustainable sources:** When buying
timber or timber-derived products, such as
paper, buy only from sustainable sources –
look for certification to prove this.

There will always be contradictions and areas
of compromise. Not all organic produce is fairly
traded, for example, and while coir is a natural,
sustainable product it is flown a great distance in
order to reach the shelves of our stores. However,
to do nothing on this basis is to miss the point.

Equally, you can no longer use aesthetics or
quality as an argument for passing over green
choices. Organic food is often better quality than
conventional options, since it won't be relying on
an arsenal of additives and preservatives, for
example; and organic textiles can be as soft and

luxurious as any other materials. In fact, going
green is now more chic then it has ever been,
so you can content yourself with the fact that
you are helping the planet at the same time
as beautifying your home and garden.

If you should find that making eco-friendly choices
in your home is both easier and more satisfying
than you thought possible, then perhaps it is time
you took these ideas and principles and applied them
to other areas in your life. Environmentally-friendly
holidays and pensions are just a few examples of
what is on offer. Hopefully, this book will set you on
a path that will take you to them and many other
planet-friendly activities in the years to come.

chapter one
back to

basics

We are all familiar with the expressions 'greenhouse effect', 'acid rain' and 'global warming', but very few of us probably realize how our actions on a day-to-day level add to these environmental problems. When we burn fossil fuels such as coal, oil, peat and gas we are making the global situation worse, not only by increasing the amount of harmful emissions released into the atmosphere, but also by contributing to the depletion of non-renewable energy sources. The greenhouse effect and acid rain are both caused by burning these precious fossil fuels to meet our ever-increasing energy demands. One of the major greenhouse gases, carbon dioxide, is also released into the atmosphere via landfill sites – those huge, ugly areas where most of our domestic waste ends up being dumped.

Some materials that can still be found in older houses are extremely hazardous and there is no doubt that the state of our homes has a direct effect on our health and wellbeing. Lead pipes, for example, are often found in older plumbing systems and they should be replaced if possible. An increase in health problems such as allergies and asthma could be a result of our unhealthy living environments: a situation known as 'sick building syndrome' (SBS). Pollution from common materials in our homes such as plastics, conventional paints and synthetic fibres can cause a number of symptoms, including headaches, general malaise and low productivity. Other factors that can cause SBS include the electromagnetic fields emitted by electrical equipment, timber preservatives, radon gas, damp and inadequate ventilation. The amount of daylight that comes into your home and the quality of the internal atmosphere are also contributory factors. All these problems are worth considering when you are looking at ways in which you can improve your living environment.

With our hectic lifestyles, we tend to rely heavily on technology and machines to do jobs that previously would have been done by hand. Time-saving devices, such as washing machines, electric bread knives, dishwashers and microwave ovens, are now commonplace. This means that most of us could cut back on the amount of fuel we use just by making a few painless decisions. A huge amount of all the energy used is consumed in our homes, which are also responsible for emitting many of the gases that contribute to the greenhouse effect. By taking some fairly simple steps, such as insulating and draught-proofing our homes, or replacing the boiler with a more efficient one, we can reduce our power consumption considerably. Heating our homes, or 'space heating' as it is known, accounts for a large proportion of the energy we use at home, which makes it a good place to start when you are in the process of changing your energy habits.

This opening chapter looks at what steps we can take on a very local level to lessen our impact on the environment. Our aim should be to replace the fossil fuels we use with renewable energy sources. Some of the ideas can be stored away for future reference when you buy your own home or move house, whereas others can be put into practice straight away. Whether you live in a high-rise block or a weather-worn farmhouse, there are steps you can take to make your home life that little bit greener.

alternative
energy

In order to repair some of the damage that has already been done and to prepare for the future, it is essential to look to renewable energy sources to provide heating and light. The phrase 'renewable energy' covers a number of diverse technologies designed to produce heat and power in a sustainable way, including solar water heating, wind energy and hydropower. The easiest natural energy source to harness is solar power. Depending on your house and energy needs, there are various ways to use the sun's energy. In the future, advances in technology will reduce the costs involved, making it a practical and desirable option.

One of the simplest ways to make a difference is by choosing a green electricity tariff from your local supplier. Although it will cost you slightly more than a conventional tariff, lots of companies offer incentives for going green, such as a quota of low-energy light bulbs. Wind power, hydroelectricity and biomass are all forms of renewable energy that governments should be supporting to provide for our energy needs. We should be aware of these options and how they affect the planet – support any local initiatives for renewable energy schemes and arm yourself with knowledge so that you can inform others.

Solar power

Passive solar power design is a way of maximizing the energy that can be directly derived from the sun. It is most effective when a new building is being constructed, when decisions about which rooms should face which direction can be made. Most of us, however, live in housing that was not built to make the most of the sun's energy. Even so, it is still possible to employ passive solar power in our homes without any cost or inconvenience. There is nothing very new about it – over 10 per cent of the space heating in an average home comes via solar energy through walls and windows.

Although this system can be best applied in new buildings when decisions can be made about the size of the windows and the materials used, as well as the orientation of the building, passive solar measures can also be applied to existing buildings to good effect. A good way to introduce passive solar energy in your existing home is to build a conservatory. This is an expensive option, but it does increase the value of your home by adding an extra living space that costs you nothing to heat. A conservatory will insulate your house and preheat the ventilation air, as well as providing direct solar heating to the intervening wall, which is then convected into the rest of the house.

Solar water heating

Using the sun to heat hot water for your home sounds like a rather impractical option at first, but there are a number of advances in this area that are making it more of a realistic option. Even in countries where the climate does not offer a great deal of sunshine, solar energy is available.

A solar water-heating system has few environmental impacts and those that are produced are generally a result of the processes involved in the manufacture of the solar panels, the most popular form of solar energy. There are different kinds of systems that can be used at home, so take a look at what is available, and consider how best you can incorporate it into your particular living space.

There are different methods of solar water-heating systems: flat-plate collectors and evacuated-tube collectors. The flat-plate collectors are basically sheets of metal painted black to absorb the sun's energy. Water is fed through the panel in pipes attached to the sheet and picks up the heat in the metal. Look for pipes made from copper for better conductivity, and that contain non-toxic antifreeze for the winter. The metal sheet is embedded in an insulated box and then covered with glass or clear plastic. The flat-plate solar energy collectors should ideally be installed on a south-facing roof – if that is not possible a roof facing south-west or east to south-east will do. The panels should be set at an angle of between 10° and 60°.

The evacuated-tube collector system is made up of a series of between 20 and 30 glass heat tubes grouped together. The tubes are insulated by a vacuum inside the glass and use a heat-transfer fluid instead of water. Like the flat-plate collector, this system needs to be situated on a southerly-facing roof in order to absorb the most heat.

Getting the **most** from **solar energy**:

- The main glazed areas should face within 30° either side of south.
- Fit large windows in south-facing walls and smaller ones in north-facing rooms.
- Avoid overshadowing from trees and other buildings.
- Build a conservatory onto your home – try to make sure it is on a south- or west-facing site that is protected from the wind.
- Avoid using net curtains and keep curtains wide open during the day to allow the maximum amount of sunshine in.
- The building should be well insulated to reduce heat loss.
- Install a responsive heating system to reduce wasted heat.

Doing it yourself

Although it might not sound like it, a solar water-heating system involves simple technology, and making your own system is not nearly as hard as you might think. Most of the components are readily available and, if you are able to put up a set of shelves successfully, building and installing your own solar water-heating system shouldn't be beyond your capabilities.

Do-it-yourself kit systems for solar water heating are available from some manufacturers. In the same way that you can buy a self-assembly table or shelf unit, self-build collectors are available from specialist suppliers (*see Resources, pages 178–83*), while components such as copper pipes and timber can be purchased from a standard building store. A cheaper option is to use radiators painted black, but, although they are a good way of reusing an unwanted item, they are less efficient than panels because they are slower to respond to sunlight and the transfer of heat.

As our lives speed up, time is often a more valuable commodity than money, but if you want to pay someone else to do the work for you, make sure you get at least three different estimates before you decide on a supplier or installer for your solar water-heating system. A standard installation would be a panel of 3 or 4 m^2

$(3\frac{1}{2}$ or 5 sq yd) with a tank of 150–200 litres (34–45 gallons). The ideal size of system depends on your actual hot water use, which the supplier should be able to calculate for you according to your particular needs.

Green tariffs are available in various countries around the world. Some countries are more active than others and some electricity suppliers are more proactive than others. It is a case of contacting your national or regional energy supplier.

Renewable electricity

Every time you flick a light switch or turn on the toaster, spare a thought for the huge amount of greenhouse gases emitted from power stations that produce the electricity. Each time you use electricity to turn on the television or microwave oven, another lump of coal goes up in smoke and carbon dioxide emissions are released into the atmosphere. This can be avoided by buying 'green' electricity produced from a renewable source. Conventional electricity produces harmful emissions such as sulphur dioxide and carbon dioxide during the manufacturing process, and these pollutants contribute to climate change as well as to acid rain. Electricity that is produced using renewable sources, such as solar, wind and water power, has minimal impact on the environment in comparison.

Start by enquiring with your local electricity supplier about the possibility of buying renewably generated electricity on a green tariff straight from the national grid. There are a range of green tariffs for domestic users, but be aware that

A solar water-heating system will reduce carbon monoxide emissions – one of the causes of global warming.

Solar water-heating systems can produce up to 100 per cent of our hot water needs in the summer months.

because they generally involve the payment of an additional premium they are often more expensive than conventional tariffs.

Green tariffs work in different ways. On some, for example, every unit of electricity bought by a consumer is generated from a renewable energy source. On others, the additional premium is invested into new renewable energy projects in the form of a fund, usually used for developing community-based renewable energy projects. As well as using sustainable power from the sun, wind and rain, some companies generate electricity using the methane gas that is produced by rotting waste at landfill sites, which is an excellent use for this unwelcome by-product of waste disposal.

Photovoltaics

Photovoltaics (PV) is the use of solar energy to generate electricity directly in a clean, renewable way. It is already being used to power satellites, and the first solar-powered spacecraft was operated way back in 1958. PV is best incorporated into buildings via panels as part of the cladding. It can be used on a small scale to provide a power supply for devices such as lights, pumps and radios. This makes it particularly useful for garden and security lighting – the sun's energy is soaked up during the day and then provides light during the night. It will save you money as well, because once the device has been installed the cost of the lighting is absolutely free. Another use for PV is to power a garden fountain – kits are available with installation instructions. PV panels last for 20–30 years and new designs are being developed to enable them to blend more easily into roofs. Though it is currently too expensive to use PV on a domestic level, this is likely to change in the future.

PV is used to charge leisure batteries such as those used in caravans (mobile homes).

Within half an hour, enough of the sun's energy is received by the earth to power all of mankind's activities for a year.

PV is already used to power a number of products, including calculators, watches, laptop computers, model cars and torches (flashlights).

The word photovoltaic originates from the Greek word for 'light'.

The bigger picture

As consumers, it is important that we know where our power is coming from. We all take electricity at the tip of our fingers for granted and rarely spare a thought for the consequences of our actions. It is crucial that we start to take more responsibility for the energy that we use and pay more attention to the alternatives, so that we can make efforts to put pressure on our governments and local authorities to change their habits.

We have looked at changes we can make in our own homes to help the environment, but it is also important that we know what is happening on a wider scale. There are various initiatives and projects around the world that are developing renewable energy sources, which unlike fossil fuels will never run out. Renewable energy sources, such as biomass energy, wind and hydropower, are infinitely safer, cheaper and less polluting than non-renewable power sources.

Wind power

There is a tremendous potential for certain countries with a suitable climate to use wind power as a source of sustainable energy. Electricity from wind can be produced at a cost comparable with electricity from conventional sources. Wind energy projects are simple, clean and cheap to maintain, but they have not been widely explored. Wind turbines are sited in the windiest areas, often offshore, and the electricity generated can be fed straight into the local grid. Wind power is one of the fastest-growing energy technologies in the world and already provides for at least some of the energy needs of some nations. It is cheap to harness and use, but the main problem is that wind turbines themselves are large and some people consider them to be a blight on the landscape.

Hydropower

The energy potential of moving water has been used by man for thousands of years. Traditionally, it was used to power wheels to drive mills and machinery. Large dam projects are currently in operation in many countries to provide electricity, but the potential of hydropower on a global scale is still largely untapped. The problem with hydroelectric schemes is that dams must be built, which can damage the environment by disturbing river ecosystems. There is also a high cost involved.

Biomass energy

Wood is the ultimate in natural resources, as long as it is grown in a sustainable way. After solar energy, the next choice for space heating is using biomass energy, a cheap, easy source of renewable energy. Fast-growing trees such as willow and poplar can be used as commercial energy crops to provide for local heating needs or they can be used

in power stations to create electricity. The heat created could also be used to provide hot water and heating for the power station itself, making it extremely energy efficient. Developing a sustainable energy source like this not only creates power but also creates jobs. It does have its disadvantages, however, the main one being the huge amount of crops that would need to be grown to create enough electricity to provide for our needs.

Waste watch

We have started to look seriously at the amount of waste we produce and the implications of disposing of that much material. Despite our best efforts to reduce waste, there will always be a substantial amount for which the best environmental option is energy recovery – using waste as a source of power and for heat generation. Much of what we throw out of our kitchens ends up in landfill sites where decomposition of the organic matter gives off methane-rich biogas. This can be collected and reused to produce electricity for our heating and power needs. This has the added advantage of preventing the biogas from seeping out into the atmosphere and damaging the environment.

We have started to look seriously at the amount of waste we produce

insulation

Making sure your home is properly insulated is crucial if you are serious about saving energy. By insulating your home well, you will be helping to reduce carbon dioxide emissions into the environment, and saving money as well as energy. A lot of the draughts that whip through our homes are a result of poor construction techniques, but there is still a lot most of us can do to reduce the amount of energy lost through walls, doors and windows. Start by checking that all your doors and windows are sealed properly and can be closed firmly against the wind and look out for plaster shrinkage that can sometimes leave a gap between windows or doors and adjoining walls.

Insulating your home to its optimum may not be one of the most exciting things you have ever done, but it will pay dividends for you and the environment. It still amazes most people when they hear that the average domestic building is responsible for wasting huge amounts of energy as heat is lost through poor insulation. Do what you can to improve the insulation in your home, especially if it is an old building. Avoid synthetic materials and choose eco-friendly insulators derived from renewable natural vegetation instead. Lagging pipes and hot-water tanks are jobs that most of us can do successfully ourselves and it can make a lot of difference to the energy efficiency of our homes.

Ventilation

Insulation does not mean that you have to seal up your home completely – ventilation is also very important if you are to avoid an unpleasant stuffy atmosphere. If you have a solid-fuel fire or gas appliances ventilation is essential as a well-insulated house will trap vapours and gases that would escape from a less insulated home.

It is also important to keep the kitchen and bathroom well ventilated so as to prevent condensation and avoid wood rot. But how do you reach a balance between the two? If you do have a problem with condensation, you could think about fitting an extractor fan. If you have a solid-fuel fire make sure you have the chimney and air bricks checked for any blockages. A ceiling fan can also be good for circulating air in both the summer and winter.

Loft insulation

This is one of the easiest and most cost-effective methods of insulating your home. Even if you already have insulation in your loft it is worth checking that it is thick enough – the general rule with insulation is that if you can make it thicker, do so. Loft insulation really needs to be at least 20 cm (8 in) thick – this might sound excessive but it is worth it as insulation this deep could save you around 20 per cent of your heating costs.

There are different types of loft insulation, such as sheep's wool, cellulose fibre, hemp (burlap) and flax – most of which you can install yourself. The material with the lowest impact on the environment is blown-cellulose fibre, which has the added advantage of being able to fill all the air gaps that can sometimes be left by solid insulation materials such as glass fibre, making it the more efficient insulator. Wool- and paper-based insulation materials have the added attraction of being free from formaldehyde.

Check that your hot-water cylinder is wrapped up, because this way the water will stay hot for longer and consequently save you money. If it is in the loft, do not insulate underneath the tank, so that warm air can rise up from the house and prevent it from freezing in the winter. New water tanks generally have built-in insulation, but installing a ready-made jacket, available from most do-it-yourself stores, is easy to do. If this is beyond you, do not despair; you can always pay someone to do it for you. If you have a jacket on your cylinder, check what kind of condition it is in and replace it if it is worn out.

You can prevent loss of heat along the length of your hot-water pipes by insulating them. The most important pipes to cover are those between the boiler and the hot-water cylinder, as well as those in the loft to stop them freezing up in the winter. This is quite easy to do yourself, but if you are paying a professional to install loft insulation for you they should also lag your pipes at the same time. If you have a choice in the matter, keep the length of pipe between the hot-water cylinder and the most frequently used taps (faucets) as short as possible.

- Once your loft has been insulated, make sure any pipes or tanks are also well insulated to avoid the problem of freezing in the winter.

- Not all cavity walls can be insulated – an installer will check whether your house is suitable.

- Once you have spent time, money and energy insulating your loft, make sure you also draught-strip and insulate the loft hatch to prevent heat loss through the opening.

- When draught-proofing, check the places where pipes enter your home and seal up any gaps.

- Add a newspaper layer beneath your carpet underlay for extra insulation.

- Trickle vents in the window frame can provide background ventilation and reduce the need to open windows to prevent stuffiness.

- Make sure you close the door behind you when you are leaving or entering a room.

Wall insulation

Many people are surprised to discover that more heat is lost through walls than any other way. If they are not insulated, your walls could be responsible for up to 35 per cent of all heat loss. If your home was built after 1930 it probably has cavity walls, which means there is an inner and outer layer with a small air gap or 'cavity' in between. Cavity-wall insulation is the most cost-effective method of home insulation after loft insulation, and can reduce heat loss through the wall by up to 60 per cent.

Insulating cavity walls is a fairly easy operation for a professional installer – they use specialized equipment to inject the insulating material into the cavity from outside by drilling small holes in the wall. If you are unsure about whether your house has cavity walls or not you can usually tell by measuring how thick they are. Cavity walls are at least 30 cm (12 in) thick, whereas solid walls are normally only around 25 cm (10 in) thick.

Insulating solid walls is more difficult and, therefore, more expensive. It should be done by a professional, who will apply a layer of render and cladding on the outside of your walls to provide insulation. It could be worth considering if your exterior walls need repairing or re-rendering. Another option is to insulate the interior of your walls when they need redecorating or repairing, but be prepared for upheaval, because it is a major job and involves removing all the skirting boards (baseboards), window surrounds and doors.

- Cover windows and doors with curtains to block out draughts.

- Use renewable materials for insulation.

- If you cannot insulate your walls, put in extra loft insulation.

- Make sure there are no gaps between floorboards and skirting boards (baseboards).

- Check for any gaps around pipes and loft hatches.

- Use stuffed-fabric draught-excluders to block draughts under doors.

- Create a buffer area between the interior of your home and the outside by adding a porch or conservatory.

Windows and doors

Statistics show that around 23 per cent of heat loss from homes escapes through windows. One way of preventing this is by fitting double-glazing; in itself double-glazing is not very environmentally friendly, but when measured with its energy-saving benefits, it is the best option. Secondary double-glazing, which is detachable in case of fire, is cheaper, and there are also new types of energy-efficient glass available, called low-emissivity glass, which can help reduce heat loss by a further 10 per cent.

If double-glazing is not an option, then invest in some heavy, thermally lined curtains, which should be drawn at dusk to prevent heat loss. Or, even better, use shutters to cover windows at night. If you live in an old house, check to see if you already have shutters, because they might have been boarded over. If not, you can quite often pick them up from a salvage firm or get new ones made by a joiner, using wood from a sustainable source.

To check for draughts, hold your palm up to a window or door to feel whether any cold air is coming in. Small gaps in windows and doors are responsible for around 20 per cent of heat loss and can be prevented by draught-proofing. Materials for do-it-yourself draught-proofing can be bought at most hardware stores and they are easy to install.

Insulating floors

The next time you decide you need to change your carpets or floorboards think about floor insulation. If there are gaps between the floor and skirting boards (baseboards) you can simply add wooden beading between them. By filling the gaps between floors and skirting boards you could save as much as 20 per cent of your annual fuel bills. There are plenty of types of tube sealants available, which can be used in the same way that you use a sealant around the edge of the bath. And if you can insulate under the floorboards on the ground floor, the room will feel warmer and you will save more money.

Natural materials for insulating flooring include Warmcel (a material made from surplus books, newspapers and telephone directories), sheep's wool and recycled rubber, which provides a softer surface to walk on, as well as providing soundproofing. Coconut fibreboard, made from the outer husks of coconuts, is a very durable and completely natural insulation material, with good thermal and sound insulation properties. These materials are available from environmentally friendly companies and builder's merchants.

Materials

There are various materials available for insulating all areas of your home. Organic materials include cork, sheep's wool, cellulose and wood wool. There are also materials derived from naturally occurring minerals, such as mineral wool, which comes in different formats, such as quilt and loose fill. When you are selecting a material there are a number of different considerations you need to take into account. A particular source, such as blown-cellulose fibre, might be a more preferable choice than a glass-fibre material because it has a lower impact on the environment during the manufacturing process. Some materials might prove to be too expensive for the size of the area you are insulating and for your budget. The best thing you can do when you embark on an insulation project is to get some expert advice from a green building company (see Resources, pages 178–83), and then weigh up your options and decide what is most appropriate for your living space.

As we become increasingly concerned about the materials we use in our homes, a growing number of companies are developing innovative, environmentally friendly materials for use as insulation. Insulation material made from recycled rubber is good for creating a softer surface underfoot when it is used underneath carpets, and it has the added advantage of offering effective soundproofing. Sheep's wool used for thermal insulation can absorb more than one-third of its own weight in moisture and can therefore help prevent timber from rotting or from being attacked by mould or fungus, and prevent metal from rusting. Make sure the wool is from sheep that have not been dipped in pesticides; it should simply be washed and treated with borax to make it resistant to fire and insects. Sheep's wool insulation comes in a felted quilt format and it can be cut with a pair of sharp scissors to fit exactly the area it is being used to insulate, so it is very easy to install.

Organic insulating materials:

Cork, which comes in slabs, tiles or granular format.

Expanded rubber for piping.

Wood fibre as insulation board for walls.

Sheep's wool, which comes in a felted quilt format.

Heraflax – felted flax quilts.

Wood wool slabs.

Cellulose loose-fill pellets.

lighting

We could all save energy and money by being more careful about the way we light our homes. Firstly, make sure that you are getting the most out of the natural daylight available to you and be aware of the amount of artificial lighting you use in your home. A house designed to save energy would have large south-facing windows and skylights to make the most of the daylight. Try to arrange your living space around the natural light that is available throughout the day – in the morning use rooms that face south or east and in the afternoon and evening use those facing west. Rooms that have very limited light or face north should be used the least.

You can also remove any obstacles that block daylight getting into your home (within reason!) such as trees and bushes. Deciduous trees are a good way of keeping your house cool in the summer without blocking out light in the winter. Make sure you can draw curtains and blinds completely away from windows to allow extra daylight in. You could also consider installing a skylight for dark attic rooms, hallways and stair areas that would otherwise require a lot of artificial lighting. If you are planning any renovations, it might be a good idea to take the opportunity to install more windows in darker areas of the house.

Light bulbs

We must all of course use some artificial light, but the choice of light bulb makes a huge difference in terms of how much energy we use to produce that light. Standard or incandescent filament light bulbs are extremely inefficient, as only around 10 per cent of the energy they use is turned into light; the rest is converted into heat. In an incandescent bulb, light is produced when an electric current passes through a filament, making the bulb glow and give off heat and light. During the winter incandescent lighting is an expensive form of electric light, and during the summer it adds unwanted heat to your home. But don't feel you have to rush out and replace all your bulbs with new ones. Try introducing low-energy light bulbs gradually – the next time a standard bulb goes, replace it with a compact fluorescent light (CFL).

Compact fluorescent lights

Compact fluorescent lights work like standard tube fluorescent lights, only the tube is smaller and folded over to concentrate the light, and the compact design allows them to be used in place of incandescent light bulbs. This can be a really good way of introducing eco-friendly solutions into your home without causing a big disruption or incurring great expense. Although energy-efficient bulbs are more expensive than standard ones, they will save

you money in the long run. Compact fluorescent light bulbs require less energy to produce the same amount of light as a conventional bulb because they convert much more of the energy to light – standard bulbs convert most of the energy to heat. They have a lifespan eight times longer than a standard bulb, so therefore save energy and raw materials during the manufacturing process and produce less waste.

It is a good idea to replace standard bulbs with compact fluorescent light bulbs in areas of your home where the lights are left on for long periods of time. To cut down on the amount of waste when you are disposing of old bulbs, you can buy compact fluorescent bulbs with an external ballast that can be used with an adaptor. You need discard only the bulb, rather than the bulb and the ballast. But bear in mind that this means you have the extra initial expense of an adaptor.

Compact fluorescent light bulbs are available in most supermarkets, hardware and do-it-yourself stores, as well as by mail order from green companies. You have probably spotted them before and maybe you did not act because you thought they were expensive and instead reached for the regular 40-watt bulb. If so, now is the time to think again.

Shape and size
As with standard bulbs, compact fluorescent bulbs come with both bayonet and screw fittings so they can be easily fitted into existing sockets. They also come in a variety of shapes and sizes so you can choose ones that are the most appropriate for each lamp and fitting. It does not really matter what

- Replace your most frequently used light bulbs with energy-saving bulbs first as these will generate the most savings, in terms of both energy and money.

- Get into the habit of always turning off lights when you leave the room and nag everyone else to do the same – after all, there is no point in lighting an empty space.

- If energy-saving bulbs are used outdoors make sure they are enclosed in a sealed unit to provide protection from cold-weather conditions.

- Compact fluorescent bulbs are not suitable for lights that are switched on and off frequently because this can reduce their life – use low-wattage standard bulbs instead.

shape or size of bulb you use, but you will find that the 'stick'-shaped bulbs give off a more rounded light, so they are good in central locations, whereas the flatter bulbs work better as wall lights, because they give off light from the top and bottom.

Compact fluorescent bulbs are available in a range of wattage, depending on how brightly you want an area lit. When replacing standard bulbs with low-energy equivalents start with rooms and areas most commonly used, as this will save more energy and money. Any lighting that is left on for long periods of time, such as outdoor security lighting, would be much more cost effective if the bulbs were replaced with energy-saving ones. But it is worth noting that compact fluorescent bulbs do not usually work with dimmer switches, timers or sensors.

If you are using a dimmer switch with standard bulbs, check with the manufacturer whether it is an energy-efficient appliance: some are, but others waste a lot of energy through heat generation – you can usually tell if this is likely to be the case because the switch will be warm to the touch.

Compact fluorescent bulbs are not appropriate for rooms that you do not use very often, such as toilets. For these rooms, the best way to save energy is to use low-wattage standard bulbs.

Strip lighting

Fluorescent strip lights, which are even more energy efficient than compact fluorescent bulbs, are often fitted in kitchens and bathrooms. Strip lights fell out of fashion for a while and most of us still associate them with kitchens in the 1970s or cheap student accommodation. But this is no longer the case today, and improvements have been made in fluorescent strip lighting that make it almost indistinguishable from standard lighting in terms of quality, colour and its ability to create a warmly lit atmosphere. It works particularly well as indirect lighting around the perimeter of a room or as task lighting above a bathroom mirror.

Halogen lamps, a form of incandescent lighting, last up to eight times longer than conventional bulbs. They are often used where high light quality is needed and are commonly used in retail stores and commercial buildings. Halogen lamps fall between standard incandescent lighting and compact fluorescent lamps in terms of efficiency. They are, however, useful where light is needed in only a small area.

ⓘ Look out for energy labelling on all light bulbs – even standard ones. This is a guide that shows how the bulb rates in terms of its energy efficiency (rated from A to E), light output, power consumption in watts and its lifespan in hours.

heating and
hot water

Heating is responsible for more than 75 per cent of the energy consumption of an average household and by controlling your heating you could save a substantial amount of money. Heating and hot water account for more than half the average fuel bill – even more if you live in an old building. There is no point spending time, money and energy on home insulation and draught-proofing if you do not heat your home efficiently. Having an overheated house can be as uncomfortable as a cold, draughty environment, so make sure you know how your heating system works.

Try turning the thermostat down a few notches – we have been conditioned to live in over-heated environments and expect to walk around in a T-shirt even if it is snowing outside. The thermostat should be set to around 19°C (66°F) for most people to feel comfortable without the room getting stuffy. Do what you can to make the most out of the natural heating power of the sun and protect your home from cold prevailing winds if possible, as this will reduce the amount of energy you need to heat it. This is not always possible, however, so use techniques like room thermostats, lining radiators and timer switches to cut down on wasted energy and to get the most out of your system.

Heating your home

Electricity is really the least energy-efficient way to heat your home and hot water because it is produced in incredibly inefficient power stations that burn huge amounts of coal or oil. When electricity is used for heating, around 90 per cent of the fuel's primary energy is lost due to inefficient transmission systems and electrical appliances. Gas is the best energy source for heating your home and hot water, but there is great scope for the use of solar power for purposes of domestic water heating (see Alternative Energy, pages 15–16). If you are planning on moving house or considering carrying out major refurbishment work to your existing home, these are ideal times for exploring the solar power options available.

Reducing heat loss

There are a number of low-cost and even free steps you can take to reduce your energy consumption levels. If possible, you should make sure radiators are placed on internal walls rather than on external ones, which has been the practice in the past. If you have no choice, then reduce the heat lost through external walls by pasting sheets of aluminium foil, shiny side in, on the external wall behind the radiator. Another idea is to place shelves (also with foil on the underside) above radiators to try to trap the heat. If you have enough room you could also consider creating a mezzanine level, which would make use of warm air near the ceiling.

One of the most effective ways of heating your home is to heat only the rooms that you are using, with different temperatures for different rooms depending on how much you use them. Our bodies lose heat through radiation – the transfer of heat from one object to another – so to reduce this it

Do not fit a room thermostat in a room that is heated by anything other than a centrally heated radiator, such as a solid-fuel fire, as this will turn off the heating in the rest of the house. In rooms with other heat sources, fit a thermostatic radiator valve.

is advisable to use natural materials in your home such as wood and fabric, rather than glass and metal, which conduct heat more rapidly.

Central-heating systems

Have a look at your heating system to see how efficient it really is. There are a number of upgrades that can be made to central-heating systems to improve their efficiency, such as controls for room temperature and the temperature of stored water; on/off times for heating and hot water; and switching the boiler off when heating is no longer required. Thermostatic radiator valves also allow you to control individual room temperatures, because they automatically turn off a radiator once the temperature has reached the desired level.

The key is flexibility, so that you can regulate the amount of space and hot water you want to heat without wasting any energy (or money). The controls of your heating system should be able to react to changes in temperature. You should be able to switch your heating and hot water off and on whenever you want. Most modern systems are able to do this, but if you have an old heating system its controls might be too simple. If this is the case, think about upgrading it and adding better controls. If you are considering updating your heating system and debating whether to add full or partial controls, you should consider the age of your central-heating system. If it is very old it might be wise to install the full range of controls, but if it is a fairly new system it might benefit by simply adding thermostatic radiator valves.

Timers and thermostats

The time switch or programmer is one of the most useful of all heating controls, because it turns your heating and hot water on and off automatically at pre-set times. Some will allow you to set timings for your hot water and heating separately. A room thermostat switches the heating off once the set temperature is reached, and then back on again if it drops below that level, giving you a constant temperature. The thermostat should be installed on the wall of the most frequently used room, away from draughts, sunlight and other heat sources. It can be wired to your central-heating pump, but it will be more economical if it is fitted as part of a complete control system that switches off the boiler to prevent so-called 'dry cycling', which is when the boiler fires up to keep itself hot even when it is not needed. You can also choose to have different heating 'zones' in your house, so that you can heat certain areas individually.

Thermostatic radiator valves enable you to control the temperature of each room separately and can be useful in rooms that are inclined to overheat, such as the bathroom and kitchen. They work by reducing the flow of water to the radiator as the thermostat reaches its set temperature.

Hints for **heating**

- Save up to 10 per cent on your heating bills simply by turning your thermostat down by as little as 1º.

- Instead of cranking up the central heating think about putting on a thicker sweater and socks.

- Use a hot-water bottle in bed rather than an electric blanket.

- Use thick, organic cotton sheets and a woollen blanket to make the bed feel warmer.

- Make sure you heat only the areas of your home you need to.

- Turn the central heating down or off when you go out.

- Set your thermostat for heating water at around 60ºC (140ºF). Don't have it scalding hot or you will have to run extra cold water to cool it down.

- Make sure your boiler is serviced regularly to maintain its safety and for maximum efficiency.

Most central-heating systems also heat your hot-water cylinder. One way of saving energy is to reduce the temperature of your stored hot water. If you have a pumped or gravity hot-water system you can do this by fitting a thermostat to your hot-water cylinder and a motorized valve to the cylinder. Or you could fit a clamp-on cylinder thermostat as part of an integrated control system.

Boilers

Most of us have had problems with boilers at some point – there is nothing worse than waking up on a cold winter's day to find out that the boiler refuses to crank into action, leaving you without heating or hot water or possibly both. Boilers generally have an efficient lifespan of around 15 years, after which they become a lot more expensive to run and far less energy efficient. Modern boilers are, however, much more energy efficient than older versions, so although investing in a new boiler is a major outlay, it will certainly save you money in the long run. Most boiler manufacturers publish the seasonal efficiency of their boilers, so make sure you get this information before investing in one. There are different boilers for different jobs, so get advice about which is the best type for your living space. This is true of central-heating systems, too – if you are installing a brand new system look around for the one that best suits your specific needs.

If you are installing a condensing boiler be aware that it will produce water vapour that is visible from the flue, known as the 'pluming' effect. This can be unsightly and unpleasant, so to avoid irritating your neighbours, site the flue away from windows and doors.

Condensing boilers are the most efficient boilers available today. They convert around 88 per cent of fuel into heat, compared with the 72 per cent managed by most standard boilers. They can be wall mounted or floor standing and are suitable for any size home, but because they are more expensive than other boilers they are particularly good for larger houses where the initial cost will be recouped more quickly.

The next best boiler in terms of efficiency is the non-condensing boiler, which runs at a minimum of 72 per cent average seasonal efficiency. These tend to be lighter and can run on a variety of fuels. A condensing combination boiler heats the central heating and the hot-water cylinder, which means they are particularly good for smaller spaces where there is no room for a hot- or cold-water tank.

Other heat sources

Alternative methods of heating your home are gas fires, convector heaters, electric storage heaters and solid-fuel stoves. Electric storage heaters work by storing heat during off-peak periods when electricity is cheaper because there is less demand, and then releasing it the following day.

Although open-log fires are very appealing they are not very energy efficient and waste around 85 per cent of the fuel they burn. An open fire uses around 15 times the air content of the room where it is situated every hour, and so to compensate it sucks in air from gaps in windows and doors, creating draughts. There are a variety of wood-burning stoves on the market. All of them produce convected and radiant heat and some of them burn wood very cleanly and efficiently. If you run a stove alongside a central-heating system you could cut your fuel bills considerably, unlike an open-log fire, which is likely to push your fuel bills up. When choosing a stove it is important to buy one that is not too big for the room, because otherwise it will be underfiring and not performing at its best. Most stoves are made from cast iron, which is able to continue radiating stored heat well after the fire has gone out. They can be used for a number of functions, including direct space heating, hot-water heating and radiator heating. Some versions even have hot plates for warming up food.

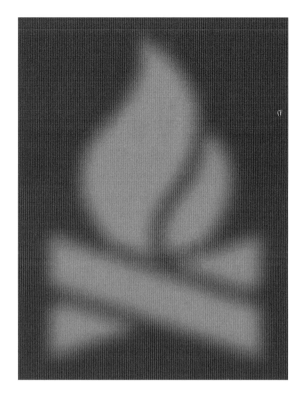

- If you have a solid-fuel stove, save twigs and scraps of paper and newspaper to start it rather than using firelighters, which are made from paraffin and other flammable chemicals.

- Wood bought as fuel should come from a renewable source, such as a sustainably managed forestry system, or recovered wood waste.

- Look in the telephone directory for local tree surgeons and construction companies, who might be willing to give you waste material for fuel.

- Keep wood stacked outdoors but under cover to keep it dry.

- Softwoods can be used for kindling as they burn very fast and hot.

- Reuse discarded packing pallets for fuel, making sure you remove nails first.

materials in the
home

A look around the average household is enough to highlight the lack of natural materials we use in our homes. We are used to soft furnishings stuffed with synthetic fibres; floors covered in wall-to-wall carpet and walls finished with paints containing petrochemicals. By incorporating more natural materials, such as wood, clay, cork and hemp, you can reduce the amount of pollutants in your home, and improve both the insulation and the quality of the atmosphere in your living space.

Using locally sourced natural materials is the best option in order to cut down on pollution caused by transportation. The average household suffers from the volatile organic compounds (VOCs) and other pollutants released by furniture made from composite boards, and synthetic fibres used in carpets and upholstery, as well as conventional paint and vinyl wallpaper. By seeking out more traditional materials such as stone and timber, you will create a home that is more in sync with the environment and better for you and your family.

Walls

Before you start thinking about how you want the interior walls of your home to look, it is important to do what you can in terms of insulation and rendering first. The walls of your home are the boundaries between you and the outside world, and as such they can have a significant effect on how warm, quiet and comfortable a room is. Consider practicalities such as insulation and heating as well – making sure your walls are well insulated will save you money as well as saving energy (*see Wall Insulation, page 22*).

If you are in the process of renovating a building or adding an extension onto your home, it is worth finding out more about in-wall heating. This kind of heating is effective at much lower temperatures and therefore saves a lot of energy. Seek expert advice from environmental building companies about costs and installers. And if you do have the opportunity, select the building material that the walls are made from.

Clay

Unfired clay is an attractive and natural option for finishing walls and floors, giving a rustic feel to the interior. It has been used for construction for many centuries because of its outstanding properties. Clay is quite literally an 'earth material'. It has natural insulation properties and therefore keeps the interior pleasantly cool during the summer and maintains a warm temperature throughout the winter.

Today there are a number of clay building materials available, which have a very low energy impact because they are made from natural raw materials available in great quantities such as earth, sand, wood chips, flax and reed. The processing procedure for clay building materials is mechanical and therefore does not use the huge amounts of energy needed to make fired clay bricks. Clay is also completely recyclable and does not contain any synthetic additives.

In addition, clay can absorb odours and is good for absorbing sound, too. All of this makes it an excellent option if you are considering carrying out any kind of renovation work – but remember that unfired clay bricks can be used only for internal partition walls unless a timber or steel frame is used for support.

The clay plasters that are available are a much better option than the gypsum-based plasters still widely used in the construction industry. Clay bricks and finishes are very good because of their ability to regulate temperature and absorb moisture. As clay can also be very attractive in its own right you can use clay plasters to finish walls without having to paint them.

Lime plaster

Plaster has been used in house building for centuries, starting with mud huts, which were finished with a thick layer of lime plaster. It was originally used to protect houses from the weather, but was also frequently used to decorate the interior and exterior of buildings. Lime plaster is one of the oldest forms of plaster. It is made from slaked lime and coarse sand granules, which are mixed with water and fibrous materials such as animal hair or chopped straw, or even cow dung. It is by no means as ecologically sound a choice as clay – lime production causes carbon dioxide emissions and the demand for the limestone causes its own problems, with bigger areas being excavated, and centuries-old limestone pavements being destroyed. But some green builders still favour lime due to its 'breathing' qualities and traditional appearance.

Use unfired clay bricks for internal partitions – but make sure it is a non-load bearing wall.

Use clay plaster for a final finish to walls rather than paint.

Make your own limewash for walls by adding water to lime putty and then passing it through a sieve – add a plant-based oil such as linseed oil for external use.

Problems with paint

The earliest paints were made using ochre – a clay-like earth material – and ground rocks to create pigments. Colourful pigments were made by grinding shells, stone and minerals to create a range of colours from red through to blue. Early oil paints contained linseed and hemp seed oil to dry and harden them. The creation of chemical synthetics meant that a whole new range of colours that had never been used before was introduced, and since then petrochemical synthetics have taken over from natural vegetable oil and resin bases for paints. Today, all paints, whether natural or synthetic, are either solvent or water based. Natural organic paints are made with solvents derived from plants such as citrus peel oil and other natural ingredients.

Synthetic paints are harmful to those involved in manufacturing them as well as using them, and they also pose a problem in terms of pollution. Synthetic paints contain solvents that give off volatile organic compounds (*see pages 42–3*) during application of the paint, when it is drying and sometimes for years afterwards. Synthetic paints are also likely to contain fungicides and heavy metals such as cadmium, and they can pose a major fire risk as once alight they will burn very quickly and emit toxic fumes.

- Avoid non-drip paints as they may contain polyurethane.

- Choose matt or satin finish paint over high-gloss versions, which contain many more solvents.

Natural paints are available for painting walls, plaster and metal, and water-based paint that can be used on wood is becoming more widely available. They are made using pigments derived from natural plants, minerals and resins, such as linseed oil, and waxes also derived from plants, which act as binders and media for the pigments. Natural paints are more subtly coloured than conventional ones and generally smell nicer as they are often made with essential oils. A word of caution: check the oils in the paint you use are safe if the room is used by pregnant women as some essential oils are not.

The paints you use should be vapour-permeable and anti-static and made without using latex or other plastic binders, as is common. The same goes for natural oils, waxes and varnishes used on panelling and floors. Natural fillers for walls are cork based – a good alternative to the silicon sealant normally used in fillers.

Solvents are widely used in the manufacture of many products, including paints, varnishes, carpets, fabrics and glues. With paints, varnishes and glues the solvents evaporate into the atmosphere in your home as they dry. Solvents have been linked with lots of health problems, such as eye and throat irritations, and they are a major contributor to sick building syndrome.

There has been much research into the effects of conventional paints on health, and studies have now shown them to be carcinogenic. This has led to an increased demand by consumers for natural paints, instead of the more commonly used petrochemical-based varieties. The manufacturing process for natural paints is less environmentally damaging than that for conventional paint production, which often uses undesirable chemicals, such as titanium dioxide, chlorine, cadmium and sulphur dioxide. The heavy metals and other toxins used to colour and bond the paints can be extremely harmful to health, as well as damaging to the environment, and they use lots of energy during their production – making them, all in all, a pretty poor choice.

- Whenever possible, opt for natural, unpainted finishes.

- Look for limewash, mineral- or plant-based paints for walls and ceilings.

- Check whether the pots are recyclable.

- Try to use paint 'kits' so you can make only as much paint as you need.

- Buy solvent-free products.

The disposal of paint pots also poses a big problem – particularly those that are not completely empty – because the toxins can leach out into the water table. Natural paints and stains are water based and are made using plant-based dyes, solvents and fillers, which are biodegradable. Typical ingredients found in natural gloss paint include linseed oil, oil of citrus peel, danmar (tree resin) and calcium octoat.

As well as improving the aesthetic quality of your home, natural paints and finishes also help to create a healthier living space for you and your family. On a practical level, they allow the walls to 'breathe', which in turn reduces the likelihood of the long-term structural damage that can result from moisture being trapped behind sealed, non-breathing, non-porous surfaces.

- Look out for low-odour paints.

- Use paints made from natural resins, essential oils, chalk, India rubber and linseed oil.

- Don't throw unwanted paint down the drain – let it dry first and contact your local authority regarding disposal.

A growing number of companies produce natural pigment paints made from plants, minerals, natural oils and resins. A common ingredient found in natural paints is shellac, a resin secreted by the lac insect, which is used to bond the paint together. Natural paints are available for general interior household use, as well as for iron work and masonry. Lots of natural paints are sold in kits so that you can mix up only as much as you need, reducing the amount of wastage.

- More environmentally friendly paints are those thinned with milk casein or natural glue.

- Be aware that water-based paints such as lime distempers and whitewash may not be very durable or washable.

If you are planning to redecorate or have recently moved house be aware of the hazards of dealing with paint. Lead is often found in old paint so take great care not to inhale the dust or fumes when rubbing or stripping down old surfaces. When you are doing this sort of work, wear a mouth and nose cover made out of an old T-shirt or sheet and keep windows open to make sure there is sufficient ventilation. The least harmful way of stripping paint is to sand it off, rather than using harmful paint-stripping chemicals.

Conventional paint strippers contain a solvent called dichlormethane (DCM), which is thought to be carcinogenic. Water-based paint strippers that are biodegradable and do not give off toxic fumes are available but they vary in their effectiveness.

Wallpaper

Until recently wallpaper had been out of fashion, but a number of designers have modernized it and it is once again a good way to cover your walls. But how acceptable is it on an environmental level? Many wallpapers are vinyl based and wallpaper paste is a solvent that often contains fungicides. Vinyl and plastic wallpaper stops the wall from breathing, which can lead to structural problems.

- It is hard to find recycled wallpaper, but wood-chip paper and lining paper are cheap, and although not necessarily made from waste products, these wallpapers use less resources than a lot of other types and are longer lasting because they can be repainted rather than replaced.

- Use borax instead of fungicide in the paste if you are papering walls.

- Throw paint shavings away in a sealed container.

- Avoid fibre-cement and asbestos-cement artificial slates.

Flooring

Indoor pollution can be caused by the very materials you introduce into your home to furnish it, so do not forget this when you are choosing the floor covering. In order to avoid the volatile organic compounds (VOCs) (*see pages 42–3*) given off by artificial fibres and synthetic materials, make sure you are aware of exactly what your new carpet is made from. An immediate indicator of how harmful it might be is the smell of a new carpet or floor covering. Although the smell does eventually fade, the carpet could continue to emit harmful gases into your home environment.

Most carpets and floor coverings are made from petrochemical-based synthetics manufactured using non-renewable resources. This makes them non-biodegradable and difficult to recycle, so they end up on landfill sites or in incinerators once they have been disposed of. Vinyl flooring, whether on a roll or in tiles, should always be avoided as it uses polyvinyl chloride (PVC), the manufacture of which is extremely hazardous to the environment.

A growing number of companies are starting to cater for people who want a greener home, and it will not be long before the do-it-yourself giants start their own ranges. In the meantime, materials to look out for are: natural linoleum, wood (as long as it is from a sustainable source or salvaged), cork and local slate. Wooden floors might seem like the most natural option and they certainly look good, but to be sure of the wood's green credentials, check where the timber is from and how it has been forested (*see Wooden Flooring, pages 40–1*).

Insulation

Before you decide which flooring you want for your home first make sure the floor is properly insulated against draughts and sound. This is a relatively straightforward, albeit time-consuming, job but well worth the effort. Lift the floorboards and fit wooden slats or netting to support the insulation material then fill the space with the insulation material – you could use anything from old pieces of carpet to compressed wood fibre – making sure you leave some gaps to allow for ventilation. You can then fit your new flooring over the top of this insulating layer. (*See also Insulating Floors, page 23.*)

Carpet concerns

None of us like to think about the amount of dust and dirt trapped in our carpets, but we all know it is there no matter how conscientious we are with the vacuum cleaner. Recent research has shown that dust mites in carpets can cause and exacerbate allergic reactions, particularly among children, so choosing environmentally friendly flooring can be beneficial both to the planet and to your family.

Buying a wool carpet might seem like a good eco-option, but not if it has been treated and dyed with chemicals, so check the processes it has been through. There are often VOCs (*see pages 42–3*) present in the binders used in the fabrication of materials such as carpet padding, as well as in the adhesives used to apply carpet padding and tiles. Natural and organic wool that has not been treated with chemicals is one option – just make sure it has not been backed with a synthetic material. Look out for woollen felt backing, which as well as being natural provides a comfortable surface to walk on and has the added benefit of offering good sound insulation.

If you cannot bear to live without it, there are a number of green alternatives to having carpet throughout your home, and it does not have to be cold, scratchy or minimalist. Environmentally friendly flooring comes in many different forms, so you could choose a different material for each room. Flooring made with materials such as cork, coir and sisal can look very good and will give your home a clean, modern style. Natural carpet materials are more costly than common carpet materials, but they are competitively priced in comparison with standard high-quality carpeting. Even better, most natural fibres are grown and harvested in traditional ways so they do not pollute the atmosphere and, crucially, are biodegradable.

Coir

Most commonly used to make doormats, coir is a 100 per cent natural and renewable fibre from the husks of coconuts that otherwise would be thrown away. The colour of coir varies with the annual cycle – coir harvested in the wet season is lighter than the summer crop. The coir fibres are softened, spun into yarn and then woven to make coarse matting, which is ideal for kitchens and bathrooms.

Cut down on noise pollution by adding a layer of acoustic insulation under floorboards or carpets. Try using coconut fibre matting or mats made from recycled rubber tyres.

Flooring made from coir is very long lasting, as well as being eco-friendly – coir was traditionally used to make rope and twine because it is so durable. Its fibres are non-oily and therefore prevent bacteriological activity, which helps to eliminate the chances of an allergic reaction, such as eczema or asthma, which can be caused by synthetic carpets.

Sisal

Sisal is traditionally grown in Mexico. Its 1 m (1 yd) long leaves are soaked until they disintegrate into tough fibres. The fibres are then spun into yarn and woven to make carpets or matting. It is the most commonly used natural fibre and makes carpets and mats of various textures and colours. However, there is some concern about the intensive cultivation methods, which can lead to soil erosion, and the effect of sisal dust on factory workers.

Jute

Jute is grown in India and then exported. The fibres are extracted from the stem of the plant and soaked in water. It is then used to make a number of products, including hessian (burlap) cloths and sacking, as well as wall coverings and backing for carpets and rugs. Jute is less hard-wearing than sisal.

Cork tiles

Cork is a sustainable, natural material, which comes from the bark of the cork oak tree. Once it is 25 years old, the tree can be harvested once every nine years without being damaged. Cork trees can live for up to 150 years and, as well as producing

cork, they also support a diversity of wildlife. As a natural product, cork is biodegradable, sustainable and non-polluting – pretty much all you can ask for.

The cork industry is currently under threat because of the increase in popularity of the plastic wine 'cork'. This is due to the large number of wines that are 'corked', or contaminated, by a faulty cork. Corked wine costs the wine industry thousands every year and there are increasing calls for producers to use plastic corks instead so as to prevent this loss. The wine industry is the single biggest user of cork, with most other products, such as tiles, being made from wine cork leftovers.

Cork floor tiles are useful in areas like the bathroom and kitchen. Cork is made up of millions of air pockets so it makes a very good insulation material, for both noise and warmth. The best option if you decide to buy cork tiles is to look out for unvarnished tiles. You can then seal them yourself with an innocuous sealant such as a water-based varnish or beeswax polish, which will also make them easy to clean. For a more colourful effect, try staining cork tiles with a plant-based stain. There is also the added bonus that you can replace odd tiles if they get spoiled or damaged, rather than having to re-lay the entire floor, so it is always worth buying a couple of extra tiles just in case. There are some interesting 'designer' cork tiles around at the moment, which really bring the material bang up to date with unusual designs and colours. While these are tempting, a lot of them are finished with a PVC laminate – one of the most toxic, non-biodegradable materials around.

Look for flooring adhesive made from natural materials when you are laying cork, linoleum or carpet.

Seagrass

Seagrass is grown in seawater paddy fields and is used to make flooring that is water and stain resistant. The seagrass is twisted and then woven to make coarse, rustic-looking flooring. Make sure that the company you are buying it from does not use chemicals such as dyes or bleach to alter the look of the fibres. Also, make sure it does not use synthetic backings on the seagrass, which defeats the object of buying natural flooring, as these are non-biodegradable. There are concerns that harvesting seagrass can disrupt the delicate eco-system it is part of, and you should also take into account the amount of energy used in transporting materials from different countries.

Linoleum

It might surprise you to find out that linoleum is another good natural flooring option. It might not appear to be the most natural of materials, but it is actually made from softwood powder, linseed oil, pine tree resins, cork, chalk and jute backing. The cork used in linoleum is harvested from the cork tree on an ongoing basis without harming the tree. Linoleum will cost more than low-cost vinyl flooring but is by far the better choice. When laying a linoleum floor try to use a plant-based adhesive rather than a solvent-based one. If you are using linoleum as a flooring material make sure that you have a damp-proof surface as moisture can damage the backing of the linoleum.

Rubber

Rubber comes from the white, milky latex extracted from the rubber tree, which is indigenous to South America. Although it is a natural substance the rubber we use today is vulcanized in a production process that is very energy consuming. It is combined with sulphur under heat and pressure to make it resilient and elastic and to get rid of any smells and stickiness. As it is tough and waterproof rubber is often used to make flooring for bathrooms and kitchens. Rubber is readily available in tiles but some people are allergic to it.

Reclaimed tiles

Unfired clay is a very eco-friendly material; in fact it is quite literally the earth beneath our feet, and is eminently biodegradable. The problem with tiles is that they need to be fired – a process that uses a huge amount of energy and causes a great deal of pollution, although some types of kiln are more energy efficient than others. The best option is to look for salvaged or reclaimed terracotta tiles. Also, bear in mind that if you are using tiles on your floor, the glazes often contain toxic chemicals and compounds, including zinc and lead. Generally, the brighter the tile colour, the more toxic the glaze.

Stone

For centuries people have used stone such as granite, slate, flint, limestone and sandstone for building. The high cost of materials such as granite is because of the rarity and quality of the stone and the fact that its transportation is very labour intensive. Transportation costs can also be high due to the weight of the stone. This means that using these materials for flooring is not very green unless it is salvaged stone from old buildings.

Stone is hard, strong and water resistant and a raw material like slate can be made into thick slabs for floors. Stone is a non-polluting, natural material that is ideal for use in kitchens and bathrooms. The disadvantages of using stone are really the expense and possible problems with radon, which materials like granite can emit, so make sure it is tested by an expert first. Natural stone can give an earthy, natural but contemporary feel to a room.

- Coir and jute are very durable and ideal for areas in the home that get a lot of wear and tear, such as stairs and hallways.

- Sisal is more delicate and would be better used in areas that have less traffic, like the living room or bedroom.

- Linoleum is ideal for use in the kitchen because drips and spills can be mopped up easily.

- Reclaimed ceramic tiles, locally produced or salvaged stone, cork or bamboo are all good choices for the bathroom.

- ⓘ Use second-hand slate if you are roofing or re-roofing your home.
- ⓘ If you are repairing a roof make sure you remove all the slate tiles intact, as they are extremely versatile and always in demand.
- ⓘ Avoid fibre-cement and asbestos-cement artificial slates.

Wood

Wood is one of the best environmental choices when selecting materials to use in your home. It is waste efficient, recyclable, biodegradable and non-toxic. But this is valid only if the wood is harvested from a renewable source. Trees stabilize climate and global temperature, so deforestation causes a number of problems, one of which is the reduction in the number of trees that soak up excess carbon dioxide. Even with sustainable forestry there is the potential problem that although it provides us with a renewable resource, it does not support the same diverse wildlife as natural woodland.

Although trees are a renewable resource there is still concern that we are using too many and that it is affecting the delicate ecological balance. Look for certified wood that has been grown under a sustainability management scheme. This indicates that it conforms to environmental criteria regarding the protection of the environment, including water resources and soil structure, as well as social issues such as the welfare of forestry workers and the rights of indigenous peoples. The certifier should indicate a link with the Forest Stewardship Council (FSC) – an international coalition that promotes a common set of guidelines used to evaluate certifying organizations. The FSC was set up in 1993 as a non-profit organization with a membership of timber traders, community forest groups, forest workers'

Trees are felled when they reach maturity, which varies depending on the species: oak matures at 100 years while ash takes 50.

The **following** are threatened tropical **hardwood species** and **should** be **avoided**:

Teak

Mahogany

Rosewood

Kapur

Ebony

Ramin

unions and retail companies across the world. It is recognized as a credible international certifier of sustainable forestry by environmental groups such as Greenpeace and Friends of the Earth.

When you are buying new timber, find out exactly what type of wood it is. If possible, buy sustainable timber local to where you live, to try to reduce the amount of imported wood, and at all costs avoid all endangered tropical hardwood species. Also avoid wood 'alternatives' like composite boards, such as fibreboard (MDF) and plywood, as they contain adhesives and formaldehyde.

Wooden flooring

Many older houses have wooden floorboards hidden beneath the carpet, which can make very attractive flooring if sanded down and polished. This kind of floor needs less cleaning than a carpet because dust can be simply swept up without the need for

Timber is divided into **two groups**:

These are softwood and hardwood (which does not always reflect the hardness of the wood). Hardwoods such as oak come from broad-leaved trees from temperate regions and softwoods such as pine come from coniferous trees. Hardwoods grow more slowly than softwoods and are more resistant to fungal and insect attacks.

a vacuum, and other dirt can be wiped away with a damp cloth. A wooden floor also has excellent insulation properties, which makes it cool in the summer and warm in the winter.

If you do choose to have floorboards you can hire a sander fairly easily and inexpensively from a tool-hire store. Look for natural, vegetable-based wood stains and polishes, and use a water-based varnish to create a smooth, easily cleaned surface. Beeswax is the best choice of natural varnishes, but it can make the floor very slippery.

Rugs make wooden floors more comfortable. They also have the added advantage that they can be shaken and aired outdoors, unlike carpets, which are there for good. To stop them slipping you can stick them down using strong tape or special grips designed specifically for this purpose. Don't buy rugs with non-slip backing, because the backing material will probably be foam or plastic. Wooden floorboards are the cheapest and greenest choice of flooring for many older buildings.

If you do not have floorboards, fitting a new wooden floor on top of the existing one is an option. Most do-it-yourself stores sell wooden blocks that can be easily fitted onto different types of flooring. This has the added advantage of insulating cold concrete floors. Always make sure that the wood comes from a renewable source – look out for companies that supply timber from sustainably managed forests. Even better, look for salvaged wood from old buildings. Try to buy untreated and unvarnished wood whenever possible and then treat it yourself using natural products. This allows the pores of the timber to stay open and enables the wood to breathe, which can help to stabilize the level of humidity in the house.

Varnishes

Traditional varnishes are based on natural resins from tropical trees such as shellac and manila, which are good for sealing. Shellac is a pure resin

Softwood is more susceptible than hardwood to water and insect attacks, so a lot of softwood timber is treated with toxic fungicides and insecticides such as lindane and pentachlorophenol (PCP). There are safer treatments, however, such as borax, linseed oil, potash and beeswax.

that is used as a varnish and can seal up to 80 per cent of the fumes emitted by chemically treated materials such as composite boards. Although many varnishes and stains are made using solvents, there are some natural stains, varnishes and waxes that use plant-derived resins and oils, such as larch or copal, with scented turpentine oil and pigments. Turpentine (white spirit) is distilled from a volatile essential oil called oleoresin, which comes from the bark of certain species of pine tree. Plant-based solvents in natural varnishes and stains allow the wood to breathe because they react with the oils and resins in untreated wood. They are less durable than chemical treatments but smell and look better.

The only treatment that is really necessary for interior wooden furniture and fittings is a finish of beeswax or linseed oil. Pure beeswax is a good option for finishing wood surfaces – it gives a beautiful shine, helps to combat static and gives the room a rich, wholesome smell. Liquid beeswax is a natural treatment that can be used as a finish on wood, clay, stone and cork.

Wood panelling is an excellent way to utilize wood in your home. Although we tend to associate it with the 1970s and with Swedish saunas, a bit of creative thinking can bring it up to date. Panelling is most appropriate for those areas of your home that need extra protection, such as the hallway, because it is a very durable material and will protect the walls from wear and tear. It is a good thermal insulator, keeping cool in the summer and warm in the winter.

Plastics

Plastic comes in a variety of different forms and it is impossible to avoid in today's world. We pack our sandwiches in it, sit on it and even wear it. It is also widely used in the construction of our homes for windows, doors and floors. Technological advances mean that it can be used to create highly original furnishings and equipment, which look great, but plastic really is an environmental nightmare.

Plastics in the **home**

- Phenol and formaldehyde are often used in adhesives and binders.

- Polyurethane is used in foam insulation.

- Polyesters are used in synthetic fabrics and carpets.

- Melamine is used for covering work surfaces and furniture.

- Silicones are found in sealants.

Unfortunately, plastic has become known as a disposable material when we should really treat it as a very valuable material due to the environmental damage caused by manufacture. Plastic is a by-product of the energy-intensive petroleum industry, so it is part of a much bigger problem. There are more than 50 different types of plastic, which fall into two main categories: thermosets and thermoplastics, both of which are produced from petroleum and natural gas.

Soft plastics or thermoplastics are among the most harmful because they can offgas (leak out) into the atmosphere and even into foods. They account for around 80 per cent of all plastics produced and include polyvinyl chloride (PVC), polychlorinated biphenyls (PCBs), polypropylene, nylon, acrylics and polythene. Thermoplastics emit harmful vapours known as VOCs, which are potential carcinogens (*see below and box opposite*). Thermosets are hard plastics that cannot be softened again, as thermoplastics can. They include polyesters, urea formaldehyde and silicones, and can be found in composite boards, paints, carpets, adhesives and certain fabrics.

The production of plastic products, along with metal manufacturing, is right up there at the top of the most energy-consuming processes. The oil that plastic is made from is itself a limited resource, and other valuable resources are used in what is an incredibly energy-intensive and polluting process. Another major problem with plastic is that only a small percentage of plastics can be recycled and, as it is not biodegradable, waste plastic will never decay (*see Plastic, page 52*). Some countries use incineration to dispose of plastic, but this is an extremely hazardous process: toxic chemicals such as dioxins are emitted, and even after this process around 90 per cent of the plastic burned remains as toxic waste.

All plastics are potential fire hazards; they burn twice as fast as, and hotter than, more traditional materials, as well as giving off toxic fumes that can kill quickly. Polyurethane foam, which used to be widely used in furniture upholstery, is a very dangerous fire hazard and its use in furniture has now been banned in a number of countries.

Avoid using clingfilm (saranwrap) as chemicals in it can be absorbed by fatty foods – use cellophane or greaseproof (waxed) paper instead. The same goes for plastic containers: look for stainless steel ones that you can reuse, or pack food in paper bags or empty bread bags. Pollution from plastics can also come from the PVC floor tiles, toxic adhesives and laminates that are common in many houses.

Volatile organic compounds

When talking about plastics it is impossible not to mention volatile organic compounds (VOCs) – pollutants given off by plastics in the home, which have been linked to a number of physical symptoms. VOCs include a wide range of plastic compounds, such as the organochlorines polyvinyl chloride (PVC) and the highly toxic polychlorinated biphenyls (PCB), which are found in many

Avoid VOCS

- **Organochlorines:** these are compounds often found in synthetic chemicals such as those used to make household cleaners and air fresheners. They include polychlorinated biphenyls (PCBs) and polyvinyl chloride (PVC), and chloroform and chloramines, which are both toxic gases. Organochlorines have been linked with skin irritation, depression and headaches.

- **Phenols:** these carbolic acids are found in plastics and disinfectants, and phenolic synthetic resins containing formaldehyde can be found in paints, plastics and varnishes. Phenols are suspected of causing damage to the respiratory system.

- **Formaldehyde:** this is widely used as a binder and preservative in hundreds of household items, including wood sheets, bed linen and cosmetics. It is also used in furniture upholstery. Formaldehyde releases toxic vapours at room temperature, which pollute the atmosphere. It has been associated with a number of physical symptoms, including nausea and nosebleeds, and it is a suspected carcinogen.

household cleaning products, paints and adhesives. These have been linked with headaches and nausea, and PCBs are carcinogenic (*see box above*).

Gender benders

A number of noxious chemicals, including DDT, lindane, dioxins and PCBs, have become known as 'gender benders'. This is because they contain hormone-disrupting compounds (HDCs), which mimic the female hormone oestrogen and can cause such disturbing and long-reaching effects as low sperm count and male infertility. Cancers and tumours thought to be a result of the effects of HDCs have been found in fish and mammals in the North Sea and America's Great Lakes.

The main culprits are: phthalates, which are widely used in plastics, vinyl flooring, paint and ink; alkylphenolic compounds, which are used in detergents, paints and shampoos; bisphenol A, used in food cans and bottle tops; organochlorines, which are widely used in pesticides, plastics and synthetic materials; and dioxins.

Dioxins are known to be carcinogenic and have been shown to affect foetal development and the immune system. Organochlorines accumulate in fatty tissue and can be passed down the food chain. These gender benders or hormone-mimicking chemicals are found everywhere in the average home – from pesticides in non-organic food to food packaging, children's toys, detergents and cosmetics.

Metals

We use a vast range of metals in our lives today, including steel, zinc, aluminium, copper, cast iron and brass. They appear in our homes in various different guises: copper pipes, aluminium gutters, steel windows and brass wiring. Metals also appear in a number of household items and appliances such as washing machines, toasters, coffee makers and aluminium foil.

We should all be trying to reduce the amount of metal we use because they are very expensive materials, manufactured in an energy-intensive way. The mineral ores from which they come are a non-renewable resource, and some metals, in particular zinc, lead, tin and tungsten, are becoming extremely rare. In addition, the manufacturing process for some metals uses huge amounts of energy and creates even more pollution with emissions of carbon dioxide and acid gases. Metals are also extremely toxic to humans – dust, fumes and particles can accumulate in the body and lead to toxic levels. Aluminium has been linked with Alzheimer's disease and lead can cause poisoning.

Around half the iron used for steelmaking comes from scrap and around one-third of the aluminium produced is recycled, but it should be much more. Recycling aluminium is much more energy efficient, as secondary aluminium requires only 5 per cent of the energy it takes to process iron ore.

- Recycle your food and drink cans.

- Choose greaseproof (waxed) paper over foil for the kitchen.

- Don't use aluminium or zinc pots or pans.

- Don't collect rainwater from lead gutters or roofs.

Steel
Steel production is one of the most energy-intensive industries, but it does create clean waste heat, which can be recovered and used. The production process causes emissions of carbon monoxide and hydrogen sulphide, as well as dioxins. Stainless steel is produced in much the same way as steel but is heated to higher temperatures. It is made mainly from recycled steel and has the benefit of being able to be continually recycled.

Aluminium
Aluminium production uses huge amounts of electricity, which is extremely expensive and polluting, producing twice as much carbon dioxide as steel. Some countries have developed hydro-electricity schemes for aluminium production. These sound quite promising but in fact often end up disrupting wildlife and people on a grand scale as villages and valleys are flooded to create reservoirs. Aluminium is made from bauxite, which makes up part of the earth's crust. While it is now in great supply, it will eventually run out. The plus points are that aluminium can be recycled using far less energy than the original production cost.

Lead
Lead is a very poisonous metal, which can attack our immune systems and can be fatal. It used to be widely used in paint but has now been phased out. Lead production involves burning off impurities from the ore, smelting and refining. Emissions produced during this process include lead oxides, zinc, mercury and copper.

Copper
Copper is produced in a similar way to lead and gives off large quantities of sulphur dioxide and nitrous oxides, which cause acid rain. As it is a very conductive material it is widely used in the home for electrical cables and water piping.

Fabric

Most of us enjoy using fabric in our homes. Decorative cushion covers and throws can be very attractive additions to living spaces, but are you aware of how your gorgeous embroidered throw has been produced? And what about the processes involved in creating the vivid colours on your favourite rug or towel? All of these issues need to be looked at carefully and this includes gaining an understanding of what is meant by 'natural' fabrics.

Textiles are an integral part of our lives – in our homes and on our backs. By reusing and recycling fabric whenever possible we can reduce the impact of the chemicals used to grow raw materials such as cotton and also cut down on the pollution caused by the dyeing process. And by passing our unwanted textiles onto charity stores we can also help to raise money for charity.

- Avoid fabrics that are labelled 'non-iron' as they may have been treated with formaldehyde and could cause allergic reactions.

- Use organic cotton, linen or hemp bedding.

- Buy items you will want to keep/wear for a long time.

- Look for vegetable-dyed fabrics.

Cotton

Many people are under the impression that cotton is an environmentally friendly fabric because it is a natural product, but this simply is not true. It is, nonetheless, the most widely used plant fibre for clothes and for furnishings. However, cotton is one of the most intensively produced crops in the world, and the cotton industry uses vast amounts of fertilizers, pesticides and growth regulators. Cotton is made from the *Gossypium* plant, which is also used for making more coarse fabrics such as rayon, as well as in papermaking. It is the intensive farming processes used in cotton cultivation that make it such a very environmentally unfriendly fabric. Insecticides, such as DDT, are sprayed on the crops throughout the growing season – cotton production alone accounts for 25 per cent of the global pesticide market. These chemicals can cause skin irritations and allergic reactions when they come into contact with our skin.

There are also problems incurred by the high demand for irrigation during cotton production, which can cause or exacerbate local water shortages. Most cotton available today has been chemically bleached and if dyes have been used they are more than likely chemically derived.

Another concern for environmentalists is the production of genetically modified (GM) cotton in some parts of the world, such as the USA. There are fears that, as with GM foods, the ecosystem will be irreversibly damaged and superweeds will be created by the growth of GM cotton crops that are resistant to herbicides.

As a solution to these problems a number of companies have chosen to start producing basic organic cotton. Buying organic is really the only way of being sure that harmful pesticides and insecticides have not been used in the production process. Organic farming also guarantees that workers are not exposed to harmful chemicals and that their working conditions are monitored. Some organic farmers are even growing coloured cotton, which eliminates the need to use toxic dyes. If you cannot find unbleached organic cotton, look for products bleached with hydrogen peroxide rather than chlorine bleaches, which is slightly less damaging in its effect on the environment.

Hemp has been **used** to **make**:

- Sails for ships.
- The first pairs of Levi jeans.
- Writing ink.
- Rope.
- Paper – the American Declaration of Independence was thought to have been printed on hemp paper.
- Dollar bills.

Hemp

Hemp is a very good alternative to cotton and linen. A totally natural fibre, it grows prolifically – it takes only four months for a hemp crop to mature, and it can do this without the use of any fertilizers. Hemp also grows in such a way that it naturally squeezes out any unwanted weeds, thereby eliminating the need for the use of herbicides. This means that it is pretty much organic without even trying. For a crop to be certified as organic, a great many other factors have to be taken into account, but by its growth habit even non-organic hemp produces a very environmentally friendly fabric that deserves to be used much more widely.

After the crop has been harvested, hemp leaves rot down and return a high proportion of nutrients back to the soil, making it an ideal rotation crop for a sustainable organic farming system. But despite its apparent desirability, hemp has had quite a chequered history in terms of production due to its close association with the plant *Cannabis sativa* – or marijuana. Cannabis contains a much higher level of the narcotic ingredient tetrahydrocannabinol (THC) than hemp, which cannot be used as a narcotic but which closely resembles one. Because of its unfortunate family connections, hemp was an illegal crop in most of the world for nearly 60 years. But it is now starting to be grown again under special government licence in some countries, including the UK and the USA.

Silk

Silk is made by the silkworm – a caterpillar that feeds on the leaves of the mulberry tree. The worm spins a cocoon made of fine, long filaments and then meets its death when the cocoons are heated in water to separate the strands. Silk is the finest natural textile fibre and it can be dyed easily. To be sure the silk has been produced in an environmentally friendly way, buy it only from ethical and environmentally responsible suppliers who can vouch for the production process.

- Avoid buying fabrics that need to be dry cleaned.

- Keep your dry cleaning to a minimum because the chemicals used are toxic.

- Buy duvets and pillows filled with natural down or feathers rather than polyester.

Wool

Conventional wool production uses far fewer chemicals in the manufacturing process than conventional cotton. Wool is incredibly versatile, and has the added advantage of being naturally flame resistant and receptive to dyes. This means that natural plant-based dyes can be used to good effect on woollen fabrics. Wool also repels dirt, so it requires less energy-consuming washing. Its role as a by-product also means that it is well suited to an organic farming system. The simple manufacturing process required for wool products means that it can be done on a small scale with minimum impact on the environment.

When buying wool products, check that they are naturally dyed, 100 per cent new wool. As most conventionally produced wool is moth-proofed with chemicals it could be possible that people who think they are allergic to wool are actually allergic to the chemicals used to treat it instead. Look out for wool that is certified as organic, which guarantees that the sheep are from farms where no organophosphate dips have been used on their coats. Once the sheep have been shorn, the wool is washed using soap flakes without the use of chemicals or bleach and it is not treated to make it flame retardant. Most certified organic wool comes from New Zealand, the Netherlands and Germany, as these countries already have organic textile certification standards in place.

Felt, which is made using wool, has become popular again over the last couple of years. It is made by steaming and pressing wool to create a durable structured fabric that can be used on walls as well as furnishings. Flax is another green fabric option – it is derived from the same plant as linseed oil, *Linum usitatissimum*, and can be used for textiles, insulation and paper.

What we wear

Most of us enjoy shopping for new clothes but the two concepts of being fashionable and being environmentally consciousness are irretrievably opposed. The kind of conspicuous consumption associated with keeping up to date with fashion can be a hard habit to break. The well-known buzz of so-called 'retail therapy' is familiar to many of us, but only by taking responsibility for our actions can we improve the ecological situation.

As well as the amount of waste produced by mass-manufactured clothing, there are other issues to take into account, such as the welfare of the workers. Sweatshops still exist where workers are exploited to push up profits. Only by buying clothing made from organic fabric can you be certain that standards regarding working conditions have been adhered to throughout the production process.

- Look out for innovative fabrics such as eco-fleece and Tencel – eco-fleece is made from post-consumer recycled plastic bottles.

- Buy fewer, higher-quality items, which will last you a long time, rather than lots of cheap, poor-quality pieces.

- Look out for hemp clothing.

- Join a sewing class and start making your own clothes, or at least customize pieces you would otherwise throw away.

The average dustbin (trash can) contains 10 per cent unwanted household textiles, clothes and shoes, which end up being buried along with other refuse in landfill sites.

production. Companies producing recycled textile wipers are often in competition with others producing disposable paper alternatives, which use bleach in their production.

Textiles are not recyclable once they have been contaminated by household waste, and tonnes of discarded textiles end up on landfill sites every year. This is a massive waste of a potentially useful resource. So don't throw out that old T-shirt with holes in it simply because you don't think the charity shop would want it. Either rip it up and use it for cloths at home or keep it until you have a chance to get to a textile bank – they are usually situated near supermarkets and in public car parks.

We could also take a leaf out of our grandmothers' books by being a lot more resourceful. The attitude then was 'make do and mend' and although this does not sound very fashionable there is plenty of scope to be creative by reusing things you might have thrown away. Instead of getting rid of an item of clothing just because you are bored with it, try to adapt or customize it into something new.

Recycling textiles

When we think about recycling it is most commonly with regard to paper and glass, not textiles. But textile banks are almost as common as bottle banks these days. They act as a collection point for unwanted textiles, which are then sorted into different categories. Items in good condition are sent to charity stores and sold to the public, or exported to developing countries. Textiles that are not reusable are sold to merchants for recycling. Woollen garments are colour sorted and sold to specialist firms where the fibres are shredded to make something called 'shoddy', which can then be respun and used to make fabric. Rags are sold to what is known as the 'filling and flock' industry. They are then shredded and used as fillers for car insulation, roofing felt, loudspeaker cones and furniture padding, among other things.

Almost every industry has a manufacturing process where 'wipers' – general cleaning cloths – are used, including car manufacturing, engineering, printing and the chemical industry. As part of the recycling process, cotton and silk fabrics are sorted and some are used to make cleaning materials or wipers, while others are used for specialist paper

- **Donate unwanted textiles to charity stores or textile banks.**

- **Scour second-hand stores for curtains and bedding – you can often find large lengths of really interesting retro fabrics, which are back in vogue.**

- **Be creative – get out the sewing machine and make some cushion covers, for example, from second-hand fabric rather than always buying new items.**

- **Learn how to knit so you can make throws and blankets with leftover balls of wool.**

recycling

Most of us could probably benefit from a major rethink about the amount of things we consume and the waste we create. Although this section is called 'recycling', it also looks at how we can reduce the amount of waste we produce in the first place, as well as how we can reuse existing items to reduce the amount of waste going into landfill sites and creating more pollution. Reusing and reducing the number of unwanted items is more important and fundamentally greener than simply deciding to use your local recycling bins. Nonetheless, recycling unwanted items is very important and something that most of us can introduce into our lives fairly easily.

Modern labour-saving devices designed to revolutionize housework are, on the whole, 'disposable' and therefore not environmentally friendly. After all, what exactly does disposable mean? Manufacturers create disposable items so that people buy more, but what right do they have to say whether it is acceptable to keep buying sponge cleaners and throwing them away a week later? The manufacture of these items contributes to the pollution of the environment, and the resources being wasted. We can happily live without them by making a few simple decisions about how to change our lifestyles.

● Look out for schemes where you can buy refurbished white goods such as refrigerators, washing machines and dishwashers. When getting rid of your old appliances see if any local groups or charities are able to use them, rather than send them off to the landfill. The same goes for old computers, though check first whether an upgrade would increase its lifespan.

Think green

Before you even start to think about recycling your household waste, why not give some thought to ways of reducing the amount of waste you create in the first place? There are hundreds of ways we can cut down on the amount of rubbish we produce each week, such as reducing unnecessary consumption and reusing and repairing items that might otherwise end up being thrown away. We have all heard the saying 'buy cheap buy twice' and it does make sense to buy fewer, better-quality items, which will last for longer and which can be repaired if they break down – this applies to everything from towels to televisions, from can openers to dishwashers. Even better, give your next purchase some real thought rather than carelessly laying out your hard-earned cash: do you really need another salad bowl, pair of flip-flops or toy for the cat? With a little effort we can all opt out of the culture of conspicuous consumption.

An essential point to remember is that it is far more important to live in a more environmentally responsible way – to introduce changes to our everyday habits and actions – than simply to practise 'green consumerism' as a salve to our environmental consciences. However, careful decision making about where to spend your money can still play a part in a greener society. Use your purchasing power to encourage large manufacturers to be more environmentally responsible and to promote recycling. When you are making big purchases, ask manufacturers and suppliers what their respective environmental policies are, and whether they use any reusable packaging or have on-site recycling facilities for staff and customers.

Transportation and packaging

When you are doing your grocery shopping take time to discover where your food products are from – why buy an apple that has had to be transported for thousands of miles when you can buy one that was grown on a tree much nearer to home? The transportation of imported goods, with its high fuel use, adds to pollution and energy waste, as well as congestion. A lot of food packaging is made from non-renewable raw materials and all manufacturing processes cause some level of pollution. The production of plastic, which is made using oil, is a major contributor to environmental pollution. There is also a health problem associated with plastic food packaging – a certain amount of toxins can be absorbed by food in cans and plastic containers (*see Plastics, pages 42–3*).

Rather than filling a cupboard full with plastic bags that you do not want to throw away but always forget to reuse, invest in a couple of good-sized shopping bags that you actually like and will be pleased to carry around the next time you go shopping. Try to use organic cotton hankies instead of tissue paper, and cloths instead of paper towels in the kitchen. They might seem slightly less convenient but once you get into the habit of using them you will wonder why you ever spent money on reams of paper towels that were used up very quickly.

Reducing **waste**

● Buy in bulk.

● Use refillable and reusable containers.

● Choose paper packaging over plastic.

● Provide your own shopping bags.

● Buy refills rather than new products.

● Swap magazines with friends.

● Use envelope reuse labels.

● Donate items to local charity stores.

- **Take part in the bottle-refilling schemes practised in some stores.**

- **Shop locally rather than always driving to the supermarket.**

- **Find out if there are any recycling schemes or initiatives in your area and support them – some will collect any recyclable items from your doorstep for a small monthly fee.**

Landfill sites

The next time you throw something away, try to picture what will happen to it once it leaves your house – this makes it much harder to dispose of things that can be reused or recycled. Almost everything we throw out ends up on a landfill site, which basically means that it will be dumped in the ground. All of the organic matter that ends up on a landfill site rots down and produces methane gas, which contributes to global warming. Organic domestic kitchen waste should ideally be used as compost for your organic garden and vegetable patch – or even flower boxes if you are not lucky enough to have a garden. You could also find out whether there is a local composting scheme in your area. (*This is explored in greater depth in Composting: see pages 126–29.*)

The rest of the rubbish in landfill sites just sits there, creating patches of polluted land unfit for use. There is also the added danger that poisonous chemicals from toxic waste such as batteries can leach into the water supply. As we begin to run out of places to dump our rubbish, the authorities are being forced to look at alternatives. One of these is incineration. This is not a very acceptable option to environmentalists because burning plastics and other products can release harmful chemicals into the atmosphere, as well as creating toxic ash, which itself must be disposed of.

Many unwanted household items can be donated to second-hand stores, but remember that it is not good enough simply to give your old clothes and books to charity if you do not buy second-hand

goods yourself – it is crucial that there is a market for recycled goods or the whole cycle would grind to a halt. People are in the habit of believing that only brand new things are desirable, but quite often you find the most original and interesting items at car boot (garage) sales and second-hand stores. When you are shopping, look out for recycled items – there are increasing numbers of plastic, paper and glass products available and even some clothing.

Create a recycling system at home using boxes that can be easily carried and emptied. Use different containers for different materials: one for paper, another for cans and so on. Stackable bins are a good idea because they take up less space.

Nappies (diapers)

So-called disposable nappies (diapers) can make up 4 per cent of total domestic waste. A lot of parents feel that their lives have been revolutionized by the introduction of the disposable nappy – no more washing and drying. But the pollutants caused by the manufacture of nappies, combined with the amount of waste they produce, is unacceptable and over the last few years there has been a move by environmentally conscious mums and dads back to more environmentally friendly nappies. These include both the old-fashioned terry towelling nappies, as well as modern reusable ones.

Reusable nappies are shaped like disposable nappies with convenient velcro fastenings so there is no need to use pins. Some companies make paper liners, which can be flushed down the toilet before the cotton is washed. As most of us have access to a washing machine, there is no need for endless hand washing. If you have a young baby there are plenty of other items that need washing, such as bedding and clothes, so adding a few nappies will not make much difference to your wash load. Cotton nappies do not have to be boiled; a machine wash at 60°C (140°F) is good enough. If you do not have access to a washing machine there are now a number of nappy-washing services available where you can pay to have them collected, laundered and then delivered back to your door. These services are also kinder on the environment than home washing. Another benefit of reusable nappies is the money you save.

Items that can be recycled:

- ⓘ Clothing and shoes
- ⓘ Paper
- ⓘ Aluminium cans
- ⓘ Plastic carrier bags
- ⓘ Cardboard
- ⓘ Plastic bottles
- ⓘ Glass
- ⓘ Household appliances
- ⓘ Aluminium foil
- ⓘ Steel cans
- ⓘ Kitchen waste

Sanitary protection

Conventional sanitary protection creates a huge amount of waste and can also cause health problems. A by-product of the chlorine-bleaching process is dioxin, a poisonous chemical that has been linked to reproductive problems, cancer and birth defects (*see page 43*). The pesticides used on non-organic cotton can also be harmful, so the safest and greenest option is to use reusable products. This might seem like a step too far for many people, but it is really just a case of adapting – our grandmothers made do with cotton rags after all. Reusable sanitary towels come with a holder and just require washing after use. Once you have made the initial outlay of buying a pack with enough towels to see you through a cycle you will save yourself a lot of money as well as help the environment. Another form of reusable protection is natural sponges, which can be rinsed out and reused.

Many women do not know the best way to dispose of their sanitary towels and tampons. The answer is to throw them away – don't flush. Sanitary protection pollutes our beaches and can disrupt sewage systems if it is flushed away. There is really no ideal way to dispose of it, but it is preferable that it is sent to landfill sites rather than flushed down the toilet into our water system. Cut down on the amount of waste in the first place by avoiding products with lots of packaging such as applicators and unnecessary wrapping. There are companies that manufacture unbleached, biodegradable protection, so look out for their products in your local healthfood store.

Plastic

Plastic really is a big problem in society today, and it has been associated with diseases such as cancer and liver dysfunction. Plastics are made from petrochemicals in polluting factories. They do not decompose and when burned they emit toxic fumes into the atmosphere, which makes their disposal a major problem. Most people already have a lot of plastic in their homes, but it is good to get out of the habit of buying and using plastic products such as food containers whenever possible. Use a metal

sandwich box rather than clingfilm (saranwrap) or a plastic container for transporting food, and use greaseproof (waxed) paper for wrapping and storing food at home.

Glass

Although glass is created from natural materials that are readily available, such as sand and limestone, the manufacturing process for glass products is very intensive and energy consuming. Try to reuse glass wherever possible – wash out jars and containers and refill them with loose foods such as breakfast cereals or rice. Look out for stores that practise a bottle refill system, such as local delicatessens and healthfood retailers. When recycling glass, make sure that bottles and jars are rinsed thoroughly clean before you take them to the bottle bank. Remove all the lids, corks and labels, and make sure you put the right colour glassware in the right bin.

Paper

Paper is made from cellulose fibre, which comes from a number of sources, including rags, cotton, hemp, grass and straw. Most of it, however, is made from waste paper and wood pulp. By recycling paper we are helping to reduce the number of trees that are cut down each year.

Try to buy recycled paper products, such as writing paper, cards, books, toilet paper and envelopes, wherever possible. Use a big container such as a basket in which to collect newspapers and junk mail at home.

Cans

When you recycle food and drink cans make sure they are clean, then crush them. It is really important to recycle aluminium cans because aluminium is such an energy-intensive and polluting material to produce. It is, however, easy to recycle and can be reprocessed over and over again. As well as cans, clean aluminium foil, milk-bottle tops and sweet wrappers can also be recycled, and many schools and charities collect these items for fundraising. Why not suggest this to your boss or local school if they do not do it already?

- When you are buying new items be aware of the amount of packaging that they are wrapped in.

- Avoid pre-packed foods and try to shop in places where you can buy loose items sold in paper packaging or reusable containers.

- Junk mail can be recycled, but ideally you should stop companies sending it to you in the first place.

- Try using a deodorant crystal rather than your usual brand of aerosol deodorant.

- Swap old clothes with friends.

- Cut down on the amount of newspapers you buy – make sure you get only one per household and read someone else's at work.

- When buying paper products and stationery make sure that they are recycled.

- Think twice about disposing of batteries. They are a serious source of toxic waste and should not be thrown in the bin (trash can) – if they end up on landfill sites they can enter the water system.

- Batteries contain a wide variety of toxic substances and it takes around 50 times as much energy to manufacture them as they actually hold.

- Find out if your council has a facility for toxic-waste disposal, or even better, invest in a battery recharger rather than throwing out batteries.

- Encourage your family to use appliances and toys that do not rely on batteries.

- Use old newspapers for composting – when you are chopping vegetables have a newspaper handy to collect the scraps, then just fold it up and throw it straight on the compost heap.

- Keep a big container handy for recycling used paper.

- Use both sides of sheets of paper.

- Encourage children to get involved with recycling at home by turning it into a game.

- Use old mugs and plates for picnics and parties rather than buying plastic ones.

- Reuse old envelopes.

- Think more carefully about everything you buy – do you really need it?

- Buy fewer, better-quality items that will last much longer and you are less likely to get bored of.

chapter two
the gree

n house

The interior of your home is very important and has a big impact on your frame of mind and general wellbeing. Once inside the average household there are a lot of challenges if you are serious about living in an environmentally friendly way. We are so accustomed to items like wall-to-wall carpeting and mass-manufactured furniture that we do not stop to consider what their impact may be on the environment and our health.

To create a green, natural home we have to look at everything – from the furniture we buy to the energy rating of our cooker. A painter and decorator who uses organic paints told me that the biggest problem we face is being unwilling to compromise on how we want our homes to look. Rather than luxuriating in plush carpet we should consider wooden or cork floors, and instead of painting the walls a deep, vivid blue we should select a lighter shade of paint, which has been made with non-synthetic, plant-based ingredients. By creating a more natural living space using materials that are more in tune with the environment we will be able to live more comfortably and be kinder to the planet.

As well as wasting large amounts of energy, the average household is also responsible for creating huge amounts of waste. From paper to plastic – we throw out tonnes of rubbish and hardly spare a thought for where it goes. This chapter looks at what to do when your refrigerator reaches its final day, for example, and what you should really be doing with those unwanted toner cartridges.

A green house should still be somewhere that you can relax and feel comfortable, so start by working out the needs of your household and make whatever changes you can accordingly. Start small – place a recycling bin for newspapers and magazines in the living room. This will get the ball rolling and has the added bonus of tidying up the room. There are plenty of other ideas in this chapter on ways both small and large scale, to change your home. Ideally, it should be fun and you will achieve a sense of satisfaction that at last you are part of the solution rather than the problem.

Although changing habits like not throwing packaging and used tea bags into the same waste bin (trash can) can seem insignificant in the great scheme of things it marks the change to a more eco-friendly lifestyle. By explaining your actions to visiting friends and family you can spread the word and set a good example to others. The last few years have seen a bit of an organic revolution reaching as far as the design world, so there is a wide range of eco-friendly products available to help you in the quest for a green home.

Whatever you do, don't get stressed. It is not productive or healthy to start worrying about the fact that your sofa could be stuffed with synthetic foam or that your washing machine is not the most energy-efficient model. Even if you make just a couple of changes, such as recycling your paper or starting a compost heap, you will be helping rather than adding to the situation.

the kitchen

At the heart of every home is the kitchen. We all have an image of a perfect kitchen, whether it be a minimalist vision in stainless steel or the romantic dream of a cat snuggled next to the Aga, a pot of soup bubbling on the hob and a cosy chair pulled up to the range. But, no matter what kind of kitchen you have in reality, there is one thing that it will have in common with most others – it is the location of many of the home's most energy-guzzling appliances and some of our least environmentally friendly habits. So it is a great place to start if you are keen to go green.

It does not take much to make a difference – you could make big changes by replacing your appliances with greener versions or doing away with them altogether, but changing the way in which you use your kitchen is just as important, especially when it comes to water and energy.

Appliances

Most people's kitchens in the developed world are crammed with appliances. Fridges, freezers, washing machines, dishwashers, tumble dryers, ovens and microwave ovens are common even in small kitchens for just one or two people. Obviously, they have become essentials for many of us and the thought of losing them fills us with dread and horror – so don't worry, we are not about to suggest a return to the good old hand-washing days of yesteryear. But the way in which we use our appliances and the type of product we buy can still have a massive impact on the environment as does what we do with them when they are no longer working. Of the over 900,000 tonnes of used electrical and electronic goods thrown away each year in the UK, for example, large domestic appliances, such as washing machines, fridges and cookers make up 35,000 tonnes – 8 million units. So disposing of them carefully and preferably recycling them is a priority.

Fridges and freezers

Other than reviving the use of the larder or 'cool room' in your home or no longer using foods that need refrigeration, there is little choice but to use a fridge and, for many of us, a freezer as well.

If you are buying a new fridge or freezer, the single most important thing to look out for is the kind of refrigerant it uses. In the past, chlorofluorocarbons (CFCs) were commonly used as cooling agents. By 1986 a quarter of all global CFC production was for refrigeration, but once the hole in the ozone was discovered and CFCs blamed, fridge makers were forced to find a new gas.

They turned to hydrochlorofluorocarbons (HCFCs) and hydrofluorocarbons (HFCs) for the coolant and in the foam insulation, but these have now been found to contribute to global warming. HCFCs are being phased out – they are illegal in all newly manufactured fridges and freezers – but HFCs are still being produced and they continue to exacerbate the greenhouse effect.

But there is a 'green' alternative developed by Greenpeace called Greenfreeze, which uses a natural gas, hydrocarbon, for the refrigerant.

Hydrocarbons have no effect on the ozone layer, less impact on global warming than CFCs and HCFCs, are cheaper and are non-toxic. The energy efficiency of these hydrocarbon fridges has also proved to be as good as, or better than, those cooled with CFCs or HFCs – they can use up to 70 per cent less energy. The most energy-efficient fridge currently produced is completely CFC and HFC free, with an energy consumption equivalent to a 15-watt light bulb.

But if you are thinking of getting rid of your old CFC-containing fridge, do remember to dispose of it carefully – around 2,000 tonnes of CFCs are contained in the 3 million or so fridges scrapped in the UK each year. Both the CFC coolant and CFCs in the insulation foam can be removed but many authorities deal only with the coolant. Contact your local government office for advice on recycling schemes and safe disposal.

Apart from the refrigerant, the other thing to look out for when buying a new fridge or freezer is its energy-efficiency rating. Friends of the Earth recommend buying fridges that run on less than 150 kW/h annually and freezers or fridge/freezers that run on 350 kW/h or less annually.

If you are not in the market for a new fridge or freezer, there are still ways in which you can improve the energy efficiency of your current model. For example:

- Minimize the number of times you open the door: for each minute that a fridge door is open it will take your fridge at least three minutes to regain its temperature.

- Regularly defrost your fridge or freezer (especially in summer): on average a fridge/freezer should be defrosted every three months and a fridge every month.

- Always cool food before putting it in the fridge.

- Make sure your fridge or freezer is not in a sunny spot in your kitchen and is well away from other hot spots such as the cooker, boiler, tumble dryer or washing machine – putting it in a cool garage or cellar helps save energy.

fridge and freezer facts

CFCs contained in old fridges s till in use will continue to destroy ozone in the upper atmosphere for another 100 years.

HFCs are at least 1,200 times more powerful in terms of the greenhouse effect than carbon dioxide.

Refrigeration accounts for 36 per cent of electricity consumed by all domestic appliances.

■ Check the condition of the seals on your fridge and freezer by trapping a piece of paper in the door when closing it; if the paper can be pulled out easily, the seal is no longer working well and should be replaced.

■ Keep the coils at the back dust free, as accumulation of dust on condenser coils can increase energy consumption by up to 30 per cent.

■ Consider insulating around the sides of your fridge or freezer, using aluminium foil (recycled if possible), to save energy.

■ Do not fill your fridge more than three-quarters full, to allow for circulation of cold air. Many items that are commonly put in the fridge may not need to be there at all, such as bread, root vegetables or fruit cordials.

■ Keep a thermometer in your fridge or freezer to check that the temperature is kept constant – 3–5°C (37–41ºF) for fridges and -18°C (64ºF) for freezers. If your appliance is not maintaining constant temperatures it needs to be serviced.

Cookers and microwave ovens

Choosing the right heating method for the job is the key when cooking your food. If you want to reheat a meal for one, then opt for the microwave oven, and if you are toasting just a single slice of bread, don't use the grill (broiler), go for the toaster instead – both will use less energy.

Although microwave ovens are more energy efficient than conventional ovens, don't be fooled into thinking that by surviving on a diet of pre-prepared and heavily packaged microwave meals you are helping the environment. The environmental costs involved in processing the food, packaging it and shipping it to your local supermarket, which you will probably have driven to, far outweigh the benefits of one cooking method over another.

When choosing a cooker or a microwave oven, ask the supplier for as much information as possible regarding energy efficiency and environmental policies. Go for a gas cooker rather than an electric one if you have a choice – gas is more energy efficient – and look out for cookers with options such as electric grills that allow you to switch on just half of the element for smaller jobs, or double ovens, so that you can use the smaller one for everything except the family roast. Glass doors allow you to check if your food is ready without wasting heat by opening the door, and fan-assisted ovens use less energy to cook your food.

Best of all are pressure cookers and, for the really green, haybox or solar cookers (*see opposite*).

The way in which you cook is also important; don't waste a hot oven – try to cook several things at once. The same goes for using the hob – try steaming some vegetables in a colander over your saucepan of simmering rice or use a tiered steamer for steaming several vegetables at once.

Choose the right size pan for the job and make sure it has a tight-fitting lid. Use only as much heat as is necessary – if you have your gas flame licking up the sides of the pan then you are wasting energy. And don't use your microwave oven to defrost frozen food; think ahead and put it in the fridge the night before you need to use it.

haybox cookery

● Haybox cookery, or retained heat cooking, has been particularly valuable in regions, such as rural South Africa, where firewood is scarce. All you need to do is boil your food in a cooking pot with a well-fitting lid then put it in an insulated box – hay is commonly used, but you can use other natural substances such as cotton, wool, feathers or crumpled newspapers. The food will continue to cook at a little below simmering point.

● Soups, stews, sauces, stewed fruits, milk puddings, brown rice and stock can all be made this way. The box can also keep food warm or cold for short periods. Obviously it will take longer to cook this way – stews will take three to five hours, milk pudding around an hour – but you will be using a fraction of the energy.

solar cooking

Another green way in which to cook is to use solar energy. It is thought that over 100,000 solar cookers are used in India and China and there are solar cooking projects in most countries. There are three basic kinds of solar cookers:

Box cookers
These are well-insulated boxes, usually fitted with one large window in the top and an adjustable reflector in the lid. Solar cookers with slanted glass windows and multiple reflectors are another form of solar box. Both can be used for retained heat cookery on cloudy days.

Panel cookers
Four or five flat panels covered in a reflective surface, such as foil, concentrate the sun's rays onto a pot inside a plastic bag or under a glass bowl – food may need to be stirred or rotated to provide even cooking.

Parabolic cookers
These concave disks focus the light directly onto the bottom of a cooking pot. However, they can be dangerous, particularly to the cook's eyes if not used with care.

Food in a single-reflector box cooker will take about twice as long to cook as in a conventional oven, but the advantage is that you can't really burn your food, so you don't have to keep watching it or stir food continuously while it cooks. Panel cookers are better for smaller portions and often cook slightly faster, whereas a parabolic cooker is similar to cooking on one burner of a conventional stove and there is the same risk of food being burnt.

Washing machines and tumble dryers

Okay, so we could all hand wash more than our jumpers but, be honest, who wants to, let alone has the time? The washing machine has freed up millions of people from the drudgery of hand washing, and few would want to sacrifice their beloved washing machine or Launderette (Laundromat).

But washing machines use phenomenal amounts of energy and water just to keep you in clean shirts all week – they can account for around 13 per cent of household electricity consumption and 12 per cent of domestic water usage. So it is best to opt for the most energy-efficient model possible, no matter if there is an initial cost premium. Design options to look out for include eco-buttons, which define wash temperatures and loading levels, higher spin speeds that will reduce the moisture content of clothes and consequently decrease the energy used if tumble drying, and automated detergent dosage.

Other tips include buying a machine with the right capacity for your needs – if the machine is too large you will be wasting energy on your small loads. And look for a machine with a hot-fill facility that uses hot water from the household water supply, preferably gas heated and with a short distance between the hot-water tank and the machine, so that heat is not lost en route.

How you use your machine, new or old, is important if you are keen to save energy. Try these tips:

■ Do a full load whenever possible – half-load options, despite their name, will often use just half the amount of water or energy.

■ Pre-soak dirty clothes in bicarbonate of soda – this cuts down on the need for detergents and allows for a cooler wash.

■ Turn down the heat – 40°C (104°F) is suitable for most items and 60°C (140°F) for very dirty clothes – since as much as 90 per cent of the energy used for washing clothes goes on heating the water.

■ Always use cold-water rinses for the same reason.

■ Wash clothes less often – a single washing-machine cycle uses up to 100 litres (22 gallons) of water and the average family uses its washing machine five times a week, amounting to 26,000 litres (5,760 gallons) of water a year.

■ Use a magnetic ball (available from certain mail-order companies) to prevent calcification in washing machines, improving the operating life of your machine and reducing the amount of detergent needed.

■ Check out eco-friendly washing powders and fabric conditioners (see pages 67–9).

When disposing of an old machine, make every effort to recycle it. If it is still working, try to find a new owner by donating it to a charity that collects unwanted white goods, such as the YMCA; otherwise sell it to your local scrap dealer. Steel can be recycled from a washing machine, offering energy savings of up to 76 per cent when recycled.

If you do not have a machine then support any green initiatives your local Launderette (Laundromat) may try to introduce. In the future these could include using computerized machines that will weigh the laundry and calculate the correct amount of detergent and water required; using waste heat from the tumble dryers to heat the washing water and the building; and using the final rinse water from one wash in the first rinse of the next wash.

Tumble dryers are not as common as washing machines and remain a luxury for many. But if you do have one it would be worth considering whether it is being used as much out of habit as necessity. Drying clothes on a line in the garden is the greenest option, but if this is not possible, consider investing in a wooden clothes dryer (using wood from a sustainable source) to spread clothes out in a warm room and make use of radiators in winter.

If you must use a tumble dryer – and remember that on average a tumble dryer will use more energy than it took to wash the clothes in the first place – make sure you buy the most energy-efficient machine available. Keep the dryer clean and free of fluff and make sure clothes are as dry as possible before putting them in.

Dishwashers

As with the tumble dryer, once you have one you probably cannot imagine how you managed without it, but you should reassess how much you actually need to use it. For the washing-up requirements of a family of four each day, the dishwasher may use less water than you would at the sink, but there is still the electricity consumption to consider.

If you cannot live without it, then follow the usual tips – run full loads only, keep it well maintained for optimum efficiency and look for machines with the best energy performance. Stopping the machine at the end of the wash and opening the door to allow air drying will also save energy.

Remember also to be sure that your dishwasher detergent is as green as possible.

Others

There are many other appliances in the kitchen that contribute to our electricity bills such as juicers, food processors, sandwich makers and yogurt makers. The golden rule with all of them is to use them as little as possible – do you really need them or are there manual alternatives?

Products exist that help you do the same job by hand, such as a mouli for puréeing vegetables instead of a blender. And remember that while most appliances appear to offer the quick and easy option, they might not be quite so convenient when you consider the time spent setting them up and washing them out afterwards.

If your heart is set on having a particular kitchen helper then try to avoid plastic if you can. Buy a stainless steel kettle rather than a plastic one, for example, and an old-fashioned, but incredibly chic, stainless steel and glass blender.

Utensils and accessories

While these may not have such an obvious environmental impact as washing machines and fridges, given the amount of washing-up brushes and kitchen cloths that we will get through in a lifetime it is still important to seek out green alternatives where possible.

The main way to make a difference is to avoid all plastic in your kitchen. Much of it can easily be replaced with wood – you can buy wooden washing-up brushes with natural fibre bristles made from sustainable resources, preferably with replaceable heads, for example. Metal, especially stainless steel, can also be more green than plastic; look for metal sieves, potato mashers, and so on. Getting rid of plastic washing-up bowls and using the metal sink is also advisable, from a hygiene, as well as a green viewpoint. Washing knives used to cut raw meat, for example, can leave a washing-up bowl harbouring particularly nasty germs.

In your quest to avoid plastic you may be tempted by natural alternatives such as bamboo mats, but do not assume that they are necessarily eco-friendly. While bamboo can be grown sustainably it is not always done so, and there are concerns about the impact of bamboo harvesting on pandas in China, for example. There is also the pollution to consider as a result of the mats having been shipped halfway across the globe, and the question of toxic treatments, such as DDT or lindane, being used on the bamboo.

Clingfilm (saranwrap) and foil

Wrapping your food in either clingfilm (saranwrap) or foil is a habit worth breaking. Not only is the production of both the low-density polyethylene, used in clingfilm (saranwrap), and the aluminium, used in foil, wasteful in terms of energy, raw materials and pollution, but they could also pose quite serious health threats.

Soft plastics contain plasticizers, which are known to be hormone disrupters (*see page 43*). These can leach into warm and fatty foods in particular and so wrapping these in clingfilm (saranwrap) is not advisable. Neither should you opt for foil instead. The aluminium can also leach into food – particularly acidic food – and it has been linked with a variety of health problems, such as Alzheimer's disease.

The safest alternative for wrapping your food is greaseproof (waxed) paper or cellophane, which is made from wood pulp. Try to do away with wrapping altogether and store your food in glass or china bowls instead. If you cannot give up on foil then make an effort to recycle it, using it again for covering foods or taping it down under an ironing board cover to reflect extra heat onto your garments.

There will still be some areas where there is little choice but to go for plastic – refuse sacks, for example. But you should recycle them at every opportunity – if the 455 million kg (1 billion pounds) of plastic refuse sacks, along with the 20 billion plastic bottles, currently used in the USA were recycled, the need for landfills would be reduced by 30 per cent. So you can make a difference by using recycled plastic or by using them more than once by keeping a large rubbish container into which you empty your sacks of rubbish. Or better still – have a compost heap.

When it comes to choosing a set of pots and pans, you should be looking for those made from stainless steel or cast iron and try to buy the most expensive set you can afford, since they are likely to last a lot longer and thus reduce waste. Aluminium is a big no-no for both environmental and health reasons (*see box left*). Non-stick coatings on pans can release toxic fumes if they are overheated, and although glass is great for casseroles and baking, it does not conduct heat that well so is inefficient as a cooking pan.

The non-plastic message applies equally to plates and cutlery – even if you are keen on picnics or have a family of small children. Stainless steel bowls will not break when tossed over the edge of the high chair and can be taken on picnics every year. Teach children to use silver or stainless steel cutlery from an early age and wrap the cutlery in a tea towel for taking on outings with you. If you would rather avoid glasses when out and about then the greenest option is waxed paper cups – at least they can be recycled. If for some reason plastic cutlery and cups are essential, do not trash them – take them home, wash them and use them again, even if it is only for storing screws or as jam spoons.

Kitchen paper and other paper products are popular kitchen accessories, but here it is essential that you buy recycled. Choose unbleached paper if available; the manufacture of white paper requires large amounts of chlorine bleach, which pollutes the waterways downstream of paper mills. It also leads to the production of cancer and disease-causing dioxins, some of which have been found at low levels in bleached paper products for the kitchen, especially milk cartons and coffee filters.

Kitchen design

Fashion has come to the kitchen. As one celebrity chef after another appears 'at home' in their own kitchen so we become ever more aspirational with regard to the design of our own kitchens. Current fashionable materials in kitchen design are stainless steel and wood – but which are the most environmentally friendly?

Cabinets

When it comes to your kitchen cabinets the healthiest material to use is untreated wood that you are certain comes from a sustainable source, preferably with FSC certification (*see page 40*). It is expensive and higher maintenance, but it is also probably the best ecological choice.

Some of the cheapest and most popular materials for kitchen cabinets are particleboards or chipboards covered in plastic laminate, but they offer mixed blessings in terms of the environment. While they often make good use of small bits of timber that are produced in sustainable forestry, the glue that is used to bind them together can contain the health-threatening chemical formaldehyde – a suspected carcinogen, which can offgas (leak into the air) around you. Up to 10 per cent of some boards' weight is made up of this glue. Look instead for formaldehyde-free board or low-formaldehyde chipboard.

Surfaces

Kitchen surfaces can make all the difference when it comes to how your kitchen looks – be it the clean, minimalist look of stainless steel or the robust but beautiful good looks of granite. But as with kitchen units, the most eco-friendly choice will probably be wood – provided it has been harvested from a sustainably managed forest.

Wood is not necessarily the most practical choice, however. With a tendency to stain and absorb water, it must be protected in some way – look out for environmentally friendly resin and oil finishes.

The hard-wearing nature of granite or slate may be more attractive to you, but the energy used in quarrying, cutting and transporting these and other stone surfaces makes them a high-cost option in

terms of the environment. Also be sure to get granite checked by the supplier for levels of the radioactive gas radon, which it contains naturally and continues to emit.

Stainless steel is becoming increasingly popular as a kitchen surface but its production is a pretty polluting process. It is, however, incredibly durable and non-polluting in the home, plus it has a high recycled content in the form of scrap steel and can be reused relatively easily.

For a more rustic look, ceramic tiles are popular but these are often glazed with toxic chemicals and the energy required to fire them is enormous. Look for reclaimed tiles and at least you will be doing your bit in terms of recycling.

Plastics, such as melamine or Formica, are a common material used for kitchen surfaces, but they are to be avoided if at all possible, since their manufacture is detrimental to the environment and impact on our health uncertain (*see pages 42–3*).

Floors

Above all, kitchen floors need to be hard-wearing and waterproof. For the best in durability and eco-credentials, opt for linoleum, which is made of natural materials (*see page 38*). But do not be tempted to go for the cheaper option of vinyl linoleum, since this is made using PVC, the manufacture of which is polluting and wasteful in terms of energy, and it does not biodegrade.

Other green flooring options in the kitchen are cork and terracotta tiles. Make sure you seal cork tiles using a 'green' product. If using terracotta, look for reclaimed tiles and again make sure they are sealed against water.

Walls

The kind of paint you use in the kitchen is important, since steam and condensation are likely to be problems. But before you reach for conventional paints designed for kitchens, which usually contain fungicides among their long list of toxic chemical ingredients, seek out organic alternatives (*see pages 34–5*). Tiles and stainless steel can also be used on walls, especially as splashbacks behind the sink.

Using your kitchen

You can have the greenest kitchen in the world, but it will not make a jot of difference if you do not behave in a green way once you are in it. In fact, the way in which you use your kitchen on an everyday basis could probably have more of an impact on the environment than all the cabinets, appliances, pots and pans put together.

Try carrying out these suggestions and you will be well on your way to green living in the kitchen.

Saving water

If you do nothing else make an effort to save water:

■ Fix dripping taps (faucets) immediately. Around 4 litres (7 pints) of water can disappear down your drains this way every hour or so, and 90 litres (20 gallons) of water if the drips start to form a stream.

■ Fill the kettle with the correct amount of water needed for your cup of tea, thereby saving water and energy; and de-scale the kettle regularly – it will be more efficient.

■ Don't leave taps (faucets) running when you are washing and rinsing dishes – running the tap (faucet) can use 10–14 litres (2–3 gallons) of water a minute (enough for a small bath in just five minutes) and washing a mug under a running tap uses about 1 litre (2 pints) of water; six mugs the same as a bowl of washing up.

■ Save water leftover from washing the dishes or fitting a new water filter – it can be used for watering the plants or flushing the toilet.

Recycling

Whenever possible, buy products that have some recycled content, such as kitchen paper, bin bags and glassware and don't forget to do your own recycling. You can tear up old T-shirts to use as dusters; use old toothbrushes for tricky cleaning tasks such as the grater and the juicer; empty jars of pasta sauce are ideal for storing dry goods such as rice or beans; and washing-up liquid or drinks bottles with the ends cut off can be used as

---

drinking **water**

● Most of our drinking water comes from rainfall, but on its way into our pipes it can pick up whatever pollution exists in the air and on the land. At the same time, it is dubious whether expensive bottled water is any better for us than water from the tap (faucet), due to the toxins absorbed from the plastic. There have also been some worrying stories recently regarding well-known brands of bottled water, which have been contaminated as a result of poor sanitation due to heavy flooding. Because of the manufacturing and transportation involved in the production of bottled water, not to mention the amount of water bottles that are thrown away each year, it is a far less environmentally friendly option. If you are determined to buy bottled water, choose large bottles made out of glass that can be recycled.

● Filtered tap (faucet) water is a much better option. There are various types of filter available, from jugs with disposable filters to special systems that can be fitted under the sink. If you use the plastic jug version make sure you change the filter regularly, to prevent contamination by the release of bacteria and heavy metals back into the water. There are different types of fitted water filters: activated carbon, reverse osmosis and distillation. A distilling filter is the most effective, but is expensive to install. Seek professional advice as to what system would best suit your needs and budget.

---

protective cloches around young seedlings in the garden. Recycle plastic shopping bags by using them to line your waste-paper basket or take them back to the shops with you.

Instead of buying new, consider car boot (garage) sales, second-hand stores or markets for unwanted kitchen items – you will save money as well.

For the ultimate in recycling consider setting up a composting system – either a traditional compost heap or bin in the garden, or a wormery indoors (*see page 130*). You will save on bin bags as you will have less than half the amount of refuse you did before and you will see your garden bloom with the help of all your leftover vegetable peelings.

For cans, glass and plastic bottles, newspapers and magazines, aluminium foil and cardboard set up a recycling system in your kitchen or look out for a local recycling service, which gives you a recycled plastic box in which to store recyclables, which it then picks up weekly.

For more on recycling, see pages 48–53.

Food matters

What you choose to fill your cupboards, fridge and freezer with has a direct impact on the environment. Make sure you buy food as near its natural state as possible, which has the least amount of packaging and is preferably organic (*see Green Food and Drink, pages 154–65*).

Ideally, you will be able to supplement your store-bought items with home-grown goods – such as tomatoes from hanging baskets and lettuces from your window box. Even the most time-pressed among us can manage to grow a few herbs in our kitchens and the pleasures of freshly cut herbs could be all you need to inspire you to greater things in your cooking.

Clean green

The pressure on modern homeowners to keep their kitchens spotless is intense. We are bombarded by advertisements promising sparkling taps (faucets), sinks and surfaces with a liberal sprinkling of whatever spray, liquid or cream that is being promoted. These days, many people have grown up thinking that a different product is required for each item to be cleaned, and thus the average home contains numerous plastic bottles full of noxious, polluting cleaning agents.

The irony is, however, that many people's kitchens are no cleaner than they used to be. Most bacteria are killed by the application of hot, soapy water – something that is increasingly ignored now there are wonder products on the market that promise shining results without the elbow grease. And the advent of antibacterial products such as scourers, chopping boards, washing-up liquids and hand wash are not a long-term answer. There are real concerns that the bugs they are designed to kill may be developing resistance to the disinfectant used (*see box below*).

With an estimated 95 per cent of UK households using bleach and 20 per cent of these using it at least once a day, it is clear that there is going to be a battle to persuade most people to change their cleaning ways. But the impact on our waterways and wildlife, our health and our purses mean it is a worthwhile change to make.

Detergents

So you have your green washing machine and you are making sure you do full loads at no more than 40°C (104°F), but you could ruin all your hard work if you do not pay attention to the detergent you use. Conventional washing powders contain many chemicals, such as pigments, fluorescent whitening agents and silicone defoamers. But

superbugs

Using soaps, toothpastes and other products that contain disinfectants may do more harm than good. Recent research has found that bacteria that is supposed to be killed by the disinfectant triclosan – commonly used in soap, toothpaste, chopping boards and so on – could become immune to the chemical in the same way that some bugs are becoming immune to antibiotics.

Triclosan affects a broad range of bacteria and fungal infections, so broad in fact that scientists had thought bugs would be unable to develop immunity. But this is no longer thought likely.

Good hygiene practices using hot water and soap will not lead to superbugs and your kitchen will still be clean.

many of these are not even listed on the packaging; a study by *Ethical Consumer* magazine found that a typical laundry detergent has 12–16 ingredients, only five or six of which are commonly listed.

The problem with most of these chemicals is their impact on the environment both when they are manufactured and after use when they are dispatched into the sewerage system and potentially our waterways. For example:

■ Phosphates and phosphonates, used as 'builders' to keep dirt from being redeposited on clothes, can cause algae blooms, which distort the natural balance in rivers and lakes; not all sewage plants can remove phosphates from the water, so they can go through to our waterways.

■ Bleaches used in most mainstream powders can pollute waterways and undermine the bacterial action that helps break down sewage in sewage plants.

■ Surfactants, such as alkylphenol ethoxylates (APEs) and linear alkyl benzene sulphonate (LAS), which reduce the surface tension of water in order to dislodge ingrained dirt, are slow to biodegrade and can damage plants and animals. Indeed, surfactants are considered by the Environmental Detergent Manufacturer's Association to be the most toxic constituents of laundry products.

■ Optical brighteners and perfumes may be harmful to fish.

Even when these products do biodegrade they can create other compounds which may be harmful. For example, the product of APEs breaking down has been shown in laboratory research to inhibit the growth of male sex cells. Some action has been taken by governments on these issues. Italy, The Netherlands and Switzerland have legal restrictions on the use of phosphates in domestic detergents, and both Belgium and Ireland recently decided to ban the use of phosphates in washing powders.

But, as a general rule, you should seek to use a phosphate-free washing powder, with as few other chemical additions as possible. Ideally,

the ingredients should be plant based and biodegradability should be rapid. Concentrated varieties are usually a better green bet since they do not contain the non-active 'filler' ingredients used to bulk-up ordinary powders and they reduce the packaging and energy used in transport.

Liquid clothes detergents generally contain two to four times as much surfactant as powders, and usually come in plastic bottles. Liquids are therefore less environmentally sound than powders.

There is an increasingly large selection of eco-friendly laundry products available, so finding an alternative should not be hard. You could also try a device that promises to help you cut down on the amount of detergent you use. A doughnut-shaped ring made of hard-wearing recycled and recyclable polyethylene, called an Aquavator, can reduce the need for detergent by 49 per cent, according to the Fabric Care Research Association. It works by rubbing against clothes, helping to remove dirt and stains, and creating a jet of water through the hole in the middle which helps lather up a detergent.

You may also like to consider opting out of detergents altogether by using a washing ball or discs which, when agitated in the machine, produce ionized oxygen which reduces the surface tension of the water, allowing it to penetrate fabrics and release dirt. You may save on detergents and feasibly dispense with the rinse cycle on your machine (if you are close enough to stop it) since there is nothing to rinse! Heavy stains will need to be treated prior to washing (*see box, opposite*), and it may take some getting used to the lack of scent in your clean clothes, but you could always put a few drops of lavender essential oil in your wash.

Other products you may currently use in your wash include fabric softeners, stain removers and bleach. If you must use them, and you really should try to avoid them, choose eco-friendly brands, with as few petrochemicals as possible.

With bleach, you should particularly avoid the chlorine variety, since it is highly reactive and can combine with other elements in the environment to create toxic substances. Opt for chlorine-free powdered bleaches if absolutely necessary.

clothes washing tips

- For mainstream brands, a washing powder is better than a liquid, and a concentrated powder better than a standard powder.

- Use soap-based detergents, or ones with a high soap content, as soap is completely biodegradable.

- Vegetable-based surfactants are better than petrochemical-based ones.

- Use a product without phosphates, phosphonates or carboxylates.

- If you cannot do without bleach then buy a separate product made of sodium percarbonate – you will be using it only when you have to, and it needs no stabilizers (which in other bleaches have been linked to toxic-heavy metal pollution in waterways).

- Don't use the manufacturer's recommended amount of detergent – half as much will usually get your clothes clean.

- Add a little bicarbonate of soda to hard water to help minimize the redeposit of dirt on the clothes.

- Look for eco-friendly alternatives to lots of detergent, such as balls, discs or rings.

- Remove stains prior to a wash by soaking clothes in a bicarbonate of soda solution or making your own stain remover with a quarter of a cup of borax dissolved in two cups of water – this is good for removing blood, chocolate, mud, coffee, mildew and urine stains. Lemon juice and vinegar can also be applied to fruit and vegetable stains.

Other commonly used detergents in the kitchen are washing-up liquids. Again, the important issue here is the kind of surfactant used – make sure it is vegetable based – and avoid any product with synthetic perfume and colourings.

Cleaners

Open the cleaning cupboard in most kitchens and you will find a veritable arsenal of cleaning products for use all around the home. Not only do these products pollute the home environment, but when you throw away the last remnants of them they continue to pollute the wider environment. In addition, greater quantities of bleach and detergent are discharged to sewers from domestic households than from factories manufacturing them. Don't forget, too, the cumulative effect of all that plastic packaging on our landfill sites, too.

Unfortunately, manufacturers are not required to list specific ingredients on labels so you do not necessarily know what you are getting. Many products not only threaten the environment but

may also cause certain allergies and diseases in those people using them and living in the chemical fog they generate.

No one needs more than one or two cleaners at most, and you could probably get away with non-toxic home-made cleaners for most of your needs. But if you do wish to buy a particular cleaning product, go for the one without synthetic chemicals, that is rapidly biodegradable, phosphate free,

Mopping it all up

Cloths and mops come in a variety of materials, most of which do not appeal to the environmentally aware. The greenest products are those that can be reused rather than thrown away, so avoid foam mops and sponge scourers, and go for cotton dishcloths and string mops that can be washed and used again.

chlorine free, vegetable oil based, unscented, dye free and concentrated. Liquid soap, for example, is a safe option, especially if it is perfume and colour free. So make sure you have plenty of the best-quality, natural soap you can afford – it will meet most of your cleaning needs.

Sodium carbonate crystals, or baking soda, used to feature in most kitchens. It is more eco-friendly than detergents and can be used to clean floors, tiles and work surfaces – just dissolve the crystals in warm water. If you add some crystals to your washing-up water you can also reduce the amount of washing-up liquid you need to use. Washing/soda crystals are also useful for cleaning fridges, freezers and plastic containers. Plus you can try soaking stained clothing in dissolved crystals before washing it to remove stubborn marks.

When you are buying household cleaners, try to purchase them in the largest possible containers, avoiding PVC packaging, and refill small pump-action spray bottles for use around the home to save on packaging.

Home-made cleaning products

It is not that long ago that homeowners had to be more resourceful when it came to keeping a spotless kitchen and home, using many items that were already in their pantry. Such traditional methods are still as effective today for those of us wishing to avoid the worst of the chemical industry.

The following are a few of the basics that it would be well to have on hand, and some of their uses:

Salt
When added to bicarbonate of soda salt can help cut through grease; a sprinkling on the inside of a bin (trash can) reduces unpleasant smells; it removes burn marks from the edges of dishes and stains from china and earthenware; it whitens discoloured wooden draining or bread boards if used with cold water as a daily scrub; it removes fish or onion smells if rubbed on damp hands; and it cleans stained cutlery if applied with a soft cloth.

White vinegar
A solution of half vinegar and half water cleans windows, tiles and mirrors and, if wiped off immediately, it can remove dust and finger marks on polished wood. Mixed with olive oil it can polish off cup rings and other stains on wood; in a stronger solution it can be a good toilet cleaner and limescale remover for sinks, kettles and irons. It will keep

Herbal furniture **polish**

Grate 100 g (3½ oz) of beeswax into a bowl containing 300 ml (½ pint) turpentine (white spirit) and stand it in another bowl of warm water on the stove until the beeswax dissolves (be careful as turpentine catches fire incredibly easily). Or leave the mixture for a few days and the beeswax will dissolve of its own accord.

Add a few drops of essential oil – try lavender, thyme, pine or rosemary. Pour the polish into a can or jar to set. Use a soft cloth to rub it onto furniture and buff with a clean cloth once dry.

You can add a herbal infusion – try mock orange, lemon balm or sweet marjoram – and around 15 g (½ oz) olive-oil based soap (melted in the infusion once it has boiled) to the beeswax and turpentine mixture, when cool.

bread fresh if wiped on a cloth inside a freshly washed breadbin; and 300 ml (½ pint) vinegar mixed with 300 ml (½ pint) boiled linseed oil, which has been allowed to cool, makes a natural polish for leather upholstery.

Fresh lemon juice

It can be used instead of bleach to disinfect surfaces and the toilet; used neat it can remove grime at the base of taps (faucets), cleans bath edges and showers and grouting. Warm water and lemon juice will polish silver as long as a piece of foil or a milk bottle top is present when soaking, in order for electrolysis to take place. A cut lemon can remove fresh fruit juice stains and smells left on chopping boards by fish or garlic, and return cotton socks back to their whitest best by boiling them in a saucepan with a few slices of lemon.

Bicarbonate of soda

It can be added to washing powder to soften water; diluted, it leaves sinks, cutlery, tiles and floors clean and very shiny; it can be added to washing-up liquid and dishwasher powder to improve performance and cut back on the amount required; a hot strong mixture dissolves grease on grill (broiler) pans; it is good for cleaning fridges, freezers and plastic food containers; it can remove stains on garments left to soak in a solution; weak mixtures can be used on cork tiles, wooden floors and paintwork; it helps clear blocked drains if followed by boiling water; it cleans brooms and brushes; and it deodorizes trainers (sneakers) if left in them overnight.

Borax

This is a naturally occurring mineral which has no toxic fumes and is safe for the environment, but which can irritate skin and eyes and should not be ingested. Mould and mildew can be tackled with a mix of borax and water – simply spray on and wipe off, and sprinkle borax on a damp cloth for wiping down baths, tiles and sinks.

Herbs

The leaves and flowering stems of rosemary, eucalyptus, juniper, lavender, sage and thyme can all be simmered in water for 30 minutes to make disinfectants, which will last up to a week if stored in the fridge. Clean metal or pewter items by soaking for five minutes in an infusion of horsetail – combine 25 g (1 oz) of herb with 300 ml (½ pint) boiling water, infuse for two to three hours, then bring to the boil and simmer for 15 minutes before straining. Rhubarb and sorrel can clean pans (though not aluminium ones) if placed in water and boiled in them. Make furniture polish using herbs and beeswax (*see box, top left*) or rub ground sweet cicely seeds on woodwork as a polish.

Pest control

As well as waging a war on dust and grime, we all have skirmishes with bugs in our kitchens from time to time, most commonly with ants and flies. Despite their small size and relatively benign behaviour, we unleash a deadly array of toxins in their direction (and usually the direction of kitchen surfaces).

There are safer and less polluting alternatives:

● Herbs can be used to deter ants and flies – try hanging sprigs of fresh sage, penny royal, rue or tansy in your kitchen cupboards to deter ants; bay, camomile, cloves, eucalyptus, elder, mugwort, peppermint or wormwood should do the same for flies.

● Mint in particular is disliked by ants and flies, so plant some by your windows and doors to stop ants coming in or sprinkle some dried catmint across their trail. Alternative sprinklers are chilli powder or borax. To deter flies, hang fresh bunches of mint from window and door frames.

● If you have found an ants' nest, mix borax with icing (confectioner's) sugar to lure the ants out, and sprinkle it on some wood placed near the nest. This mix can also deal with cockroaches if left in shallow dishes.

● Feverfew flower heads will poison most insects on contact so bunches should be hung around the kitchen, and sage is another unpleasant herb as far as most insects are concerned, so have some dried bunches hanging around, too.

● Dried bay leaves in flour, rice and pulses keep weevils away.

● Mint and tansy hung or strewn in cupboards will deter mice, and peppermint oil was traditionally used to drive rats away.

For outdoor insect repellents, see pages 152–3.

Pet care

Most of us are crazy about our pets, but do we love them enough to care about what chemicals we are putting in and on their bodies? Sadly, commercial pet foods, pest controls and pet medicines all contain some pretty unfriendly ingredients, so it may be time to integrate your pets into your green living plan.

Pet food

With regard to food, the same rules that apply to humans also apply to pets – organic food is the best bet for the environment and their health; it should also be as fresh as possible, and appropriate for the particular species' needs. Organic certification does apply to pet foods, so look out for the relevant symbols or numbers on packaging (*see page 160 for more on certification*); the choice is growing ever wider.

The added bonus is that organic pet foods do not have the artificial colourings, flavourings and preservatives that are so prevalent in conventional pet foods and which have been implicated in a number of animal diseases. There are over 100 permitted chemicals approved for inclusion in pet foods by the European Commission.

It is best not to feed your pet on a diet of prepared food only; supplement it regularly with fresh food. Most animals will do well if they are fed on organic fresh vegetables, while some birds will thrive on organic fresh fruits, and organic hay is a must for rabbits and horses.

As with human food products, choose pet-food packaging that can be recycled or reused. This means leaving those brightly coloured, individually packed foil sachets on the supermarket shelf and instead buying food in paper bags or cardboard instead. Pet foods in cans are estimated to contain 60–85 per cent water, which means that you will probably need to buy twice the amount to satisfy your pet, generating twice the amount of waste. And when feeding your pet, avoid using plastic feeding bowls and opt for ceramic, clay, stoneware or enamel bowls instead. Not only is plastic bad for the environment but the chemicals and dyes used can leach into the pet food and harm the animal.

Pest control

Fleas are probably the number one pet pest and the cause of more chemical use on pets, via sprays, collars and injections, than any other problem. Over 50 million flea collars are bought and eventually dumped each year, leaching often highly toxic insecticides into the environment. Common pesticides include the organophosphate diazinon or carbamate carbaryl – both of which are nerve poisons and are also suspected endocrine disrupters, potentially causing cancer, reproductive disorders and various other ailments. In addition, many flea collars are made from PVC, which has its own environmental cost (*see page 42*).

There are greener alternatives, such as herbal flea repellents, but regular flea combing, the use of flea traps, washing your pet when you first see the fleas and disinfecting the house through washing and vacuuming should be your first and more environmentally friendly line of attack. For dogs, regular bathing in diluted tea tree oil or eucalyptus oil – 20 drops to 600 ml (2 pints) of water – should help you keep on top of the fleas. You could also try adding yeast or garlic to your pet's food, or cider vinegar to its water, in order to put the fleas off biting in the first place. Other deterrents include spraying your pet with citronella, eucalyptus or citrus peel essential oils well diluted with water, and putting penny royal on a fabric collar.

If you must use chemicals to sterilize your house in order to prevent reinfestation, use a pump-type spray to apply the pesticide where it is needed rather than an aerosol 'bomb' that coats all surfaces. Follow directions and be careful not to mix pesticides.

Cat litter

Most litters are mineral-based absorbents which are not generally considered an environmental threat, but try to buy ones without added scent to mask odour, as these are unnecessary chemicals. Also look out for litters made from recycled ingredients such as card and paper.

Pet health

Pets cost their owners dear in vets' bills and the environment dear in terms of the manufacture and disposal of animal medicines. So it would be great if you were familiar with green pet first aid.

Obviously prevention is better than cure, so a good organic diet and plenty of exercise is the first step. But there are also many supplements that you could consider adding to your pet's diet. These can prove particularly effective when treating conditions like arthritis or in building up the immune system prior to winter, for example. There are books that provide advice on specific herbal and dietary supplements and there are an increasing number of pet remedies in the areas of aromatherapy, flower remedies, herbalism and homeopathy.

A few handy items for a pet first-aid kit include: aloe vera gel and spray for cuts and burns; arnica tablets and cream for shock, bruises, swelling and most kinds of injury (although the cream should not be applied to broken skin); tea tree oil and grapefruit seed extract for disinfecting wounds; and comfrey tincture or ointment for healing wounds and helping broken bones mend.

Should the problem with your pet prove too serious to solve then consult a vet, but try to find one who is qualified in natural medicine and nutrition, such as a homeopathic vet.

First-aid kit

Knives, hot saucepans, boiling water and naked flames – most people's kitchens are an accident waiting to happen, so it would be as well to have a first-aid kit handy. But don't be tempted to reach for the same old chemical products; this is your chance to try out natural medicines – such as herbal remedies, aromatherapy, homeopathy and flower remedies – which are safer for you, your family and the environment.

But just because they are 'natural' does not mean they are necessarily green. With up to 80 per cent of medicinal herbs gathered in the wild and many herbs now appearing on lists of threatened species worldwide, it is important to find out where your remedy actually comes from.

Always pick the organic variety, if available; plants used in herbalism, aromatherapy, flower remedies and homeopathy may all have been bombarded with an array of toxic chemicals, unless they were grown organically. And conventional growers may ignore natural environmental conditions, cashing in by planting huge areas with a popular plant, with little care for the impact on local flora and fauna – something that organic growers are unlikely to do.

Try to use the least-processed form of remedy possible. Fresh herbs and home-made herbal teas or tinctures will have had less added to them and have taken less energy to produce than tablets, for example. And keep an eye on the packaging of the product – homeopathic tablets should be stored in glass, but can now be found sold in foil and plastic blister packs or plastic and glass dispensers. Suppliers with clear environmental objectives will make an attempt to use recycled materials and/or package their products in something that can itself be recycled.

So armed with this knowledge, you are now ready to go out there and stock up on the remedies required, or even better to start growing your own in the garden or window box!

Below are some key plant-based remedies for treating minor ailments:

Migraine and headaches

The herb feverfew is widely used to treat migraines and headaches – eat the leaves or make a tea with them. It is best taken regularly as it has a cumulative effect. Lavender and valerian may help reduce tension if this is a cause of headaches. Essential oil of peppermint rubbed on temples can suppress nerve pain, while willow bark supplies the same chemical as aspirin to help relieve pain and inflammation – try taking the tincture.

Minor burns

Aloe vera is the remedy to have on hand for minor burns. If you have a plant then cut a leaf and slice it down the middle; apply the inside surface to the cut Aloe vera can also be bought in gel form, so if you do not have your own plant, pop a tube of gel in your kit and get a tube of calendula ointment or cream while you are at it – it is soothing and especially good as the burn heals.

Stomach upsets

Camomile tea can soothe an upset stomach; to relieve nausea try freshly grated ginger or powdered cinnamon steeped in boiling water – this will also help with diarrhoea. Peppermint has antispasmodic qualities so it will help stop vomiting when your stomach is empty – again, try drinking it as a tea.

Cuts and bruises

Arnica – which is so useful that it should be in everyone's first-aid kit – is great for treating bruising and shock. Use it in ointment form (on unbroken skin only) and consider also investing in calendula and comfrey ointment to speed healing. A fresh comfrey leaf poultice will also greatly help any bruise or strain, so head for the garden.

For cuts, reach for another first-aid favourite: tea tree oil. It is antibacterial, antifungal and antiviral so will see off any bugs that might have got in through the cut. Use either the diluted essential oil directly on the cut or buy a tube of tea tree oil cream for such an occasion. Use St John's wort oil to help ease the pain and diluted echinacea tincture to disinfect the wound if infection seems likely.

Insect bites and stings

Peppermint and lavender oils are the remedies to have handy, should you get too close to some insects, and tea tree oil can also be soothing – all of them can be applied directly to the bite or sting. For wasp stings try applying onion slices or vinegar on the spot and once you have removed a bee sting you can dab the inflamed area with bicarbonate of soda dissolved in icy cold water. Chickweed from the garden can soothe a sting if it is rubbed between the hands first to release the juices.

Coughs and colds

Echinacea is a must in all first-aid kits. At the first sign of a cold, start taking the echinacea, preferably in tincture form, and follow it with elderberry tincture to tackle any flu bugs. If this fails and the cold takes hold, use eucalyptus, peppermint or bergamot essential oils in steaming water as inhalants for a blocked nose and a cough; liquorice tea is one to consider for a cough and marshmallow root tea can work wonders for a sore throat. Try to build resistance to colds by drinking rosehip tea, which is high in vitamin C.

Digestive problems

Drinking a cup of peppermint tea after meals can help you avoid indigestion, and chewing aniseed, caraway, dill and fennel seeds after a meal is a common digestive remedy in India. For constipation try chewing liquorice root, eating flax seeds or taking syrup of figs.

Allergies

Hayfever is one of the more common allergies, and millions of people pump chemicals up their nose each summer. An alternative and more natural approach is to take bee pollen throughout winter to build up resistance to pollen, to drink nettle tea, and to bathe the eyes in diluted eyebright tincture to soothe inflammation.

Hangovers

Good old peppermint tea crops up again here – have a cup when you wake up to ease your aching head and dodgy tummy. Milk thistle is the herb beloved of all serious party goers as it supports liver function – have the tincture on hand for when you need it.

It is very important that you check with your doctor before taking any natural remedies if you are already taking any prescribed medication, if you have an existing medical condition and/or you are pregnant.

Consult only qualified herbalists, aromatherapists, homeopaths or other natural practitioners for advice on natural, alternative medicines and for remedies tailored to your individual needs.

the living
space

The living space in a home should be a place for people to relax and unwind together. It will probably host a number of activities, such as watching television, listening to music, talking and eating, as well as the odd party now and again. This means that careful consideration needs to be taken so that it does not become a cramped, cluttered and unhealthy environment but one that is calm and comfortable.

The problem is that the modern Western living room is full of synthetic materials such as wall-to-wall carpeting and furniture upholstered with synthetic fabrics. Do your best to eliminate all synthetic materials in the room and create a natural, pollution-free space in which you and your family can relax. The materials you should aim to include in your living room are wood, cork and clay, and natural fabrics such as wool and cotton.

Furniture

A large proportion of sofas and armchairs were at one time made using polyurethane foam as part of the upholstery, which is a serious fire hazard. Although this particular foam has now been banned in many countries in the world, buying new furniture made from synthetic materials can still be hazardous as they might contain chemicals that offgas into the room and pollute the air. For example, formaldehyde is routinely used in the production of a lot of furniture upholstery (*see box, page 43*). Try to limit the furniture you have in your living room to pieces made using natural fibres and with natural fillings, such as wool and cotton.

Good, solid, well-made furniture will last much longer than modern, mass-manufactured items. The most environmentally friendly items of furniture are simple pieces made without energy-intensive manufacturing processes.

Car boot (garage) sales and auctions are good hunting grounds for interesting old items such as lamp shades and stands. But be careful that you do not leave with a load of extra stuff that you do not really want and that will clutter up your home until you get rid of it at the next sale.

If you are buying new pieces of furniture look for items made from timber with natural finishes, or even better, unfinished pieces you can treat yourself using natural stains and varnishes. Choosing furniture with natural fillings such as cotton, linen or hemp (burlap), and upholstery made from natural fabrics, will help to maintain a good level of humidity in the room because they are more porous and absorbent than synthetic materials. It will also help to combat static caused by electrical equipment like televisions and stereos.

If you have a generous budget there are some really interesting examples of furniture design using green and recycled materials like recycled drinks cans, but as with anything 'designer' they will cost more than standard furniture. Another idea is to visit wood salvaging centres where you can sometimes find beautiful pieces of wood which are offcuts from saw mills and that you could use to make unusual shelving with a bit of sanding and waxing. An offcut of walnut or cherry wood from a saw mill needs only

- Have a large basket in the living room in which to dump old magazines and newspapers before they are sorted for recycling.

- If you have a solid-fuel fire buy a log-making machine. This squashes wet newspapers into 'bricks', which will burn for up to an hour.

- Look for second-hand items of furniture and have them reupholstered using natural materials.

- Look for wooden furniture made with traditional joints such as dovetails rather than metal hinges.

- Visit design students' graduation shows for original items – lots of students are exploring environmentally friendly design for furniture.

- Second-hand office furniture shops are good hunting grounds for interesting leather chairs and stools.

- Check out local auctions, car boot (garage) sales and house clearances for interesting pieces. Look for furniture made from recycled items, too.

planing, sanding and waxing; it can then be made into an unusual table or even a breakfast bar. It is far more satisfying to have furniture in the room that you have created rather than something that has been bought from a store. Wooden pallets can be used to create coffee tables or CD racks. Once they have been stained or painted they will be quite unrecognizable and are certain to be the talking point of the room.

Televisions, stereos and videos

Televisions, stereos and videos in the living room contribute to atmospheric pollution and use a lot of energy. The plastic used in the production of the components and casing of electrical equipment can contribute to pollution in the room. All electrical equipment generates electromagnetic fields (see page 86), radiation and static, so try to eliminate the amount of equipment you have in any one room. Natural fibres rather than synthetic carpet will help reduce static. It is also important to make sure the room is well ventilated, as this will cut down on static and pollution.

All electrical equipment is subject to fashion and new technology develops rapidly so we are always looking to have the latest model. With the advent of digital technology there have been lots of changes in home equipment and we have seen the arrival of yet more machines to include in our homes, in the form of DVD and MPeg3 players.

● Visit record fairs and second-hand shops for unwanted vinyl and CDs.

● Use your local library to borrow CDs and videos rather than always buying them.

● Use your local video rental shop.

● Swap CDs, records and videos with friends.

In the not-too-distant future it is predicted that most households will have a central station where the occupants can watch television, check their e-mail, surf the Internet and play computer games. This will be an improvement, as long as we do not end up with one of these stations in every room of the house rather than one per household.

There is also the problem of what to do with defunct electrical equipment so that it does not end up on a landfill site. (See page 49 for information on recycling electrical equipment.) Try to have electrical equipment serviced regularly to maintain it in good working condition and always see if it can be repaired before getting rid of it.

Conservatories

If your living room faces south and leads into the garden you might want to consider building a conservatory, which is a great way to use passive solar energy. A conservatory is a cheap way to insulate your house because it acts as a protective zone between the house and the outside. It traps the sun's heat and can be warm and comfortable even on winter days – so you can make the most of the sun's non-polluting free energy.

The conservatory should be as large as you can make it and the floor should be well insulated.

Always switch electrical equipment off rather than leaving it on standby as it still uses around a quarter of the energy used when it is fully operational. Arrange the room so that you are sitting a good distance away from the TV screen and do not let children sit close to it.

Make sure, too, that it has adequate blinds to shield against the sun on really hot summer days. By adding a conservatory onto a house you are essentially creating another room which can be used in the winter and summer.

Walls

Both clay and lime plaster have good insulating and breathing qualities, which makes them ideal for walls. Natural plasters can look good as a room finish, rather than painting or wallpapering over the top. You will be cutting back on buying unnecessary items, which saves money, and you will achieve an original and individual look. Unpainted plaster can really bring out the best in a room furnished with natural materials; use different colours and textures of plaster to create a decorative finish. It is also possible to add pigments to the plaster to alter the tone and create effects like marbling.

If you decide to paint your living room, use natural paints made with natural solvents and pigments to avoid offgassing of VOCs (*see page 42–3*) by petroleum-based paints. If you use the kind of natural paint where you add the pigment yourself make sure you mix more than you need for any particular room – it is worth taking exact measurements of how much pigment you added just in case, though. The last thing you need is to have to start the job all over again because you cannot match the colour.

Another decorative option for wall finishes is to use a natural fabric such as hessian (burlap), which absorbs more noise than uncovered walls and also helps to insulate the room. Wall hangings made from natural fabrics are also good for protecting and insulating your walls. You can sometimes find rolls of retro wallpaper straight from the 1960s and 1970s in specialist and second-hand shops, which can look great as long as you do not overdo it. Try putting large sections in a wooden frame for an unusual look. Old maps, architectural plans, postcards

Green
Do-it-yourself

- Use plant-based products.
- Keep windows open even when using natural paints or varnish.
- Don't throw waste paint down the drain.
- Wear gloves and a mask when dealing with solvents.

and Chinese paper all make interesting, inexpensive wall coverings. Make sure you use a plant-based adhesive to stick them down.

For more on walls, see pages 33–5.

Lighting

When you are lighting the living room try to do it according to the different activities that take place there. For example, there is no need for a bright overhead light when everyone is watching

Make the most out of your windows and the natural daylight you get in the living area. If you have enough room, build a window seat where people can read or enjoy the view. Make sure your windows are well insulated for the winter months and use shutters and heavy curtains to block out draughts.

Use aromatherapy candles made with soya or vegetable wax to create soft ambient light and burn your favourite incense to create a relaxing atmosphere.

television. If someone enjoys reading or doing other close work such as needlework in the living room place a directional light where they usually sit. Energy-efficient bulbs come in lots of different sizes and can be used in lamps as well as the main light fitting in the room.

For more on lighting, see pages 24–7.

Flooring

The flooring you choose for your living room should be comfortable and practical. Wooden flooring is a good idea – just scatter rugs where people might want to sit on the floor to add colour and comfort. Sheepskin rugs are great because they can be washed in the washing machine. Otherwise, look out for pure new wool or felt rugs. Even better, learn how to make your own rag rugs – not the most fashionable thing but very environmentally friendly. You could also try making your own bean bags using some thick, hard-wearing fabric like hemp (burlap) filled with a mixture of dried beans and wood chips so it is not too heavy – you could even add some dried herbs to make it smell good.

Instead of synthetic carpets choose a floor covering made from sisal – a plant indigenous to Mexico. The tough fibres from sisal are woven into mats or carpets that look simple and beautiful and give the room a fresh, natural smell. If your living room gets

a lot of wear and tear and is the scene for gatherings and parties, think about laying a wooden floor as it is a more hard-wearing surface.

For more on flooring, see pages 36–8.

Fragrance in the living room

Smell is a very evocative sense and pleasant smells can help to create an inviting environment. As well as burning aromatherapy candles and incense you could make your own potpourri. Although it has a slightly dated image, home-made potpourri is a wonderfully natural way to scent a room – far better than the odd mixtures of ingredients, covered in synthetic fragrance, which you can find in some shops. As well as smelling good, potpourri can be practical – for example, certain flowers and leaves, such as rosemary, act as insect repellents.

Another good way to scent a room is to use bunches of flowers and herbs – they also add colour and life to a room. Try to use flowers that have been grown organically, ideally in your own garden – these will not cost you anything and will be free from chemical pesticide treatments. Fresh herbs in a flower display make it more interesting and add to the fragrance – try rosemary or mint. Place herb-filled cushions (*to make your own, see page 109*) on the sofa so that the fragrance is released whenever someone sits down.

> **Plants are good for maintaining a good degree of humidity in the living room. Another method is to use bowls of water – these could have flower petals, herbs or candles floating in them for decoration.**

> **Freshen up floors and keep them free of germs by adding six drops of a mixture of essential oils such as tea tree, lavender and pine to 300 ml (½ pint) water. Put the mixture into a water spray container and spray it onto the floor after vacuuming.**

ⓘ Home-made potpourri can look amazing and smell wonderful.

To make a relaxing **potpourri** for the **living room** take a handful each of:

- dried lemon verbena
- dried rose petals
- dried lavender flowers
- dried calendula petals
- dried camomile flowers
- angelica root
- orris root

Combine the dried leaves and flowers in a bowl. Sprinkle on some essential oils of your choice, mixing between each drop, and then place the mixture in a sealed container. Store this in a dry dark place for six weeks and then display in your favourite ceramic or wooden bowls.

Warming up

The idea of having a solid-fuel fire in the living room is very attractive. Socializing with friends and family around an open fire is very enjoyable. A 'real' fire looks very inviting and can act as a centrepiece for the living room. The problem is that open fires are not energy efficient and, therefore, do not really have much of a place in the natural home. However, if you take measures to maximize its efficiency and do not use it all the time, having a solid-fuel fire is not unacceptable.

Remember that domestic fuel use for an open fire adds to atmospheric pollution. It can release gases such as benzopyrene into the indoor air and on a wider level adds to dioxide emissions that cause global warming. In order to make an open fire as efficient as possible keep the chimney clean at all times.

Open fires are very inefficient and most of the heat goes up the chimney with only around 10 per cent making it into the room. You can, however, improve

Stone such as granite, slate, flint and limestone has been used in building for centuries and is still used for fireplaces and flooring. There are environmental problems associated with stone: quarrying disfigures the landscape and there are high transportation costs involved in moving such a heavy material. It is natural, however, and has a place in the natural house as long as it is of local origin, salvaged or reclaimed.

If you have a **solid-fuel** fire:

- Don't overinsulate the room against draughts.

- Keep the chimney clean.

- Use only smokeless fuel.

- Buy a log-making machine for your old newspapers.

- Don't use firelighters made from paraffin.

- Keep warm by putting on extra layers.

- Have handy a soft, pure wool blanket to wrap up in when it is cold.

- Use natural materials like wood, fabric and cork in the living room, which help maintain an even temperature.

If you have a solid-fuel fire you could add a couple of drops of essential oil to the fuel before you place it on the fire – do this when it is not burning too fiercely, otherwise most of the aroma will go up the chimney.

the efficiency of a solid-fuel fire so that it is better for you and for the environment. Invest in a well-designed fireplace with a flue, smoke shelf and air dampener under the floor duct, which brings in air from outside. Incorporate a heat-storage system to make the most of the heat it generates. Remember that heat loss is greater from a fire on an external wall. If you have the choice build the fireplace in the centre of the house as a heat store, or in the middle of the living room. Use solid masonry for the fireplace and chimney as it stores heat more efficiently than bricks. High-performance stoves have lower emissions and create more heat. They can be refitted into existing chimneys and may be a good option to a solid-fuel open fire. The best overall choice is a heat-storage woodburning tile stove, which can be charged up once or twice during the day using fast-burning sticks and will give off heat gently between firings. Avoid burning damp or unseasoned green wood, which releases a mixture of carcinogenic fumes and contributes to the production of acid rain.

Interior decoration

When it comes to choosing art and ornaments for our homes we tend to forget about whether they fit the green criteria or not. We look for original items that are often sourced from far-flung parts of the world, which mean high transportation costs in terms of pollution and energy use. Try to train your eye to look for natural and recycled objects. Lots of young designers are experimenting with recycled materials to create new desirable objects. Be original – buy what you like rather than what the interior design magazines tell you to. On the whole, ceramics, glass, wood and metal are good materials to decorate your living room with. Avoid plastic furniture and lamp shades – choose Japanese-style paper ones instead.

Even better, have a go yourself at making some organic decorative pieces for your home. Use pieces of salvaged wood to make a sculpture, try printing with natural dyes, make a collage out of old letters, drawings and wrappers, or learn how to weave a wall hanging for your living room – you never know, you might discover some hidden talents you never knew you had.

the home
office

We all spend a large proportion of our lives indoors, whether we are relaxing, working, cooking or sleeping. It is important to make our living and working space as green as possible for the benefit of our health and the environment, as the two tend to go hand in hand.

An increasing number of us now spend at least some of our time working from home. Changes in the structure of our society and the traditional family unit; the number of women in the workplace; and growing demands from men to have more time to fulfil their paternal responsibilities have forced companies to be more flexible about office working hours. These factors, and an increase in the number of people working on a freelance basis, mean that the home office is becoming an increasingly important part of our living space.

Modern communications systems such as the Internet and e-mail mean that it is now easier for people to work outside the main office. This trend for teleworking is definitely here to stay. Many school children now use computers on a daily basis and this has led to a growth in the home computer market. This section looks at how you can make your home workstation greener and at the same time a more efficient and attractive environment in which to work.

The basics outlined previously regarding ventilation, heating and reducing the amount of synthetic materials are just as relevant in the home office, where you may also have the added hazards of electrical equipment such as computers and printers, as they are in the rest of the home. A chaotic surrounding does nothing to improve concentration levels and it can take quite a lot of careful planning to create a home working space that is both efficient and healthy.

If possible, your work environment should be a separate room so that at the end of the day you can close the door and not be constantly reminded of it by the sight of your computer in the corner. If this option is not realistic due to space restrictions, it might be worth using a screen to cordon off a section of whichever room your desk is in. Japanese *shoji* screens, made of natural materials like paper, wood and glass so they do not block out light, make very effective and attractive room dividers. Another possibility is to convert an attic or shed into your home office, or even build an extension if you plan to work at home in the long term.

> **Keep the room as light, airy and open as possible to allow energy to flow and air to circulate freely.**
>
> **Having plants in the office area will bring vital energy into your work space and also help to counteract the negative effects of computers and printers.**

There are some basic principles you should remember when deciding where to position your desk. Feng Shui experts suggest having your back against a wall and making sure that you face the door as this promotes a sense of relaxation. They also warn against sitting under or near a draught and underneath harsh overhead lighting – they recommend that you use desk lights instead. Flowers, plants, colourful pictures and photographs all help to stimulate you and to counteract the negative effects of electronic equipment, but take care not to overdo it to the point where your desk is groaning under the weight of family portraits and there is nowhere to put your diary.

As with every other area in your house, it is important to keep synthetic materials and finishes to a minimum in order to avoid sick building syndrome. Carpets, petroleum-based paints and varnishes, and poor ventilation have all been linked with a variety of symptoms such as headaches and nausea. When this is combined with the hazards of staring at a computer monitor for hours while sitting on an unsuitable chair, you have a real recipe for back problems, possible repetitive strain injury (RSI) and increased stress levels. On top of this, PCs generate radiation, electromagnetic frequencies (*see page 86*) and static, while laser printers give off ozone – none of which is good for you or the environment.

Changing your habits

Working at home can, however, be an enjoyable experience if you are prepared to reassess your working conditions and make a few changes. If it is possible move your office space to an area that is bright and airy – try to position your desk near to a window to make the most of the available natural light, preferably one that looks out onto something stimulating such as a garden. Research has shown that people working in areas well lit by natural light have increased productivity, which is another bonus.

IT equipment is as susceptible to fashion as clothes and food, which explains the popularity of attractive computers like the range of iMacs from Apple Macintosh. They are colourful and take up less space on your desk due to the integrated processors, and they may even improve your frame of mind, but how green are they? The only really green IT purchase is to buy a reconditioned machine, but as the whole IT world is marketed as dynamic, shiny and new, people naturally find it hard to get excited about second-hand machines. It is, however, possible to buy reconditioned, branded and boxed machines with new keyboards and software that even come with a warranty and, as the market for these machines grows, more manufacturers will start doing the same thing. Avoid getting sucked into the marketing hype and believing that you must have the newest, hottest model. If you choose your computer equipment carefully it should last you a good few years, depending on what you are using it for.

Look out for computers and monitors that carry the Energy Star® mark, which was developed by the American Environmental Protection Agency and has been highly successful internationally. If your machine has this mark it means it has the ability to 'sleep' when you are not using it, thereby cutting energy usage by up to 65 per cent. So-called screen savers are, unfortunately, not energy-saving devices at all.

- **Make the most of natural daylight.**

- **Make sure there is good ventilation and windows that can open near to your workstation.**

- **Avoid harsh overhead lighting.**

- **Install a ceiling fan for air circulation.**

Electromagnetic frequencies

In this highly technological age, a vast proportion of us spend the majority of our lives surrounded by electrical equipment without giving much thought to its effect on our wellbeing, let alone the consumption of non-renewable resources necessary to produce the electricity powering all these machines. There have been concerns that living in close proximity to power cables and lines can increase the risk of certain cancers in children and this has led to health fears about the levels of electricity in the home.

Sitting in front of a computer subjects the user to a constant barrage of strong electromagnetic fields (EMFs) and to low-frequency electromagnetic fields (ELFs), which have both been linked with eye strain and headaches, as well as high blood pressure and stress. We are also exposed to EMFs from power cables, the radio and television, as well as IT equipment, and although there is no proof that they are harmful the amount of research is growing. You can reduce the ELFs and EMFs in your home by making sure that you switch off and unplug all unused electrical equipment.

- **Sit well back from the screen but not to one side as this is where radiation is leaked.**

- **Use natural materials to maintain a good level of humidity in the room to counteract the dry air and negative ion depletion that is caused by electrical equipment.**

- **Keep computers and IT equipment away from sleeping areas.**

- **Reduce the physical strain of working in front of a monitor by using an anti-glare screen.**

Ionization

Ions are positive and negative electrically charged molecules and in a natural balance there should be slightly more positive ions in the atmosphere. All electrical devices alter the level of negative ions in the air and too many positive ions in an atmosphere are thought to have a detrimental effect on your health and have been linked with hay fever, migraines and increased stress levels. Certain weather conditions such as thunderstorms also cause negative ion depletion and are thought to evoke feelings of irritation and restlessness.

The best way to avoid this kind of atmospheric pollution is to limit the amount of electrical equipment you have in your office. Using natural materials and making sure that there is adequate ventilation can help to minimize the effects of a positive charge. If you spend a lot of your time around electrical equipment it might be worth investing in an ionizer, which generates negative ions and is thought to improve the quality of the air. Although ionizers themselves are not very expensive, an even cheaper way to improve the atmosphere is to add plenty of indoor plants.

Static

Computer screens emit forms of high- and low-frequency radiation. This is why good ventilation in a home office is essential. Good ventilation also stops the build-up of static electricity, which is caused when weak charges of electricity cannot be earthed due to the presence of insulating materials such as rubber flooring and synthetic carpets.

You can avoid a build-up of static by using more natural materials such as wood and leather, which are conductive and allow the static to disperse. As metal is a good conductor of electricity it can become charged. It is therefore best to avoid having your bed near to your computer if it has a metal bed frame or springs.

Energy saving

Computers, printers and fax machines all use up energy so it is crucial that you turn them off when you are not using them. It is tempting to think 'I'll leave it on standby while I stop for a quick lunch to save time restarting' but for the amount of effort involved there really is no excuse in letting it run. If you are investing in a new computer find out what its energy rating is and what energy-saving features it has. Flat screens such as the ones used for laptop computers use less energy and emit less radiation than standard monitors – they also have the added bonus of freeing up more space on your desk.

- Use multifunction equipment when you can, such as a telephone/answer machine and a printer/fax machine/scanner, as these use less resources and take up less space.

- Send e-mails rather than letters when possible.

- Use a solar-powered calculator rather than one that takes batteries.

- Set up your own paper recycling system.

- Choose a company that operates a take-back policy for used printer cartridges.

- Keep and reuse envelopes and packing paper.

- Turn off and unplug equipment when you are not using it.

- Reduce energy waste by ordering in bulk.

Stop the strain

The increase in the number of computer-related health problems over the last few years should be a warning to make sure you take precautions against injuries like Repetitive Strain Injury (RSI).

It also makes sense to stop regularly for breaks – most experts recommend that you take a ten-minute break at least every 40–50 minutes. Another good idea is to adjust your depth of vision every 30 minutes or so by focusing your eyes on far-off objects. This should help with the 'blurring' that is associated with VDU work, which is caused by the muscles in the eye becoming tired after focusing on short-range screens for a long time.

Make sure you keep your mouse clean, as a build-up of grease and dirt can slow the mouse down and make it harder to use, thereby increasing the risk of developing RSI. Try to use the keyboard commands

- Take frequent and regular breaks away from your computer.

- Place a book under your feet in order to raise your knees to the same level as your thighs.

- Make sure your chair supports the curve of your back – use cushions to fill the gap if necessary.

- Place printers away from your desk.

- Look away from the monitor at regular intervals and focus on a distant object to avoid eye strain.

- Keep your desk as uncluttered as possible and make sure that it is large enough for everything it needs to hold.

- Buy a wrist rest to support your hands.

- Take up a yoga class.

Your desk should provide enough space for your monitor so you can sit about 50 cm (20 in) from the screen, with the top of the screen slightly below eye level. Curved desks are very good because they stop you having to stretch for paperwork, which can put a strain on your back and upper body.

Avoid desks made with synthetic materials such as composite boards; choose one instead from a company that uses Forest Stewardship Council (FSC) certified timber (see page 40). Furniture made from chipboard, medium-density fibreboard (MDF), plyboard and particleboard is hazardous because it contains formaldehyde, which is present in the resin binder. Furniture made from composite board is often coated with laminates, which may contain PVC to give a wood-effect finish. This is definitely best avoided as it can offgas VOCs (see page 42–3) into the room and is a major source of pollution during its manufacturing process.

Some companies are looking at alternative materials to composite board and are creating new materials for furniture construction made from natural non-wood fibres like hemp (burlap), flax and sugar cane, which are by-products of existing production processes. One of the most innovative materials is Tectan, which is manufactured by a German company using post-consumer waste drinks cartons. It is a good alternative to chipboard and can be used to make office furniture, but is not yet available to buy. Or have a desk made from reclaimed wood. If you are lucky you can find really interesting pieces of salvaged wood that cost only a fraction of what you would pay at a timber yard – and a joiner could make them into a desk for you.

A supportive chair is one of the most important items for working at home. Avoid chairs made from inflammable polyurethane foam, which

rather than the mouse. Position the mouse at the same height as your keyboard to avoid shoulder strain and allow yourself enough desk space to use the mouse comfortably. A wrist rest positioned in front of the keyboard can also help to reduce the risk of RSI – use a light touch and keep your hands and fingers relaxed. To avoid sore eyes, keep some eye drops at hand and remember to blink and look away from your monitor at regular intervals. As often as possible, move away from your screen and do a few stretching exercises or go for a ten-minute stroll.

Office furniture

More companies are now designing ergonomic furniture for the home and office. Curved lines that reflect nature and allow for more comfortable working positions are becoming increasingly popular, but if you cannot afford to buy the latest desk and chair designs there are still ways to improve your working environment.

Your computer should be positioned so that it is at eye level, to avoid eye strain by looking up or down. Try to keep your work space clear and free from unnecessary clutter. Have plenty of filing cabinets at hand so you can put papers away immediately rather than have them lying around.

ⓘ Avoid using a laptop computer for long periods because although the flat screens use less energy and emit less radiation than conventional screens they put more of a strain on your eyes.

poses a serious fire hazard. If you intend working from home for long periods it is worth investing in a good-quality office chair, which is designed to support the small of your back so that you are not slouching. The height and backrest should be adjustable and the chair should have castors to enable easy movement. A good idea is to check out second-hand office furniture shops for old office chairs and filing cabinets.

Office products

Avoid using plastic office equipment such as trays and files. Choose metal trays, which last longer and are less harmful to the environment, and wooden filing cabinets for your work. Instead of buying boxes of disposable pens invest in a beautiful pen that you love to use and that will last for years. Look out for water-based correction fluid and marker pens rather than ones that contain toxic solvents. Use old CDs as coasters for your desk and dining table, and look out for unusual office accessories such as mouse mats and CD holders made from hemp (burlap) and recycled plastic.

> Try to find natural glue made from animal products such as bone or casein (soured milk) or vegetable products like gum arabic.

Recycling

If you are working from home you have to consider how to dispose of used office equipment such as printer ink cartridges, paper, pens and floppy disks, as well as the computer hardware. There are a growing number of companies that have take-back policies whom you could consider contacting, and some of them make it even easier for you to recycle by providing envelopes for returning used toner cartridges.

This take-back policy extends to some responsible manufacturers of PCs and photocopiers, so if you are thinking of investing in new equipment it is worth making a few phone calls first to find out which companies deserve your support. If you are considering getting rid of an old computer find out

- Set up an infrastructure at home for the collection of recyclable materials using crates and boxes.

- Join a local scheme and arrange for regular collection of materials for recycling.

- Create space to store materials in your home before they are collected or you take them to the recycling bins.

if there are any IT recycling schemes in your area before you throw it out. Another option is to advertise it in your local paper or to offer it to a school or community centre.

Recycling paper

The major source of waste from the home office, and indeed the average domestic home, is paper. Household paper products such as newspapers, magazines, telephone directories, pamphlets, coloured paper and cardboard can all be recycled. It takes around 28 per cent less energy to produce recycled paper than virgin paper, and by recycling you will help reduce the waste-disposal problems.

● Be aware of your use of paper – don't use more paper than you need.

● Try to use both sides of the page.

● Buy recycled paper for your printer and photocopier.

● Recycle the waste paper from your home office.

● Look out for notepads made from recycled paper or old maps.

Although recycling paper does not save trees because saw mill waste and tree tops – by-products from the building and furnituremaking industries – are generally used for papermaking, it can certainly play a role in reducing energy and waste. Paper is made from cellulose fibre obtained from wood pulp, textiles, cotton, grass and straw. The amount of paper we use is increasing, partly because it is a very attractive material to use – it is biodegradable, comes from a renewable source and is recyclable. The problem is that we often take it for granted and do not take care to recycle the paper products consumed by us on a daily basis. But there is nothing particularly new about recycling paper, since papermakers have traditionally bought their raw materials from waste-paper merchants. What is new is that individuals and companies have now started to take responsibility for the disposal of the waste paper they create.

Set up your own recycling system for your home office. Use wooden boxes or baskets to separate the different types of paper for recycling and have them near to your desk to make it as easy as possible. A stacking system of containers or boxes for different grades of paper is a good idea because it takes up less floor space. Almost all paper that is used in the home can be recycled but it is important to keep different types separate as this will affect the quality of the recycled paper.

There are nine different grades of recycled paper, ranging from top-quality waste which can be used to make new paper, down to the lower grades which are used to make the middle layers of packing boards. Make sure the paper you plan to recycle does not become contaminated by other waste, such as wax, vegetable matter or glue, as this makes it unsuitable for recycling.

Contact your local authority to find out where your nearest recycling points are situated and whether it operates a kerbside collection scheme in your area. It is also worth looking in the telephone directory for community-based schemes that collect paper and other waste for recycling for a monthly fee – probably not much more than the cost of petrol to and from the recycling bin if you add it up.

Other options are to take your waste paper to a paper bank – usually situated in car parks near to supermarkets or public amenities. The three main types of waste paper are white, newspapers and magazines, and it should be indicated which bank is appropriate for each type. Once the paper is in the bin (trash can) the next stage is for it to be collected by the local authority or paper merchant and sorted into different grades. It can then be delivered to the paper mill where it is reprocessed into different kinds of paper. This process cannot, however, go on forever, as paper can only be recycled about four to six times before the fibres lose their papermaking qualities.

Recycling your own waste paper on its own is not enough; it is important that you also buy recycled paper. Many suppliers offer a range of recycled stationery, including envelopes, fax paper, mailing labels, files and document wallets, flip charts, storage boxes and sticky marker tabs.

IT equipment

The production of computers uses natural resources and involves the use of toxic chemicals. PCs are made up of modular parts, each of which has different components, quite often produced by different manufacturers. This makes it an incredibly wasteful and unenvironmentally friendly industry which produces tonnes of toxic waste. In a recent report on the PC manufacturing industry, *Ethical Consumer* magazine stated that 'industrial illness is three times the average for other industries'. Unwanted computers make up a huge amount of waste – in the UK alone, IT equipment accounts for around 39 per cent of the electrical equipment discarded by householders and commercial groups. A great deal of electronic equipment ends up on landfill sites, contributing to environmental pollution. The overall range of substances found in electrical equipment and the fact that many of them are toxic causes more problems.

Ideally, you should be able to upgrade your computer easily by adding extra memory or a larger hard disk. If you are planning to invest in a new computer, find out about the scope for upgrading. If, however, your computer is still working but you are unable to upgrade satisfactorily you can extend its life by donating it to a community group or a school. Alternatively, there are companies that buy and sell computers for refurbishment or spares.

Recycling IT equipment can be very complex, due to the mixtures of materials involved. This means that a huge percentage of disposed IT goods cannot be recycled. A growing number of companies practise take-back schemes whereby customers can sometimes take their old PCs back into the store and they are then dismantled and recycled. If there are no such schemes near you the best option is to contact your local authority and ask for advice on the best way to dispose of IT products.

Mobile phones

Mobile phones have become one of life's essentials and these days it is more surprising when someone

does not own one. But what happens to unwanted cellular phones when the user moves on to the latest version? Currently, only a very small percentage are recycled and most unwanted phones end up on landfill sites. There are a number of problems caused by unwanted mobile phones – the rechargeable battery and LCD screens are both toxic. Some manufacturers have started take-back schemes but there is still a long way to go.

Toner cartridges for printers

Discarded toner cartridges are a real problem, but thankfully some companies are addressing it. The surplus ink from the production of the cartridges is remilled and reused where possible, but a large amount does end up being disposed of in landfill sites where it is classified as 'difficult' waste. Remanufactured and refillable cartridges for ink jet, lasers and toner are now available and some companies claim they give a better print quality than the original cartridge. Many companies offer free collection services for used cartridges – they are also often cheaper than original cartridges. In order to be remanufactured the used cartridges have to be collected, dismantled and cleaned, and any faulty parts replaced. They are then refilled with fresh toner and sold on.

Software solutions

When you start considering how much waste the average home worker creates, the list seems endless and brings up questions about all sorts of things that you probably had not even considered before, such as computer disks. What happens to the millions of disks that get thrown out every day? Less than 30 per cent of packaged software is recycled and most of it ends up in landfill sites where it can take any time up to 450 years to degrade (source www.greendisk.com) and will eventually leach oxides into water supplies. Another possibility is that disks are incinerated and then become a contributing factor to acid rain.

There are, fortunately, a growing number of new initiatives which aim to tackle this problem and reuse unwanted disks. Most recycling schemes work by removing the information that is on the disks magnetically and then disassembling them so that the plastic and metal components can be recycled to make new toner cartridges, as

● When choosing IT equipment look for items that can be upgraded.

● Check if the company you are buying from operates a take-back system.

● When something stops working try to repair it before thinking about disposing of it.

● Contact your local authority for information about reuse and recycling schemes for IT equipment near you.

well as other items. Instead of throwing out your old cartridges, collect unwanted ones and find out if there is a recycling scheme in your area.

Lighting up your work space

The type of lighting you have in your working environment can make a lot of difference to your comfort. Harsh, overhead lights causing awkward shadows are not conducive to long periods of work. Standard tungsten filament lamps, also known as incandescent light bulbs, are very wasteful of energy because around 90 per cent of the energy produced is converted to heat rather than light. There are other problems associated with conventional lighting, too – when incandescent bulbs heat up they can cause pollutants to be released from their plastic fittings into the atmosphere.

It is a good idea to experiment with lighting your work area to make sure that you are using the right amount of lighting. Try out different levels of lighting to see what best suits your needs so as to avoid using more energy than you need.

The best kind of light on an environmental and personal level is natural daylight. Make the most of the light in your office space by positioning your desk near a window. Make sure you can pull blinds or curtains away from the window to allow the greatest amount of light in. If at all possible you could think about installing a skylight, which is an effective and attractive source of natural light.

- Turn off lights when they are not in use.

- Install a timer or remote-controlled lighting system.

- Use low-energy light bulbs for areas that need to be lit for long periods of time.

- Use less powerful task lighting instead of having a stronger lamp further away.

- Keep bulbs clean to maximize their light output.

Low-energy lighting

When you do need to have some artificial lighting there are a number of options. Low-energy light bulbs come in a range of different shapes and sizes for different fittings. One of the most recent environmentally friendly lighting designs is the low-energy 'e.light', designed by the Italian company Artemide Spa. It uses only three watts and will last up to seven years, even when used up to eight hours a day. It is also fully directional, which makes it the perfect desk lamp, and also looks good so it would be an extremely useful and valuable addition to your work environment.

Fluorescent strip lights are energy efficient but they can give off a harsh light that is far from pleasant. Some people complain of irritability, eye strain and headaches when exposed to fluorescent lights. Many old fluorescent lights have starting devices containing polychlorinated biphenyls or PCBs, which can leak and pollute the atmosphere in the room. However, considerable improvements have been made to the quality of fluorescent lighting recently, and the latest fluorescents have better colour rendering and reduced energy consumption. It is therefore wise to replace your old bulbs with the new, improved versions.

One of the most energy-efficient types of lighting are compact fluorescent light bulbs (CFLs), which are efficient, economic and long lasting, and have low heat emission. These bulbs use a fraction of the energy used by standard bulbs and last for much longer, saving you money. They come with bayonet or screw fittings like standard incandescent bulbs and so will fit most lamps (*see Lighting, pages 24–7*). They are best used in areas where the lighting is left on for long periods of time so they are ideal in a home office space and they could be used for more general lighting in conjunction with task lighting on the desk.

Tungsten-halogen lamps are a new type of incandescent light. The quartz glass bulbs give a bright, white light that resembles daylight. There are two types of these lights: high-voltage lamps which are good for general lighting and low-voltage halogen lights which are ideal for task lighting. They are more expensive than other lamps but very cost effective in the long term.

the bathroom

For most of us our bathrooms are our sanctuaries. You can close the door on the noise and demands of your day-to-day life, fill the bath, light a few candles and suddenly you are in a serene world of your own. But just how relaxing would that long hot bath be if you knew that the bubbles around you contained a detergent so strong that it is used to degrease engines? And while you brush your teeth, consider that the toothpaste in your mouth may contain artificial colours, flavours, sweeteners and aluminium again!

In fact, almost every bodycare product in your bathroom probably contains a long list of chemicals – many of which could be toxic to you and the environment. Add to this the amount of plastic packaging that comes out of your bathroom in the form of toothpaste tubes, toothbrush packs, shampoo bottles, pots of body lotion and so on, the water wasted and the power used to heat your bath and shower water, and the environmental impact of your bathroom becomes very clear. Your days of stress-free bathing may be over unless you start making some green bathroom choices.

Decor

Avoid using conventional paints for bathrooms, as these are likely to contain fungicides and other chemicals that can offgas into the room. They are often also impermeable and therefore likely to trap moisture, potentially causing damp. Instead, go for water-based microporous paint that will let your walls breathe, dispersing moisture and aiding drying. Or another wall choice is wood panelling. It can help regulate the bathroom climate if it is treated with a porous finish such as beeswax.

For floors, the choice is similar to that for kitchens since moisture levels and heat are the main factors in both rooms (*see page 65*). Natural linoleum, cork and terracotta tiles are the most suitable floor coverings in the bathroom.

The bathroom suite

As with every other part of your house, try to avoid plastic when it comes to choosing a bath, basin or toilet. Alternatives include porcelain or enamel bathroom suites, which both hold the heat of the bath water better than plastic or fibreglass. Choose the best-quality fixtures you can afford as they should last longer.

Avoid power showers, as these are heavy users of energy, but be sure to have at least a shower attachment that fits to your bath taps (faucets), as normal showers are huge savers of water (*see box, page 96*). Installing water-saving shower heads can save you even more water, and opt for an electric shower which heats the water only as it is used, thereby saving energy.

Don't go for the biggest bath you can squeeze into your bathroom – think of the water and power that will be wasted (and the cost on your heating bills) in just getting it half full. Remember that the less surface area of water exposed to air the less heat that will be lost, so go for a short but deep bath tub if possible. In fact, you could dispense with a bath altogether – a shower will do the job and save you acres of space, too.

Your taps (faucets) should ideally be low flow and sensor controlled, turning on only when your hands or toothbrush are beneath them. But if these are

beyond your budget, choose mixer taps, which use a minimum amount of water to get the right temperature. Spray taps save water, too.

When it comes to toilets the golden rule is to choose low-flush models, as toilets use the most amount of water in the home (54 litres [90 pints] per person each day; 33 per cent of all household water use). New toilets are now required to use no more than 7.5 litres (13 pints) of water in their cisterns, but most existing toilets use at least 9.5 litres (16 pints), if not more. Look for a valve flush, rather than the less water-efficient siphon flush, and check out the latest models, some of which have 6.5 or even 3.75 litre (11 or 6 pint) cisterns. There are also dual-flush models that allow you to choose how much water you need for each flush. The cisterns can be bought separately and fitted to your existing toilet.

For the determinedly green, there is no better option than the compost toilet. This uses no water and creates a valuable garden fertilizer out of your waste. Contrary to popular belief, compost toilets are not smelly if they are properly looked after and you can now buy compost toilet systems specifically designed for domestic properties.

Finally, say 'no' to a bidet. They are not really necessary and will waste yet more water when a shower would do the job just as well.

Water-saving tips for the bathroom

- Don't have a bath or shower just to wash your hair and remember you do not need to wash your hair every day – in fact it is better for your hair if you don't.

- Have showers rather than baths – a bath uses around 170 litres (37 gallons) of water compared with 80 litres (18 gallons) for a five-minute shower, so if you had a shower every two days instead of a bath, over a year you would save 17,000 litres (3,740 gallons) of water. In addition, a shower uses only 40 per cent of the hot water needed for a bath.

- Get leaking taps (faucets) fixed as soon as possible, as up to 4 litres (7 pints) of water can disappear down your sink every hour this way. A dripping hot tap (faucet) can waste 31 hot tanks of water each year.

- Find out if you have a leaking toilet cistern by putting vegetable dye in the water. If it appears in the toilet bowl without flushing, you know there is a leak, which needs to be fixed straight away.

- Recycle a plastic water bottle by filling it with water and putting it in your toilet cistern. It will fool the cistern into thinking it is full and therefore save on water use.

- Flush your toilet less. One-third of an average family's water use is flushed down the toilet – the equivalent of two baths of water per day. If you are the only one in the house do you really need to flush it every time?

- Investigate water-saving systems – there are various ways of collecting rainwater for use in your toilet and saving greywater from your bath for use in the garden. You will probably need advice from experts on the best system for your needs.

- Make use of the water in your bathroom air by growing humidity-loving plants in your bathroom, such as ferns.

- Turn the tap (faucet) off! Leave it running while you brush your teeth and you could be wasting 4.5 litres (8 pints) of water.

Bath and shower accessories

The look of your bathroom is defined by the accessories – a truly green bathroom will have no plastic in sight and the accessories (and those that are only absolutely necessary) will all be made from natural materials, such as wood.

So resist the urge to use a plastic shower curtain and have a glass screen instead. Don't buy a plastic non-slip bathmat unless you are really unsteady on your feet or have small children, and don't clutter up the place with a lot of unnecessary plastic soap holders, plastic storage boxes and plastic toothbrush holders. If you really do need all of these bits and pieces seek out those made of sustainable materials. Otherwise opt for items made out of stainless steel, which can be recycled and is, incidentally, very fashionable.

Use a flannel (wash cloth) rather than a sponge. Real sponges are taken from the sea disturbing precious natural habitats, whereas artificial sponges are another product of the plastics industry. Cotton flannels (wash cloths), preferably organic and unbleached, can be washed time and again, and used around the house for other cleaning tasks when they are past their best.

Unbleached, organic cotton towels are the most eco-friendly and if you have linoleum flooring you may want to look out for organic cotton bathroom rugs as well. Or make your own bathroom mat by sewing together the best bits of old towels or by gluing leftover cork tiles onto a piece of hardboard.

For scrubbing under your nails, reaching the middle of your back or giving your skin an all-over brushing to help detoxify, choose wooden brushes with natural-fibre bristles. Check that the wood comes from a sustainable source – likewise for toilet brushes. You can also buy wooden duckboard-style slatted mats for stepping onto when you get out of the bath. As always, check the source of the wood before you buy.

Avoid plastic in other areas of your bathroom, too. Don't buy disposable plastic razors – use metal ones with replaceable but durable blades, or an electric shaver. Look out for recycled plastic tooth-brushes – now available in the USA made from yogurt pots – and make the effort to recycle your toothbrushes. An old toothbrush makes a great cleaning aid for hard-to-reach areas around your taps, on bicycle chains and under your nails.

And, although it is not strictly an accessory – more of an essential item – when it comes to toilet paper there is no excuse for buying anything other than recycled paper. The quality and softness are now the equal of most other papers.

Health tip

If your skin is dry and flaky, and your hair dull and lifeless, it could be due to the chlorine in your water. Chlorine is commonly added to water supplies. You can absorb it through your skin and, as the water is heated, it can give off vapours that you then breathe into your lungs. It has been estimated that during an average shower you absorb as much chlorine as you would by drinking eight glasses of chlorinated water.

You can remove the chlorine from the water in your shower by fitting a dechlorinating shower filter. Alternatively, remove it from all water in your house by using a whole-house water purifier.

Green cleaning tips

Here are some green solutions to a few of those tricky cleaning challenges in the bathroom:

Limescale on taps (faucets): rub with half a lemon, rinse thoroughly and dry.

Limescale on tap (faucet) nozzles: tie an old plastic bag filled with white vinegar around the ends of your taps (faucets) until the scale is dissolved, then rinse.

Blocked shower head: remove the head and soak it in a bowl of warm, neat vinegar. A needle will help clear blocked holes.

Hard-water deposits in toilet bowl: apply a paste of borax and white vinegar, leave for a few hours, then rinse.

Hard-water deposits on shower doors: wipe with white vinegar, leave for 30 minutes, then rinse.

Mildew on shower curtains: prevent mildew by soaking curtains in salted water before hanging, and scrub with a bicarbonate of soda paste and water, then rinse.

Mould around shower: wash down with borax and do not rinse – the borax residue will fight mould growth.

Fungus on tile grouting: apply a paste of bicarbonate of soda and water, leave for an hour, then rinse with warm water.

Bath stains: light stains can be treated by rubbing with cut lemon dipped in salt, darker stains should be removed by applying a paste of borax and lemon juice – leave for an hour, then rinse.

Drip marks in a bath: rub with warm vinegar, then rinse with warm water. Repeat this daily until they disappear.

Energy-saving tips

- If you have a problem with condensation in your bathroom then you will need to consider ventilation. The most eco-friendly way of airing your bathroom is obviously to open the window, but if feeling a draught around your ankles while you stand in the shower does not appeal then you will almost certainly require an extractor fan.

- To save energy, it is best to use a wind-operated fan in your window that draws air out of the house using the difference in pressure alone. If you do not have a convenient window then you are likely to need, or already have, an electric extractor fan. Often these come on automatically when you switch on the bathroom light, but to save energy install a second light in the bathroom, say above the mirror, which can be switched on without the extractor fan going on as well. You can use this light when you are just brushing your teeth or putting on your make-up – use the main light (with the extractor) only when you are having a bath or shower.

- Finally, you will want to be sure that the bathroom door is well draught-proofed to prevent all your valuable, centrally heated, warm air being drawn out along with the condensation.

Bodycare

Today bodycare means big business. There are products aimed at the moisturizing, cleansing, toning and all-out pampering of almost every part of your body, and men are now just as well catered for as women. But behind the alluring promise of beauty lies the ugly reality of thousands of chemicals polluting the environment, millions of plastic bottles sitting in landfills, and the earth becoming ever more depleted of diminishing resources. So if you want to make a world of difference in one quick and easy step, make sure you buy only what is absolutely necessary and always check that it is as natural as possible. But beware: the term 'natural' is used somewhat loosely in the bodycare world; in many countries very few ingredients need to be natural for this term to be applied to a product.

What you should be looking for are ingredients that are plant based, rather than petroleum based, since these are theoretically sustainable, non-polluting and better for our health (see box, page 100). It is also advisable to avoid as many manufactured chemicals as possible, which come in the form of fragrances, preservatives, detergents, chelating agents, thickening agents, colorants, antimicrobials, emulsifiers, and even UV absorbers to stop the chemical dyes in some products from fading in the sunlight (i.e. chemicals to protect chemicals!)

Bodycare products are notorious for their long list of bewildering ingredients, so it can be hard to distinguish which are good or bad among them. Read as much as you can on the subject (see Further Reading, pages 184–5) and, if in doubt, choose the product with the least number of ingredients of any kind.

Always choose certified organic bodycare products or products that at least contain organic ingredients. Again, beware of the hype here – the term 'organic' can be freely used on bodycare product labels in many countries without it meaning anything at all. Look for certification of individual ingredients as a guarantee that they were grown organically and check what percentage of the product contains these ingredients. In the future you may also be able to purchase organically certified bodycare products rather than just those that have some organic ingredients – standards are currently being developed in the UK, for example.

Finally, try to avoid using as much packaging as possible. Aim to bulk buy, refill and recycle at every opportunity. You will then reduce waste and save yourself some money, too, while you are at it. And make sure that you let those manufacturers that consistently overpackage their products know that this is one of your reasons for no longer buying the product.

ⓘ Over 3,000 chemicals are registered with the European Commission for use in cosmetic and beauty products.

Health hazards

- The chemicals in most bodycare products are not just putting an unnecessary strain on the environment; they are also putting our health under pressure. Our skin absorbs around 60 per cent of what is put on it – hence the success of Hormone Replacement Therapy (HRT) and nicotine patches – so in a year the average woman is estimated to have absorbed up to 2 kg (4 lb) of chemicals from bodycare products. While there are government bodies assessing the risk from these chemicals, they are usually looked at in isolation or in the formulation used in the product, so the potential risk from the reaction of chemicals from one product with those from another is being overlooked. The net result can range from allergies to cancer.

- The list of risky ingredients is long and instantly forgettable unless you have an aptitude for chemical names; inadequate labelling also makes their detection in a product difficult. So the best approach is to avoid as many synthetic chemicals as possible – you can do this either by making your own products or buying 100 per cent plant-based products that have no added chemicals.

Green buying guidelines

Soap

Buy your soap in bars rather than bottles and save leftover scraps – they can be put in a jar with boiling water to create a soapy liquid for use elsewhere or can be stuck onto the next bar. You really do not have to buy conventional chemical-laden soaps these days; natural, handmade, vegetable-oil soaps are widely available. Look for those that use essential oils and herbs for fragrance and therapeutic value or bran and seeds for a good scrub. Alternatively, you could give ground soapnut a try. Derived from a tree grown in India and used there for thousands of years, soapnut can be used for washing more than just your body – it can be used for cleaning clothes and even the car!

Bathtime

A plethora of products claim to offer relaxation or invigoration with the addition of essential oils, but most of them have too few oils of too low a standard to offer any real therapeutic benefits. In addition, their main ingredients will undoubtedly be detergents, foaming agents and preservatives. Go for bath oils instead by either mixing your own (*see page 103*) or buying them from a reputable source, such as a healthfood store. (Remember that vegetables, nuts and essential oils can be certified as organic, so pick these if available.) The bonus of using essential oils is that many are natural preservatives – just remember to keep them stored away from sunlight, preferably in dark glass bottles. Bath salts are another green alternative – try Epsom salts for swollen ankles and volcanic mineral salts for muscular aches and pains.

Powder

Don't use talcum powder after your bath – in recent years it has been linked with female reproductive cancers and it could be contaminated with asbestos fibre. If you need to use powder choose cornflour (cornstarch) products instead.

Haircare

Shampoos, conditioners, dyes and other treatments are packed full of synthetic chemicals that place a heavy burden on our sewage system and our health. Don't be tempted by offers of gleaming, shiny locks; instead cut back on your hair products consumption. You do not need much shampoo to clean your hair and you do not need to wash your hair every day. Try making your own products using organic herbs and essential oils (see pages 103–4) or look for natural products from healthfood stores.

Toothpaste

Avoid pump-action toothpaste tubes first of all – these contain even more plastic than regular tubes. Next take a look at the ingredients. Do you really want to put petrochemicals, artificial sweeteners and flavours in your mouth? And just how important are those green stripes, because they are achieved only by the addition of artificial colours (some of which should be avoided if you are concerned about hyperactivity in your children).

Natural vegetable-based alternatives abound and there is even an organic standard for toothpaste in the UK – the first non-food product in the world to be accorded legal organic status. Some natural products contain fluoride and the detergent and foaming agent sodium lauryl sulphate, so check the ingredients panel if you want to avoid these.

For the ultimate green toothpaste, go back to the good old days, when canned bicarbonate of soda was routinely used (see page 104).

Facial care

Cleanse, tone and moisturize – the three magic steps to fabulous skin are drummed into most women from an early age, but try to keep it simple. Use home-made products as much as possible (see page 102); otherwise choose the least packaged, and least complex product you can find. Shop in healthfood stores or the increasing number of specialist natural bodycare stores for natural products that make minimal use of petrochemicals and other toxic chemicals.

Don't be fooled into thinking that the latest chemical ingredient is going to wipe your face free of wrinkles – nothing can do that, other than cosmetic surgery! Instead the chemical could agitate sensitive skin and will have wasted energy and possibly created pollution in its manufacture.

Shaving

Aerosols are still prevalent in this area, but these should be avoided at all costs due to their use of propellants. The best option is to do away with shaving foam or gel altogether and just use soap and water, but if you feel you need more, choose a plant-based product, preferably as a cream in a bowl, which you lather yourself with a brush (made of sustainable wood and natural bristles). Look out for refillable bowls to save even more on packaging.

Anti-perspirants and deodorants

Again these are still commonly sold in aerosol form – a real environmental baddie. There are also health concerns about the impact of using anti-perspirants which prevent your body sweating on a regular basis, especially those with aluminium as an ingredient. There are natural alternatives, like mineral rock crystal deodorants. If you do buy a conventional product, look for plant-based ingredients and choose a roll-on to save packaging.

Eyes

Contact lens solutions clutter up many people's bathrooms, with a huge cost in terms of waste packaging. If you wear lenses choose the simplest possible lens-care system available and buy in bulk. Best of all, go back to glasses!

Sanitary protection

With most sanitary protection the main environmental issue is how it is disposed of. Flushing a tampon or sanitary towel down the toilet is the worst thing you can do, since it may well end up bobbing up and down next to you when you next take a dip in the sea. The other environmental concerns come from the materials used – cotton and plastic mostly – so do your best to avoid non-organic, bleached cotton products and choose the brand with the least amount of plastic packaging; in particular avoid individually wrapped towels. Green options include rubber cups and natural sponges for non-disposable solutions. (See also page 52.)

For information on cosmetics, nail varnish and perfume see Bedrooms, pages 114–16.

Do-it-yourself bodycare

It is infinitely cheaper and less worrying to make your own bodycare products – you can then be sure of exactly what is in them. You do not need many ingredients and if you have your own herb patch or window boxes you may have most of your ingredients already. Here follows some home-made preparations to start off with.

Note: If you are pregnant, suffering from high blood pressure or a heart condition, or if you are taking regular medication, check first with your doctor or a qualified herbalist or aromatherapist before using essential oils or herbal extracts or supplements. Always do a patch test first to test for an allergic reaction and remember, a balanced organic diet, plenty of water, rest and relaxation will do more for your skin, hair, eyes, teeth and general good health than any product in the world.

Skin creams and lotions

■ Assess the type of skin you have and experiment with some of these herbs: lemon grass, witch hazel, elderflower and sage for oily skins; comfrey, rose and camomile for dry skin; and coltsfoot, borage and fennel for sensitive skin.

■ Make a cleanser by pouring a cup of boiling water over 4 tsp of your dried herb of choice. Leave it to stand for 10–15 minutes, then add 2 tsp of the herbal infusion to 1 tsp honey and 1 tsp almond oil (which should have been warmed in order to dissolve the honey). This can be rubbed on the face and then rinsed off with warm water.

■ A cleansing milk for dry skin can be made by gently heating half a cup of full-fat milk with 2 tbsp camomile flowers for 30 minutes. Cool for two hours, strain and keep in the fridge for up to a week.

■ To cleanse dry skin, blend half a small pot of natural yogurt with ½ tbsp lemon juice and 1 tbsp almond oil until smooth.

■ Cotton wool soaked in cold milk can be used as a gentle but effective make-up remover, as can sweet almond oil.

■ Mix 300 ml (½ pint) milk with some puréed cucumber and use it as cleanser for oily skin. It will keep in the fridge for three days.

■ Oily skin will also benefit from regular gentle exfoliation. Try a daily scrub with a handful of bran, oatmeal or cornmeal.

■ Mix 1 tsp cider vinegar with a herbal infusion to make a great toner. Keep it in the fridge and dab it on with cotton wool or spray it on your face. Herbs to try include yarrow, sage, mint and fennel.

■ Give tired skin a lift by steaming your face over a bowl of hot water infused with two handfuls of fresh herbs such as borage, calendula, comfrey and nettle. Cover your head in a towel to keep in the steam and stay put for five minutes. (Don't do this if you suffer from flushing or thread veins.)

■ Natural yogurt can be blended with finely ground oatmeal and a herbal infusion to make a face mask. Mix the herbal infusion with 2 tbsp yogurt and then add enough oatmeal to make a paste. Oatmeal can also be used to soften the skin – soak a handful of oats overnight then use the strained liquid as a face rinse in the morning.

■ Another nourishing face mask can be made by beating the white of an egg, applying it to the skin and leaving it to dry before washing it off with warm water. Add 1 tbsp honey or 1 tsp olive oil to the frothy mixture if you have dry skin and 1 tsp lemon juice if you suffer with oily skin.

■ The yolk of one egg left overnight in a hole made inside half a lemon can be applied to the face and left for 15 minutes before rinsing. It will cleanse and tone your skin.

■ For sensitive skin try mixing 2 tbsp bran with 1 tsp runny honey and 3 tbsp of a camomile infusion. After ten minutes rinse the mask off with more camomile infusion.

■ Try applying a good-quality mayonnaise on your face at night to help combat fine lines and wrinkles.

■ Another kitchen moisturizer can be made by blending a ripe avocado with 1 tsp honey, ½ tsp lemon juice and enough natural yogurt to make a stiff cream. Once cool it can be applied and left on the face for a few hours.

Baths

■ Use three or four herbal tea bags or wrap some loose herbs in a muslin (cheesecloth) square and hang it beneath the running hot tap (faucet) to make a herbal bath infusion. Herbs to try include: camomile, lavender, valerian and hops for relaxation; lemon verbena, basil, bay and pine for stimulation; calendula, comfrey and yarrow for healing; and clove, cinnamon, thyme or ginger to boost circulation in winter. Squeeze the tea bag or muslin gently underwater to encourage the essences to be released.

■ Powdered full-fat milk can help soften the skin: put 3 tbsp in a muslin (cheesecloth) bag and put it in your bath while you are running the water. You can also add herbs to the bag – try using 125 g (4 oz) of fresh elderflower, camomile, rose petals, sage or lemon balm.

■ Make your own bath oils by adding a few drops of essential oil to a quarter of a cup of carrier oil such as sweet almond oil or apricot oil. Try lavender for soothing, jasmine for relieving tiredness, and sage to ease anxiety. You can also add a few drops of essential oil directly to the running water in your bath or mix it into a paste with milk powder first. However, some essential oils can be dangerous, so do not use them if you are pregnant or suffer from high blood pressure without consulting a qualified aromatherapist or a doctor. Always read the label and use only the recommended drops.

■ Make your own herbal oil by infusing the herb of your choice in almond oil on a sunny window ledge for a couple of weeks. Use it in your bath and in the kitchen!

■ If you shower rather than bath, you can still reap the benefits of naturally scented products. Either add a few drops of essential oil to a neutral shower gel, or make up an oil solution as for a bath and pour a small quantity onto a flannel (wash cloth) and rub it vigorously over your body.

■ Exfoliating your skin will help you get the most benefit from your herbal or essential oil bath – try rubbing sea salt mixed with a little water over your body, or brushing the dry skin with a natural bristle brush. You can even use the rice bran or oatmeal that has been soaking under the hot tap (faucet) in your herbal bag – take it out halfway through your bath and rub it on your moist skin.

■ For irritated skin and aching muscles try adding a cupful of cider vinegar to the bath.

Haircare

■ Cider vinegar in warm water applied daily to the scalp can help combat dandruff. Another dandruff treatment is to rub lemon juice into hair roots and scalp.

■ Identify the herbs that best suit your hair type – lavender, rose and rosemary for normal hair; burdock, elderflower, parsley and sage for dry hair; calendula, lemon balm, mint, sage and yarrow for greasy hair; comfrey, nettle and willow bark for dandruff; horsetail, rosemary, nettle and sage for lifeless hair.

■ Give your hair a home made herbal boost by adding a herbal infusion to the mildest, least chemical shampoo you can find. Make the infusion by steeping 6 tbsp fresh herbs or 3 tbsp dried herbs in half a cup of boiling water for ten minutes. Then, every time you wash your hair, add 1 tbsp of infusion to 4 tbsp of the base shampoo.

■ Make your own shampoo by pouring 600 ml (1 pint) of boiling water over 25 g (1 oz) dried soapwort root. Let it steep for 12 hours, then bring the mixture to the boil and simmer for 15 minutes. Remove the pan from the heat, add 25 g (1 oz) of your chosen herb, cover and cool. Strain the mixture and keep in the fridge for up to four days.

■ Use herbal infusions to make an after-wash rinse. Add 1 tbsp of the infusion to 1 tbsp lemon juice or cider vinegar before adding 600 ml (1 pint) warm water. Try camomile or yarrow if you are blonde; lavender, nettle or rosemary if you are dark; calendula or witch hazel if you are auburn; and mint or sage if you are brunette.

■ If blonde, try a cold tea or diluted lemon juice rinse; if brunette, try diluted malt vinegar.

■ Make your own hot oil conditioner using almond or apricot oil into which you can add either 2 tsp of your herbal infusion or a few drops of an essential oil such as tea tree oil, which is especially good for treating dandruff. Heat the mixture gently, before carefully massaging it into your scalp and wrapping your head in a hot, damp towel. Wait for at least an hour before washing off to allow the treatment to work.

■ Mayonnaise can also be applied to the hair, left for an hour and then washed off, followed by a cider vinegar rinse, to recondition dry hair.

■ Comb rosemary hair oil through your hair prior to washing if your dark hair needs some shine. Mix 2 tbsp of strong rosemary infusion with 6 tbsp almond oil and 30 drops of lavender oil.

Teeth

■ Bicarbonate of soda makes a great toothpaste. Just mix 1 tsp with a few drops of peppermint essential oil and enough water to make a paste.

■ Oil of cloves has been used for years to help ease toothache. Apply a few drops to sore gums.

■ If you have any sage in the garden, try giving your teeth and gums a polish by rubbing a sage leaf over them. Sage tea is also good as a mouthwash for ulcers and bleeding gums.

■ Herbal infusions can be used as mouthwashes. Start with a mint and rosemary recipe – add 1 tsp fresh mint and the same quantity of fresh rosemary and aniseed to 600 ml (1 pint) boiling water. Steep for 20 minutes, strain, cool and then use as a gargle.

■ To remove stains on teeth try dipping your toothbrush in lemon juice and some sea salt and brushing as normal, but remember to rinse thoroughly. Or rub the wet side of half a lemon over your teeth (strawberries can also be used in this way).

■ Try chewing on some fresh parsley to sweeten your breath.

■ Keep your lips smooth with a home-made lip balm. Gently melt 1 tsp of beeswax in a baine-marie and add 1 tsp each of apricot and calendula oil, stirring constantly. Remove the mixture from the heat and add a few drops of orange or lemon essential oil when it has partly cooled. Pour into a jar or small pot to set.

Eyes

■ Refresh tired eyes by placing a damp used tea bag over each eye for ten minutes, then rinse with cold water. You can use regular tea bags, or try camomile or rosehip bags.

■ The herb eyebright can help soothe sore, strained eyes and give relief from hayfever symptoms. Try boiling 2 tbsp fresh herb or 2 tsp dried herb in two cups of water for 20 minutes. Cool and thoroughly filter the solution three times through a coffee filter paper before using in an eye bath.

Babies in the bathroom

From ducks in the bath to baby lotion in the cabinet, the arrival of a baby brings many new products into a bathroom, but which are the greenest?

Toys

Plastic ducks, boats and cups litter most children's baths, but the best option is to avoid plastic altogether. Failing that, look out for toys that are PVC free as the dangerous chemicals in PVC can leach into your baby if these toys are chewed regularly. The best option of all is to think creatively about what is already in your home – recycle plastic yogurt pots to make water scoops, for example.

Bodycare

Baby skincare is big business, and most products sell themselves as being the gentlest available. But if you take a look at the ingredients they often contain a long list of chemicals which are bad for the environment and completely unnecessary for babies.

Baths are fun and can help babies to relax before they go to bed, but most babies do not need bathing daily because they are not terribly dirty. Therefore, detergents and other strong cleaning agents are unnecessary. A splash around in lukewarm water will suffice or, as your baby gets older, you can use a natural olive-oil based soap or one of the increasing number of natural products for babies – but be sure to check the ingredients lists and look out for organic ingredients.

Equally, there is no need for special lotions and powders to care for your baby's skin, unless it is especially dry or if your child suffers from a particular problem such as eczema. In these cases seek out natural, plant-based products such as organic almond oil for dry skin. To heal nappy (diaper) rash, review how often you are changing nappies and let your baby go nappy free for as long as possible.

Nor is there a need for chemically saturated wipes in order to cleanse a baby's bottom when you are changing a nappy. Some warm water on organic cotton wool will do the job just as well, or make your own wipes using organic or undyed cotton squares (which can be bought from some cloth nappy companies). They can be dipped in a home-made solution of 50 ml (2 fl oz) distilled water mixed with 1 tbsp vinegar, 2 tbsp aloe vera gel, 1 tbsp calendula oil and a few drops of lavender and tea tree essential oil.

Nappies (diapers)

Your choice of nappy (diaper) can make a big difference to the environment. Disposable nappies can take between 200 and 500 years to decompose and in so doing they can emit noxious methane gas into the environment. They also contain all sorts of chemicals such as bleaches, perfumes, plastic and additives, which are not great for the environment either. In addition, 7 million trees are felled annually to meet the demand for the absorbent pulp in disposable nappies and some of these trees are from mature forests in Scandinavia, Canada and the Baltic States, rather than sustainably managed plantations.

There are plenty of alternatives to disposable nappies, including real washable nappies, nappies with a disposable inner liner and a washable outer, and greener versions of disposables – using recycled pulp, for example.

Many of these organic options will save you money and, if you decide to use a laundry service (look for a company that uses eco-friendly laundry detergents), will not generate any extra work for you, if this is a concern.

If you really cannot bear the though of giving up disposable nappies, then at least stop using plastic nappy sacks. With all those nappies filling our landfills the last thing we need is to have them all individually wrapped in their own plastic bags as well. Anyway, it is far better to keep soiled nappies outside in a bin (trash can) than to leave them inside the house in artificially fragranced bags that will lose the fight against smells within a few hours anyway.

Nappy (diaper)
statistics

According to the Women's Environmental Network, the production of disposable nappies uses 3.5 times more energy, 8.3 times more non-renewable resources, 90 times more renewable resources, generates 2.3 times more waste water and 60 times more solid waste than real nappies (diapers).

the bedroom

Your bedroom should be a place of tranquillity and relaxation – your retreat from the outside world (and perhaps from other members of your household). Due to restrictions like space this is not always possible and we often have to compromise. In this section you will find practical advice and ideas on how to create a greener and, hopefully, more serene sleeping space where you can rest easy.

It is important to have one room where you can relax and rest, free from the stresses and strains of the day. If you have the option, select a room at the back of the house, away from roads, so that it is as peaceful as possible. Try to avoid having the bedroom next to areas like the kitchen or bathroom, which might house noisy equipment such as washing machines or dishwashers.

Work out what your main activities are likely to be in the bedroom and organize the room accordingly. You might want a quiet place to read, in which case placing a low table or seat near the window to make the most of natural daylight and the warmth of the sun would make sense.

As with the rest of the house, it is important to use as many natural materials as possible. It is also worth remembering that it is better to buy fewer, beautiful items that you love because even though they may cost more they will last much longer and are less likely to fall out of favour or fashion. There should be adequate ventilation so the air stays fresh and unstuffy – avoid overheating the bedroom. The best temperature is around 15°C (59°F), slightly warmer for children and the elderly.

Avoid having electrical equipment such as televisions, stereo systems and radios in your sleeping space if possible because of the EMFs given off by such equipment (*see page 86*). Make the bedroom a telephone-free room so that you do not risk being woken with a phone call and do not feel obliged to take calls when you are resting and do not want to be disturbed. Keep whatever electrical equipment you do have in your bedroom as far away from the bed as possible.

Sweet dreams

A good night's sleep is crucial to our wellbeing, especially when you consider that we spend around one-third of our lives in bed. We all know that an interrupted night's sleep makes us, at best, bad-tempered and, at worst, unable to cope with the slightest problems that might occur during the day. To get a good night's sleep you really need a good mattress and bed base. If you can afford to invest in only one good piece of furniture make it your bed. Even if it feels like a massive initial outlay it will be economical in the long term as a good mattress should last you between five and ten years, and the bed base much longer.

There are two main types of mattress – those with springs and those without. Within the sprung-mattress category there are two types: open sprung and pocket sprung. They are made by attaching layers of padding to the spring unit. The mattress should ideally be pocket sprung – particularly if you share your bed – and made from natural fibres. Make sure that it is not too soft or hard as both can cause back problems in the future. Pocket-sprung mattresses are exactly that – each spring is sewn into a separate pocket of fabric. Poorer-quality

- Save space by using a foldaway bed or a futon.

- Use Japanese-style *shoji* screens to create separate spaces within the room.

- Try making your own bed base using discarded packing pallets.

- Invest in a mattress made with an all-natural filling.

- Avoid metal bed frames as they can pick up EMFs (*see page 86*) from electrical equipment.

mattresses tend to have fewer layers of padding, and some cheaper mattresses are made using synthetic foam, which can contain formaldehyde and other toxic chemicals – not something you want to be lying next to all night. The ideal covering fabric for a mattress is organic cotton but the majority of outer covers are still made using synthetic fabrics such as viscose or polycotton mixtures, and natural versions can be expensive.

Mattresses made with natural materials are less likely to cause allergic reactions (although natural fabrics do trigger allergies in some people). Natural fibres used as fillings in mattresses include coir, horse hair, hessian (burlap), cotton and pure new wool. There are three different types of mattress finishes: panel tops at the cheaper end of the market, quilted tops and tufted mattresses which are at the top end of the market. Latex is a foam made using natural rubber foam and can be a good option because it is non-allergenic.

However, even an expensive mattress falls prey to dust mites, which are attracted by the skin particles we shed in our sleep, so it is recommended that you turn the mattress over once a week. Using an under-blanket can help to protect against dust mites and their faeces, which can cause skin irritations. Another good tip for guarding against dust mites is to vacuum your mattress regularly.

As for the bed base, choose one made of wood with solid slats, which allows the air to circulate. There are a growing number of companies and cooperatives making use of reclaimed wood and sustainable timber so it is a good idea to browse the Internet for ones in your area – try to buy locally to cut down on pollution caused by transportation. Another good idea is to use some locally salvaged wood. Even unwanted packing pallets, which can be found in salvage yards and even skips if you are not too proud, make great bed bases with a bit of work. Imagine the satisfaction of knowing you have an original, one-off bed for roughly the price you would pay – or even less – to have a new one delivered.

Fire safety

The use of polyurethane foam in mattresses in the past proved to be a serious fire hazard, but it has now been banned in many countries. Synthetic fabrics are more of a fire hazard than natural materials as they set alight quickly and burn very fast at extremely high temperatures while emitting toxic fumes. Mattress manufacturers in many countries are legally bound to add highly toxic fire-retardant chemicals to mattress covers, but some of the more environmentally aware companies have managed to get around this by adding a very thick cotton cover or a layer of pure new wool, which is naturally fire retardant.

Futons

Futons were traditionally used in Japan, although today you would probably find that most Japanese people sleep in Western-style beds. Futons are useful beds, however, particularly in areas where you have limited space as they can be folded up to act as sofas during the day or even packed away to create more room. Before the invention of sprung mattresses most people slept on some form of futon-like mattress, which was filled with cotton or straw. Today, futons are made to be much thicker and more comfortable than their traditional counterparts.

Futons are more likely to have been treated with fire-retardant chemicals than many bed mattresses because they are classified in some countries as furniture, which is subject to stricter regulations regarding fire precaution. It is worth finding a manufacturer that makes its futons using cotton and pure new wool for the filling. Look out for futon bases made from sustainable timber and without metal hooks and hinges. Try to buy an untreated base so that you can choose a natural stain and varnish for it, or look for ones finished with a natural sealer such as linseed oil.

Bedding

Once you have chosen your natural mattress and bed base it makes sense to choose bed linen made from natural, organic fabrics. Cotton, although natural, is not very environmentally friendly unless organically grown (see page 45). Around 25 per cent of all the pesticides used worldwide are employed in conventional cotton production so it plays a large part in polluting our rivers and atmospheres. And nobody wants fabric treated with potentially carcinogenic pesticides next to their skin.

Choose unbleached, undyed organic cotton, hemp (burlap) or linen pillow slips, sheets and duvet covers. Hemp is a fantastically green fabric and is becoming more widely available despite attempts by various governments around the world to outlaw it (see page 45). It is a great fabric for items that are frequently washed because it gets softer every time.

Brushed organic cotton blankets are cosy, soft and warm, and organic cotton waffle bed linen looks very good as well as being comfortable. It is important to wash new bed linen, even if it is organic, before use to get rid of any smells and loose particles.

- Avoid synthetic fabrics.

- Look out for unbleached, undyed, organic fabrics.

- Choose hemp (burlap) bed linen.

- Avoid pillows and duvets that have synthetic fillings.

- Use a pure new wool underblanket for warmth.

- Look for duvet covers that use wooden buttons or cloth tie fastenings.

Make your own
aromatherapy pillow:

Use an old pillow case made from natural fabric such as cotton or linen. Cut it to the size pillow you want and fill it with your choice of herbs. Dried lavender flowers are very good for relaxing, or you could try rose or camomile. Add a few drops of the appropriate essential oil and sew it up. Place in among your pillows for a heavenly sleep.

Duvets

Duvets and pillows should be made with goose feathers or down, which are warm but light fillings and can be covered with a cotton dust- and mite-proof case. They are produced without polluting the environment and have very good heat-insulating properties. The feathers should ideally have been gathered from the ground rather than plucked because the live plucking of the feathers can cause injury and distress to the birds.

This, however, may be preferable to synthetic fillings made by large chemical companies with bad track records as far as environmental issues are concerned. The greenest type of bedding is to avoid manufactured duvets altogether and instead use second-hand blankets acquired from your local charity store. You might be lucky enough to find a beautiful old eiderdown or patchwork quilt, which will be unique and well made, as well as lovely to look at. Or why not make your own from scraps of fabric? Another way to enhance sleep is to use an aromatherapy pillow – try a lavender one if you have problems falling asleep (*see box above*).

Electrical equipment

It is probably impossible for most people to avoid all electrical appliances in the bedroom – what about the alarm clock, bedside lamp and hairdryer? But all electrical equipment gives off EMFs and ELFs, which are thought to have a negative impact on our health and wellbeing (*see page 86*). It is therefore best to avoid non-essential electrical items, such as a television, in your bedroom.

There are some greener alternatives to items like radios, which are often in the bedroom. The range of Freeplay wind-up radios designed by Trevor Baylis will give you hours of play time without costing you anything for the electricity. They were originally designed for communities in developing countries without an electricity supply. They do not require any batteries or mains supply and are powered by winding and solar energy – perfect for taking on picnics and camping trips. The latest version can store up to 15 hours of electricity, so you will hardly notice the difference between it and a conventional radio.

Instead of using an electric alarm clock look for a traditional clockwork alarm that simply requires winding. These have the added advantage of being much nicer looking than the average black or white plastic electric alarm and you also avoid the risk of sleeping in if there is a power cut or the electricity runs out during the night.

If you do use a battery-powered radio or alarm clock you could think about investing in a battery charger. They are fairly inexpensive and often come with a selection of reduced toxicity batteries, although there are chargers available that will work with most battery brands. Depending on the type of charger, batteries will last from ten to 50 charges.

- **Buy a battery recharger.**

- **Look for products that do not require batteries.**

- **Keep electrical equipment away from sleeping areas.**

- **Turn off unused electrical equipment and switch it off at the mains.**

- **Choose a hot-water bottle instead of an electric blanket.**

Fabrics in the bedroom

We are used to living among a variety of different fabrics dyed a myriad of bright colours. In order to live a greener lifestyle we need to wean ourselves off these synthetic, dyed fabrics and look to unbleached, organic fabrics in soft hues instead. Many natural fibres are treated with chemicals such as pesticides and fungicides so natural does not always mean green – organic is always the best option. Cotton, and to a lesser extent linen, crops are treated with vast quantities of pesticides. In some parts of the world DDT, a hazardous chemical that is widely banned, is still used in cotton production.

In the bedroom we want to be surrounded by soft, comfortable materials like cotton and linen, particularly when they are next to our skin – like bed linen and nightwear. So choose unbleached organic cotton waffle towels, which are very soft and absorbent. A number of textile designers are experimenting with organic dyes and it should not be long before vegetable dyes are readily available. Some companies are even experimenting with growing coloured cotton crops, which eliminates the need for dyeing.

Wool is a very versatile fabric, which keeps us warm in winter and cool in summer (*see page 46*). To make sure that it is not mixed with other fibres check that it has the official wool mark – most certified organic wool comes from New Zealand where organic standards are in place. Felt, which is made by matting together woollen fibres, is currently quite popular and fashionable. It can be used for rugs, wall hangings and furnishings. Other natural fabrics that can enhance our homes are silk, hemp (burlap), jute, sisal and animal skins – although there are other ethical issues involved in using leather and suede.

Avoid synthetic fabrics such as nylon and all crease-resistant and non-iron fabrics as these are likely to have been treated with formaldehyde. However, not all synthetic fabrics are a big no-no. Rayon is a synthetic fibre made from cellulose from trees and plants. It is similar in texture to cotton and is a good example of an environmentally sustainable synthetic fibre.

Mothproofing

It is common for both cotton and wool to be mothproofed using toxic chemicals so try to buy untreated fabrics. Moth balls often contain para-dichlorobenzene, which is highly toxic and carcinogenic. You can buy natural moth repellents based on essential oils – moths do not like lavender or cedarwood. Look out for them at your local natural products store.

Clothes

Fashion is anathema to environmentalism: it relies on a quick turnover of hundreds of different styles whereas 'eco-chic' relies on fewer, long-lasting items made from natural fabrics. Don't worry though, you can be green and still have fun with clothes; you just have to be creative. Root through your local second-hand shops for curtains, good-quality blankets and items that can be adapted to make new clothes. A handful of fashion designers, such as Sarah Ratty of Conscious Earthwear, make eco-friendly yet extremely desirable and innovative pieces of clothing.

- Keep dry cleaning to a minimum.
- Avoid crease-resistant items.
- Organize a 'clothes-swap' with friends session, with a few bottles of wine.
- Choose clothes that are easy to care for.
- Use aromatherapy bags to freshen clothes instead of fabric conditioner.
- Use wooden coat hangers.
- Avoid ironing when possible.

ⓘ Green clothing does not have to mean smocks and sandals – look for exciting eco-fashion from innovative earth-conscious designers.

Linen, hemp (burlap), cotton and wool are the most versatile natural fabrics and although expensive, linen is very durable and sometimes looks better the older it gets. Hemp is a very environmentally friendly fabric and there are a number of clothing manufacturers who are starting to use it, particularly for items such as jeans as it is incredibly hard-wearing but actually softens each time it is washed. There are some innovative new clothing fabrics available today such as Tencel, which is made from cellulose, and fleece made from recycled mostly post-consumer plastic bottles. This is a good use of waste plastic but it should not be seen as a solution to the problems created by plastic production.

Animal skin, particularly fur, is a bit of a problem area. Fur is one fabric that we can do without entirely. Some people feel that it is acceptable to wear second-hand fur, but this kind of attitude does nothing to change awareness that wearing fur is cruel, selfish and totally avoidable. If you do not want to risk having red paint thrown at you, avoid fur completely. If you buy designer clothing it is worth checking that the designer does not use fur in any other ranges he or she might produce, such as couture where a large amount of fur is used. Boycott designers who use fur in any of their collections. Many vegetarians choose not to wear leather or suede either, even though these are by-products of the meat industry. Perhaps organic leather biker jackets are not too far away?

Give your underwear a pleasant fragrance by placing small home-made herb and aromatherapy sachets in drawers and pockets (*see box, page 109 for how to make a 'pillow'.*) This is also a good idea for combating smelly shoes and trainers (sneakers).

Shoes

Leather shoes are essentially green because they biodegrade but a lot of chemicals are often used to treat the leather before it is used. Some companies are exploring more environmentally friendly shoe design and have created footwear with soles made from recycled car tyres. Other good ideas are wooden clogs and shoes made from felt with cork soles; they are biodegradable and very comfortable due to cork's natural insulation qualities.

Dyes

Fabric was traditionally dyed using natural colourings such as camomile, and techniques like weaving were used for decorative effect. Today we have a huge array of vivid, synthetic dyes at hand, which are incredibly harmful to the environment. We are used to bright colours and the way they lighten up our lives but if we are going to live more organically we have to get used to less vivid colours, and fabrics in their natural undyed state.

A good way to make individual furnishings or clothing is to buy lengths of unbleached fabric and dye or print it yourself using vegetable dyes. This is also a good way of livening up old T-shirts and trousers that you are bored with, although it will only work for pale items. Vegetable dyes can be quite hard to get hold of but some specialist companies do make them and it is an area that will expand as the market grows. Some companies are experimenting with low-impact biodegradable dyes, which are more fade resistant than vegetable dyes.

Blinds, shutters and screens

Different types of window covering are required in the bedroom throughout the year, depending on the season. In the summer months you will want to make the most of natural sunlight and in the winter you will need to block out the cold for a cosy night. As well as using curtains you could think about alternatives such as wooden shutters, blinds or screens. Wooden venetian blinds are great for letting in plenty of light, but they can also act as a sunscreen on very bright days.

Reeds and grasses such as straw and bamboo are good materials for the natural home, and a lot of eco-friendly houses are being made with grass roofs. These materials are very versatile and can be used for blinds, wall coverings and floors. Bamboo is the world's fastest growing plant and can grow up to 1 m (1 yd) a day. It is grown without the use of pesticides and is incredibly versatile – it is so strong that it is used as scaffolding in parts of Asia. If you choose to have bamboo blinds make sure the bamboo comes from a managed source – where the canes are cut leaving the young shoots to reach maturity, rather than being mechanically cut.

- Look for second-hand curtains made from retro fabrics.

- Change your window coverings according to the seasons.

- Look for salvaged shutters that can be adapted for your windows.

- Use bamboo blinds in the bedroom to cover up untidy areas such as shelves for clothing.

Even though it is a natural material, rattan should be avoided unless it is bought from an ethical trader because it is being overharvested and some species, along with certain species of bamboo, are in danger of disappearing. Other issues you need to consider are the production processes, because once harvested these materials are often treated with chemical finishes. Look for lighter-coloured bamboo, which is far less likely to have been treated than darker varieties. It is also always preferable to use materials that are produced locally, as shipping products around the world is far from ideal, no matter how natural they are.

The Japanese use *shoji* screens to cover windows, which still allow some light to come in, and they are an unusual alternative to blinds. They can also be very effective when used to separate rooms into distinct areas, such as the sleeping area and an area for clothes storage.

Underfoot

Good flooring materials for bedrooms are natural and warm enough for bare feet. Wooden floorboards are great and you can use rugs to soften them. There is nothing nicer than stepping down onto a sheepskin rug in the morning. Take inspiration from the Japanese again and use *tatami* mats, which are springy underfoot and absorb sound, to cover the bedroom floor. Natural sisal carpet is also a good option for the bedroom – but check it does not have a synthetic backing (*see page 37*).

Softening up

The bedroom is no place for harsh lighting – use low-wattage bulbs for lamps and choose light shades made from paper, which give off a diffused light. Many people enjoy candle light in the bedroom, as it is intimate and gentle. But many candles are made using petroleum and some still use lead in the wicks, although this has been banned in some countries, such as Australia. This means that burning conventional candles contributes to pollution on two different levels: during the manufacturing process and during the burning time.

The reason some companies still put lead in the wicks of candles is to make them last longer. Metal wicks are most often used for scented and ceremonial candles – the metal in the wick makes the candle burn slower but as the wick gets hot lead is released into the atmosphere. There is an easy test to see if the wick contains lead: simply drag a piece of white paper over the wick. If a dark line shows up – similar to that drawn by a pencil – the wick contains lead. As with most metals, lead is a non-renewable resource so it should not be overused. The manufacturing process for lead is also very harmful to the environment, and it is incredibly toxic. Lead has been known to affect the central nervous, cardiovascular and blood systems, and can lead to anaemia and kidney damage. So do you really want to be burning it in your bedroom?

Many companies today, however, make candles using natural ingredients such as soya wax, palm and coconut oil, unadulterated essential oils and unbleached papercore wicks. These are preferable for a number of different reasons – they are made from a non-petroleum renewable resource, they contain no pesticides or herbicides, and they are biodegradable and safe.

Rather than using products made with synthetic fragrances, which can cause skin irritations, as well as headaches and dizziness, look for candles made using only essential oils. Some companies try to get away with using fragrance oils rather than 100 per cent essential oils – to be sure, look on the label to check the oil used is labelled as 'absolute' or 'pure'. Other things to watch out for are additives and dyes – buy candles in natural-looking colours rather than ones made using lots of vivid colours. Some companies are developing vegetable candles coloured with vegetable dyes such as beetroot, paprika and turmeric.

Incense

Along with candles come incense – the perfect combination for creating an ambient atmosphere in your sleeping space, whether you are preparing for bed, reading or meditating. Natural incense is made using plant resins, essential oils and aromatic wood powders. Be suspicious of any scents that are not attributable to any flower or plant you can think of – these are synthetic smells created using chemicals. Many ancient cultures have used forms of incense in prayer, ceremony, medicine and celebration, and it was often thought of as a way of contacting the gods. Today we use incense to help us relax or to stimulate us and to make our living spaces smell beautiful. Incense is also commonly used to aid meditation and creative visualization.

Stick incense is usually made using bamboo (*for more information on bamboo, see page 113*) to aid the burning process, although some green companies are making bamboo- and chemical-free incense sticks now. Cone incense is made using sawdust compressed into the cone shape and saturated with essential or synthetic oils – the best ones are made using sawdust from a naturally aromatic wood such as sandalwood. Look out for

Make your own **incense**:

- 14 tsp pure charcoal (you can buy this in chemists – don't use the stuff you put on the barbecue)
- ½ tsp saltpetre
- 3 tsp dried, powdered herbs such as juniper leaves or lavender flowers
- 1 tsp natural resin such as frankincense
- 1½ tsp essential oil such as bergamot or ylang ylang
- binding agent – this can be made by mixing 1 tbsp gum arabic with 2 tbsp boiling water to form a paste

Grind the charcoal, saltpetre, herbs and resin to a powder in a mortar. Add the essential oils and mix, adding the binding agent a little at a time until you have made a paste. Knead it onto a piece of oiled greaseproof (waxed) paper and form into cones or patties around 2.5 cm (1 in) tall or wide. Store them in a dark ventilated cupboard until they are completely dry.

incense that is made using only pure essential oils. It is possible to make your own incense (*see the recipe in the box above*).

Cosmetics

The bedroom should be a sanctuary from the rest of the house and, as such, is often the room chosen for the application of make-up, which can be a self-indulgent, therapeutic and enjoyable process. The international market for natural cosmetics is a major growth area. Growing concerns about the environment, combined with an increased awareness regarding health issues, mean that a lot of people are looking for natural, plant-based make-up products that are kind to the planet as well as our skin. Conventional make-up is full of artificial colourings, preservatives and fragrances, some of which ends up being absorbed through the skin. As awareness and demand grows for organic food and drink more people are also starting to question what they put on their skin and hair. Women in particular are realizing that because of the amount of cosmetics absorbed by our skin, wearing organic cosmetics is as important as eating organic food.

The number of ingredients found in cosmetics can be quite staggering but we often do not look much further than the glossy packaging. I was shocked recently to find out that my favourite natural skincare producer put hydrogenated vegetable oil in its lip balm! The wearer of lipstick or lip balm will consume a certain amount of it while she is using it, which could amount to as much as three sticks of lipstick in a lifetime. This highlights the importance of paying attention to the cosmetics you buy as well as the food you eat.

Cosmetic companies have vast budgets to spend on marketing their products and they are adept at selling us an image. Many of these manufacturers use minimalist packaging with words like 'natural' and 'organic' on the labels, to tap into the growing market for natural products, which can be very misleading. It is always worth investigating further to find out whether they really are natural.

- Check the labels carefully for synthetic fragrances, colours and preservatives.

- Avoid using very brightly coloured cosmetics – choose more subtle, natural tones instead.

- Don't buy products containing petrochemicals.

- Avoid overpackaged products.

- Always use refillable products whenever possible.

Most cosmetics, such as foundation, lipstick, eyeshadow and eyeliner, are made using natural or petroleum-based waxes, preservatives, colourings and thickeners. Look out for products made using natural waxes like beeswax or carnauba, rather than the commonly used petroleum-derived waxes such as ceresin. Synthetic fragrances can cause all sorts of symptoms, from dizziness to skin problems, so it is essential to read the labels of scented products carefully. Be aware that products marked as 'unscented' may use chemicals to mask unwanted smells and try to use products that are naturally fragranced with essential oils instead.

It pays to be cynical, however, especially in today's market where multinationals know there is money to be made in the natural cosmetics industry. Products claiming to be natural and organic or made from essential oils may not be as pure as you would like. Always read the labels carefully and if there is something you do not recognize contact the manufacturer. The only reason manufacturers will change their products is if they know there is a demand for them. In Europe and the USA a product can call itself natural even if it contains only 1 per cent natural ingredients, so until strict organic standards are in place it pays to be careful.

Most natural cosmetic manufacturers produce only a small range of colours, unlike their conventional counterparts, because they are catering for a smaller market. This generally means that choosing to wear natural make-up means you have to be prepared to compromise and cannot expect to find the latest, most fashionable colours – which will be out of vogue in a couple of months in any case and which will end up being thrown away.

Nail varnish

Our nails can tell people a lot about what kind of person we are. Whether they are gnawed down to the quick or stained yellow with nicotine, well manicured or kept short, neat and clean – they are all indications to our personality.

Most nail products such as varnish and polish remover are chemical based. Nail polish removers contain solvents that dissolve the polish to remove it but they also dissolve the natural oils from your nails and the surrounding skin.

- Look for fragrances free from petrochemicals and based on essential oils.

- Make your own fragrance using a base oil, such as almond, with a few drops of your favourite essential oil.

They often contain formaldehyde, which can cause a number of allergic reactions. It is, however, easy to find polishes that do not contain formaldehyde. Don't be fooled by brands claiming to have added proteins and vitamins, as these cannot be absorbed by the nail and so are useless.

Instead of using nail polish to protect your nails from breaking, try rubbing a good oil or moisturizer into them at night to nourish and strengthen them. It is worth remembering that nails kept at a reasonable length will have less chance of snapping than long talons. A good way to clean nails stained by cooking

with fruits or vegetables is to dig them into a slice of lemon – make sure there is no broken skin first though or it will sting badly.

Smells good

There is big business to be made from perfumes and scents, mainly because you are once again buying into a brand name and image. Most perfumes are made from petrochemicals, and labels claiming that products are made using natural fragrances can be misleading. Around 5,000 chemicals are used in the manufacture of fragrances and some reports suggest that around 95 per cent of these are made from petroleum.

When you start to consider that the fragrances that you wear can be absorbed through your skin, you will begin to understand that the fragrance industry is as bad for your health as it is for the environment. Synthetic fragrances can cause all sorts of symptoms, from dizziness to skin problems, so it is essential that you read the labels of perfumes and scented products very carefully.

Baby bedrooms

The precautions you might take with your own room are even more important when you are dealing with a baby's bedroom because babies are much more vulnerable than adults. When they are planning for the arrival of a baby many people rush out to buy brand new things for their newborn. Filling the room with new toys, and buying new furniture and carpet is not a good idea, however, as these will emit toxic chemicals into the atmosphere.

As with any room in your home try to use only natural materials. Use only organic paints and fabrics. Look for a wooden cot that has not been treated and then finish it using beeswax. Choose a mattress made with a cotton filling and use a rubber undersheet rather than a plastic one. It is also worth asking around first to see if friends or family can donate any items or even lend them to you temporarily. Choose flooring that you can clean easily such as natural linoleum or wood, with a couple of washable sheepskin, wool or felt rugs for comfort. Keep the room free of electronic equipment and make sure that it is well ventilated.

(i) **The majority of perfumes are made almost entirely from petrochemicals.**

chapter three
green and
and

growing
eating

A green home isn't complete without a touch of nature in the form of some green leafy plants. On a primeval level we need plants in order to exist, but most of us need plantlife in a spiritual sense, too. It connects us to nature, reminds us that we are part of a complex web of life and it is thus a fundamental part of green living.

By nurturing nature in our own homes we are also contributing to the planet's biodiversity, no matter how small this contribution may be. From a shiny-leaved houseplant in the living room to a herb-filled window box outside the kitchen, even the smallest of homes, in the most concrete-filled urban centres, can play its part in the greening of our environment.

Should you be lucky enough to have a backyard, a small garden or even several acres at your disposal then there really is a huge amount that you can do to help nature on its way. And should your green growing ambitions exceed the space available to you, then there is every chance that your area may have a community garden, allotments or disused land that could provide a larger arena for your green fingers to do their work.

But it is not only the environment that stands to benefit from your gardening efforts. Imagine the satisfaction you will feel serving your friends a plate of steaming buttered asparagus, knowing that you grew it yourself. And think how much happier you will be eating food that you know has not been drenched in chemicals. The health benefits of all that fresh air and exercise are an added bonus, too.

Creating a garden is a wonderfully life-enhancing act in itself. Nature is not something that can be rushed or pushed ahead, it teaches us that there are natural rhythms and slows us down when every other part of our lives is speeding up.

It is a way of bringing creativity into our lives, accessing parts of our minds that may not have been used since we were children. And for children, there is nothing more exciting than seeing a tiny seed turn into a gigantic sunflower (and nothing more enticing than large amounts of mud and wriggling worms!).

Finally, your garden can be a sanctuary from the pressures of twenty-first-century life. Using natural materials, water features and atmospheric aids such as wind chimes, you can create a meditative space free from the telephone and television, where you can reacquaint yourself with thoughts and sensations that have long been forgotten in your day-to-day life.

Simply being outdoors working with the soil is a basic human pleasure, and so, too, is eating. And again, as with gardening, there are green options when it comes to food. It does not get much better than growing your own, but for those foods you cannot grow yourself, the best choice is to 'go organic'. You can then relax in the knowledge that you are supporting environmentally-friendly agricultural practices and that you are buying food you can trust. So get out your garden table and chairs, invite some friends over, light a few candles and cook an organic summer supper that proves once and for all that green can be gorgeous.

the green
garden

The very act of growing plants would be considered by most of us as doing something green. Growing plants brings the experience of nature closer to our families and local communities, provides a home for a wealth of living organisms, and each and every one acts as a filter for the air we breathe, thereby contributing to a cleaner global environment.

But gardening can be an activity that is far from green. For many people, their gardens become an arena in which they wage war against nature through the liberal use of highly toxic pesticides. Others think nothing of using products that have been created at the expense of precious natural resources, like peat from the fast-diminishing peat bogs and garden furniture made with wood plundered from tropical forests. And many gardens are grown with the help of excessive amounts of water drawn straight from the tap (faucet), despite the hundreds of gallons that fall from the sky each year and go uncollected in most areas.

The good news is that this environmentally wasteful approach to gardening is no longer in vogue. Gone are the days when a good garden was meant to be regimented in design, with uniform plants grown in weed-free, dark peaty soil surrounding a perfect sprinkler-watered lawn, without a daisy or buttercup in sight.

The new wave of gardening recognizes that a good garden is a complex ecosystem, with each element having a role to play. Native plants are now just as fashionable as exotics and are much more of a hit with the local wildlife. Unruly borders and meadows filled with wildflowers are now just as keenly cultivated as any neatly tended bed of roses. The modern gardener accepts nature and works with it and in so doing produces naturally healthy plants in an efficient and safe way.

Whether your gardening aspirations stop with a cheese plant in the corner of your living room, or stretch as far as a vegetable patch, some fruit trees and perhaps a chicken or two roaming about, this eco-friendly method offers you the chance to get truly close to the natural world and to put something back into your environment.

With domestic gardens making up many millions of hectares of land worldwide, the combined efforts of green gardeners can produce the largest nature reserve on the planet – and you will have your very own slice of Eden on your doorstep.

Reasons to go green in the garden

- You can grow food that you trust – free from chemical sprays and other contaminants that have been implicated in health scares worldwide (*see pages 155–6*).

- You can save the environment from the polluting effects of transporting fresh produce to you by growing your own.

- You are sparing the environment from the impact of pesticides, which kill many beneficial insects, birds, plants and animals, can pollute our water supplies and harm our children.

- You can teach your children where food comes from and the wonder of nature in a safe environment.

- Your garden will become a haven for wildlife and be safer for your own pets.

- By growing rare or unusual seeds you can contribute to global biodiversity and introduce new flavours to your diet.

- It gives you the chance to recycle in one of the most exciting ways, turning your food scraps and garden cuttings into compost, which, in turn, will support the growth of further food.

- Gardening is great exercise and fun for all the family.

- You will save money by not having to pay for fertilizers, pesticides, compost and so on, and by growing your own food. Recycling will also prevent you spending a fortune at the garden centre.

- You will be saving fragile areas of natural beauty from further ravaging by no longer buying peat-based composts and limestone, and by making sure that your garden furniture and other wood products are from sustainable sources.

- Green gardening puts you in touch with nature and its cycles, aiding relaxation and giving you an outlet for and sanctuary from the frustrations of your busy day.

Green gardening – **do's** & **don'ts**

DO:

- Set up your own composting system or use locally produced organic compost – as much as 40 per cent of household waste can be composted.

- Grow plants that are native to your area and that are suitable for your garden's conditions – both climate and soil type.

- Grow traditional varieties of plants – newer hybridized crop varieties can provide little by way of food for birds, butterflies and other wildlife and are often lacking in taste, whereas older varieties are under threat of extinction.

- Use natural methods for reducing pest problems and boosting soil health.

- Recycle wherever and whatever possible.

- Set up a water-collecting system.

- Learn to be a little untidy – too much order in a garden is unnatural, makes useful bugs and animals homeless, and removes valuable food for birds and other types of wildlife.

- Buy local, buy sustainable and buy natural.

DON'T:

- Buy seeds, plants or bulbs that have been harvested from the wild – many areas of natural beauty are being devastated by commercial plant and seed collectors who are stripping the land.

- Use peat-based growing media or sphagnum moss as lining for hanging baskets – peat bogs are being mined out of existence in order to meet gardeners' demands.

- Buy timber products without certification that the wood is from a sustainable source (*see page 40*).

- Rely on chemicals for pest control and to maintain soil health.

- Burn leaves in autumn – this contributes to pollution and wastes a valuable natural resource.

- Use sprinklers and neglect to collect rainwater in a water butt and waste water in your house.

- Throw things away – there are uses for many household objects in and around the garden.

The basics

Green gardening is based on organic principles: minimizing pollution, promoting sustainability, working with nature and natural cycles. On a practical level, this means not using chemical fertilizers and pesticides, recycling and creating diversity in the garden. But it is about more than a collection of do's and don'ts. This kind of gardening is essentially a 'state of mind'; it requires the gardener to think in a sustainable way and to work in harmony with nature. It does not matter how large or small the space you have available for your gardening aspirations – whether it is a tiny window ledge or several acres – nor how much time you would like to spend achieving your aims, these principles can work in any situation for every type of gardener. By adopting them you stand to gain in so many ways.

Without toxic chemicals, your garden will be a safer place for you, your family and your pets to relax in. The food you grow will be safer to eat (*see Green Food and Drink, pages 154–65 for more on this*) and your garden will attract and support a greater diversity of wildlife. You will be doing your bit for the global environment by saving water, planting traditional seed varieties that are under threat and reducing demand for peat and wood from threatened forests. You will reduce your household waste and save money by using natural resources. But, above all, it is fun and immensely satisfying to nurture a garden using age-old methods and your own creative ideas.

So how do you get started? There are a few basics that every green gardener needs to master, beginning with composting.

Composting

Nothing excites a green gardener more than composting. It is the ultimate form of recycling, turning household waste such as old newspapers and vegetable peelings into valuable organic matter that will reinvigorate the soil and in turn

aid the cultivation of plants. And, if you grow your own fruit or vegetables using this compost, then the whole reuse cycle is complete.

Such is the value of composting in terms of savings on waste disposal and benefits to agriculture that many local authorities will provide you with composting bins and help and guidance on composting. Even if you have no intention of gardening, you could seek out a local composting project that will accept your household waste, since 40 per cent of household waste could be turned into fertile soil instead of contributing to the problem of polluting landfill gases.

But composting does more than just save on waste-disposal costs. Garden compost improves soil structure in many ways – helping sandy soils retain water, contributing to drainage in clay soils, and inoculating the soil with healthy microbes, some

Getting started **tips**

- Join an organic organization – they offer support such as advice helplines and mail-order services for organic gardening products (*see Resources, pages 178–83*).

- If you do not have a garden but have a need to get growing, find out about allotments or community gardening projects in your area.

- Visit organic gardens or farms for inspiration. Your local gardening organization might have details of gardens in your area that are open for visits. Alternatively, contact an organic certifier (government agricultural departments should be able to provide contact details) to find out about local organic farmers who would be happy to show you around and pass on tips.

- Decide what you want from your garden before you start. A chill-out zone with minimal work? Enough vegetables to provide you with salads throughout the summer and a soup or two in the winter? Flowers and a lawn for the children to play on? Or maybe a place for entertaining on summer evenings? A garden can be many things, and they can all be green.

- Look around you. You will fare better if you create a garden in accordance with the local conditions for light, soil and weather. This goes for the type of plants you grow, too. It is easier to grow plants that are indigenous to your area; you should require less artificial aids and such plants will benefit the local wildlife.

- Assemble a few basic bits of kit: a water barrel, a compost bin or similar, and tools for weeding (these should be from recycled or sustainably produced sources).

- Get going with your compost first, since healthy soil is the root of successful green gardening.

- Choose disease-resistant varieties of plant in peak condition.

- Plant and harvest according to the seasons.

- Read all you can on organic gardening and talk to other gardeners – they are the best source of advice and tried and tested tips.

of which help plants take up more nutrients from the soil and also help improve their resistance to pests and diseases. No matter what soil you have to play with, it will always benefit from compost and you can also use the compost to make up your own growing media (*see page 129*).

Setting up a composting system is relatively straightforward. You can choose between buying a composting bin – preferably made from recycled plastic – or make your own by wiring together four wooden pallets and lining them with cardboard, or drilling holes in an old plastic or galvanized dustbin (trash can) if you have a spare one. Whatever your choice of container it should be covered, with either a lid or some old carpet, to keep out the rain and keep heat in. It is also best to site it near your kitchen so you have no excuse when it comes to depositing your kitchen waste on the heap.

Once you have allocated a site for the compost heap or bin, you are ready to embark upon what many in gardening liken to alchemy. There is no shortage of composting 'experts' who will be only

British **peat bogs**

The rapidly diminishing peat bogs in Britain provide a good example of how gardening can do more harm to the environment than good. These areas of primeval wilderness formed by the decaying remains of plants, such as sphagnum mosses, are home to many threatened species of animals and plants such as the great sundew (Britain's largest carnivorous plant) and the golden plover bird.

Peat bogs are an archive of the past 10,000 years in which ancient boats, trees, pollen and even human bodies (such as Lindow Man) have been found. And there is more – peat lands remove carbon from atmospheric carbon dioxide and thus help reduce global warming.

It would seem idiotic to destroy such unique and valuable land for the sake of some garden compost and hanging basket liners, but that is exactly what is happening. The UK gardening public buys 2.7 million m³ (3.5 million yd³) of growing media, soil conditioners and mulch annually, most of it peat-based. Currently, less than 6 per cent of Britain's original lowland raised peat bog habitat remains in a near natural condition.

There are few signs that the message is getting through to gardeners, since in the last few years of the twentieth century the use of peat by gardeners has increased by 50 per cent, with 70 per cent of all peat used in the UK being bought by gardeners, according to the Royal Society for the Protection of Birds (RSPB).

But some good news comes in the form of a decision taken by the National Trust to phase out the use of peat in all of its gardens, and to request that all of its commercial plant suppliers use peat-free compost only.

There are alternatives to peat. For potting and seed composts, coir fibre can be bought in bricks or discs, which expand to make compost when water is added. There is a good range of organic composts made from recycled waste on the market, and an increasing number of local authorities are also making garden compost from recycled waste, which will sometimes be delivered for a small fee.

Peat-free composts have not been in development for as many years as those based on peat, so be patient when you try them. Some may not be as stable as peat, but you should be able to find a compost to suit your needs.

Leaf mould, bark and manure can be used instead of peat to improve soil condition, and pine needles or composted heather or bracken will increase acidity if necessary. Or you can make your own compost (*see opposite*). When sieved and mixed with perlite or sharp sand, this can be a decent alternative.

For hanging basket liners, you could try using specially designed coir mats, compressed waste-paper liners, wool liners or highland moss liners, which come from farmed conifer plantations. Or you could make your own using hay, newspaper, an old black bin liner with holes cut in it for trailing plants, or an old woollen sweater. All have their strengths and weaknesses, but you should find one that is to your liking and you will be doing your bit to save the peat moors at the same time.

Making compost

Things that can go in:

- **Urine:** dilute it with water first.

- **Chicken manure:** ideally from organically reared chickens.

- **Comfrey:** rich in many nutrients, especially potash, but contains almost no fibre.

- **Lawn clippings:** but mix them with dry material first, such as damp straw, weeds or leaves, as grass clippings can be too soggy on their own.

- **Kitchen waste:** including tea bags, coffee grounds, cooked pasta, fruit and vegetable trimmings.

- **Farmyard manure:** again ideally from horses or cows bred on organic farms.

- **Seaweed:** a great source of trace elements.

- **Garden waste:** chop it first to help the decomposing process.

- **Weeds:** especially stinging nettles which are high in nitrogen (treat in the same way as lawn clippings), but they should be young weeds that have not formed seeds.

- **Bracken:** but avoid handling when it is producing spores as it is carcinogenic.

- **Straw:** should be damp and ideally already partly rotted.

- **Woody prunings:** shred them first.

- **Newspaper, cardboard:** use sparingly, shredded or torn up and dampened, and avoid materials with coloured inks.

too ready to blind you with science on their particular tried-and-tested method. However, the basic principles are simple. You need to provide food, air and water in order for billions of microbes (fungi, bacteria and so on), worms and insects to turn your waste into compost.

The food you add should be a mixture of high-carbon and high-nitrogen materials. Wood, paper and leaves are high in carbon but left alone would decay too slowly, and may deplete nitrogen in the soil. Grass clippings and fruit and vegetable waste, which are rich in nitrogen, break down much more easily but can create slimy, smelly compost heaps. A suitable mixture might include: dry, dead plant material such as straw, autumn leaves and wood chips – usually moistened first; fresh plant material such as green leaves, fruit and vegetable scraps from the kitchen, tea bags and coffee grounds; and fresh horse manure (ideally from organically fed horses). You can also add newspapers in small amounts and cardboard cereal boxes. (*See boxes above and right for further suggestions.*)

Things to avoid:

- **Cat litter or dog faeces:** both of these can carry disease.

- **Meat and fish scraps:** they smell as they rot and may attract rats and other pests.

- **Diseased plant material:** diseases can spread through the compost.

- **Perennial weeds and weeds in seed:** they may continue growing in the compost, especially if it is not hot enough to destroy the seeds.

- **Plastic, tin, glass and other synthetic materials:** they do not decompose.

Top **composting** tips

- Always protect the compost heap from rain with a waterproof cover.

- Make sure you can remove the bottom layer easily.

- Turn the heap every few months to introduce air into the mix.

- Dampen any dry material such as straw or autumn leaves first to aid its decomposition.

- Shred items like leaves, newspapers, cardboard and weeds to speed up their decomposition.

- Mix fresh grass mowings and fruit and vegetable leftovers with dry material to stop the pile becoming too sodden.

- Make sure you have broad mixture of materials in the pile and layer them evenly.

- To avoid attracting flies and insects to kitchen waste, make a hole in the centre of your compost pile and bury the waste.

- For best results, mix equal quantities of materials high in nitrogen (such as clover, fresh grass clippings and livestock manure) and those high in carbon (such as dried leaves and twigs).

- If you want a quick start to your composting you can purchase compost activators or accelerators containing organic material designed to kick-start your compost.

- If you have large quantities of leaves, it may be worth composting them separately in a wire mesh container or in plastic sacks (*see opposite*).

- Check on any local or state regulations for composting in urban areas – some communities may require rodent-proof bins.

The ideal method for making compost is to make a heap in one go, but to do this you need to collect bags of waste for several weeks or months. If you add material gradually, it may take at least eight to 12 months before it is ready to use, whereas in summer a newly constructed, complete heap would take around two months to turn to compost. A gradual heap may also not reach high enough temperatures to kill off weeds or diseases.

With either method, it is a good idea to layer the different materials, spreading them evenly and adding water if the material is dry, before covering the heap. Make sure your compost heap does not become too dry or wet. Soggy compost smells bad and takes a long time to break down; dry compost is also slow to decompose as microbes prefer damp conditions. To speed up decomposition, turn the compost with a fork every six to eight weeks.

Maintaining a high temperature is important to kill off weeds and diseases – your pile should be at least 50°C (122°F) (often not possible if composting gradually). If you are using a compost bin it should be at least 1 m³ (1 yd³) in size in order to achieve high temperatures and you can also help by lining the bin with dry autumn leaves or hay.

The compost is ready to use when it is a dark colour, smells earthy and the original ingredients have almost gone. Remaining straw, twigs and sticks can be picked or sieved out. The final result can be used on gardens, lawns and house plants. Dig it into the soil or leave it on top for the worms to do the work for you. It is best applied in spring when the weather should be more conducive to its staying in the soil – heavy rain can wash the compost away before the worms can do their bit.

But if you are new to gardening and all this talk of creating your own compost has put you off making a start on your own garden, take heart – there are various green options that do not require you to devote a part of your garden to a decomposing pile of waste. Your local authority may well be running a community composting scheme or composting green waste from its parks and gardens, which it will deliver to you for a small fee, for example.

Growing media

Home-made compost can be used to make your own potting compost or growing media but it does take some time and effort. The quickest – but more expensive – option is to buy your growing media and there is now a wide range available that satisfies the demands of the green gardener.

The key thing to avoid when buying a potting compost is peat (*see page 126*), but there are many good peat-free options, including those made using coir and added nutrients such as seaweed extract. There is also a peat alternative that does not use peat mined from peat bogs. Instead it uses peat that is a by-product of the water industry; it is picked up by rainwater running down mountain sides and then collected in filters before the water enters reservoirs. Find out the source before you buy.

As with all things, be sure to check with the suppliers what is actually in their composts – manure should ideally come from an organically reared animal, for example. Beware also of the term 'organic' when it is applied to growing media. Check with an organic certifier to see if they approve the compost for use in organic growing systems.

Be patient: peat-free and 'green' composts are still in the early stages of development and it may take a while for you to find one that suits. But the countryside will thank you for making the effort.

Other green soil helpers

In addition to the positive effects of compost, the green gardener has a wide variety of other soil-enhancing products at his or her fingertips.

Green manures
These are plants that are grown to enrich and protect the soil. They reduce the harmful effects of wind and rain, reduce weeds and can provide nutrients when dug back into the soil. The idea is to grow them on bare soil in winter or between different crops of vegetables in the summer. The types of plant used produce a mass of weed-smothering foliage quickly. They include: alfalfa, mustard, buckwheat, clover, fenugreek, field beans, annual ryegrass and phacelia.

But you should note that seed germination may be inhibited by decaying green manure, so you should leave a gap of at least one month between digging the green manure in and sowing seed.

Leaf mould
This can be used as a mulch (*see page 131*), but it is also valuable for digging into the soil or in a seed-sowing or potting compost. Since leaves need more light and less air to rot down than other compostable materials, it is best to compost them in their own container. You can make this using four wooden stakes at least 1 m (1 yd) high, driven into the ground with chicken wire stapled around the outside. Be warned: it can take up to three years before you get good compost from leaf mould, but it is well worth the wait. If you need more leaves, ask your local authority if they could donate some from their autumn sweepings – or collect them yourself.

Manure
Although manure is likely to contain hormones, pesticides and other nasty elements if it comes from a conventional rather than an organic farm, it is thought that if manure is stacked for at least a year these contaminants will not present a problem.

Spent mushroom compost
Again, this will need to be left for at least a year to make sure any chemicals used in mushroom-growing leach out. Don't use it on acid-loving plants, but it is good for improving heavy clay soils.

Fertilizers
Occasionally, through a lack of readily available compost or severe deficiencies in your soil, you may need to resort to a fertilizer. But even then, there is no need to reach for the synthetic chemicals. There

Worms, wonderful worms

If you really have very little space, you may still find some room for a worm composter. Worms will eat their own weight of waste each day, producing rich liquid and dark spongy compost as a result. You can buy the whole thing or make your own worm bin and either collect or buy in the worms. The best time to start your worm bin is late spring or summer when the worms are more active.

Making your own:

- Find a plastic bin (an old plastic dustbin/trash can will do) with a tight-fitting lid.

- Drill some air and drainage holes in the top and bottom of the bin and put a tray underneath it to catch the liquid.

- Line the bottom of the bin with a 10 cm (4 in) layer of small stones from your garden and some sand – this layer should then be watered until water seeps out of the bottom of the bin.

- Next, add a 10 cm (4 in) layer of mature compost, manure or leaf mould that has been mixed with shredded paper or cardboard and moistened. This layer forms the 'bedding' for the worms.

- Now you can add the worms to your bin. Red worms are recommended and these can be found around the edges of compost heaps, or you can buy them from anglers' shops or mail order. You will need around 100 worms to start off an average wormery.

- Provide the worms with food, such as well-chopped vegetable peelings, tea leaves, coffee grounds, crushed egg shells and shredded newspapers, but do not add fat or meat products or a large quantity of citrus fruit – the worms cannot digest these. After the initial feed, leave the bin for at least three to four weeks before adding any more food as too much at once may cause the material to rot. After this initial period you can add waste daily or weekly, but never overfill the bin.

- Keep the bin in a dark location, at between 18°C (64°F) and 25°C (77°F) and make sure it does not dry out.

- Depending on the number of worms, the amount of food you add and the time of year, you should expect the worms to have eaten their way through the bedding and the food waste and changed it into compost in around six months. Once they have no more food they die and become part of the compost or you can tempt them to the surface with fresh food and remove the bottom layer of compost.

- If you are having problems and you are sure the bin is not too dry or too wet, is warm enough and that you have not added too much food at once, then you could try adding protein to the worms' diet, such as grain or fishmeal. You could also add a sprinkling of calcified seaweed to stop the compost becoming too acidic.

- Take care when you are using the compost and the liquid that has drained off, as both are highly concentrated. Dilute the liquid and scatter the compost lightly on the top few centimetres or inch of soil.

is a wide range of organic fertilizers on sale in both garden centres and by mail order, including: seaweed meal, fish bone and blood, gypsum for heavy clay soils, and hoof and horn. Animal-free products are also available if this is an issue.

Liquid fertilizers or feeds are often used in container gardening and for the green gardener there is a choice of fish emulsion, liquid manure and comfrey liquid (which is highly recommended for tomatoes and peppers). Seaweed extract is also sold as a soil and plant tonic. You can make your own comfrey liquid by growing the plant, soaking the cut leaves in a container with a tight-fitting lid for four to six weeks, and then straining off the liquid.

Mulches

A mulch is a layer of material spread around plants on the soil surface to protect the soil from erosion, reduce water loss and smother weed growth. Some mulches are also biodegradable and therefore able to improve soil structure as they decompose. These organic mulches, which include grass clippings, compost, leaves, bark chippings, straw and manure, are preferable to inorganic mulches like black polythene, carpet or woven plastic. There are also purpose-made mulching fabrics available, including flax or hemp (burlap) fibre matting.

If you use grass clippings, it is best to dry them out in the sun first before applying a layer 5–7 cm (2–3 in) deep, as otherwise they can be too slimy and may suffocate plant roots. Sheets of newspaper can be placed on the ground, covered lightly with grass clippings or another mulch to anchor them, but take care on a windy day! It is best to shred autumn leaves with a lawnmower or shredder first and then compost them over winter (*see page 129*) before using them as a mulch.

Water

No garden can survive without water, but gardeners are some of the worst offenders when it comes to wasting water. For example, in half an hour, a garden sprinkler uses as much water as a family of four does in a day, about 600 ml (1 pint) for every two seconds it is in operation, or 650 litres (145 gallons) per hour. The average gardener uses 10 litres (2½ gallons) of water daily on the garden, but on hot dry summer evenings this can go up to as much as 50 per cent of the total domestic water supply used each day by the household – an average of 150 litres (33 gallons).

With global warming, water will become an ever more precious commodity. Scientists have estimated that by the year 2080 there will be reductions in UK summer rainfall of 10–20 per cent – and this is, of course, when demand for water is also at its highest. A priority for any green gardener is therefore a water-saving strategy. This should include the following:

◼ Water plants only in the evening or early in the morning when the water will not simply evaporate in hot sunshine.

◼ Don't use a sprinkler or hose pipe – water the garden with a watering can instead.

The benefits of **mulching**

● It protects the soil from the elements, preventing it from eroding and compacting in heavy rain and drying out in windy, hot conditions.

● It helps maintain a stable soil temperature.

● It prevents weeds from growing up and establishing themselves.

● It can help keep fruits and vegetables clean and does the same for your feet when you are tramping around your beds in wet weather.

● It can help feed the soil.

▓ Don't water lawns, as overwatering can weaken your lawn by encouraging roots to seek the surface; any brown patches will soon disappear when the rain arrives.

▓ Collect rainwater by installing a water butt (made from recycled plastic) with a system of pipes that collects run-off rainwater from flat roofs and gutters. Cover the butt to prevent insects taking up residence and contaminating the water and to prevent evaporation.

▓ Use an efficient irrigation system, such as a porous soaker hose allowing seepage along its length, or trickle-and-drip systems that deliver small amounts of water directly to the soil, reducing evaporation from plant leaves. (Speak to suppliers of such systems for advice on setting one up and the type of system suited to your needs.)

▓ Grow plants that are adapted to dry conditions if lack of water is a problem in your area, such as: alyssum, aubretia, catmint, sedum, yucca, Spanish broom, yarrow, nasturtium, Californian poppy, moss rose, juniper, artemisia, lavender, sage, iris, thyme, crocus, New Zealand flax, rosemary and evening primrose.

▓ Grow indigenous plants, since they will be best suited to your local natural conditions and should require less additional watering (although this will also depend on the soil you are growing them in).

▓ Use mulching to prevent water loss through evaporation and wind.

▓ Add garden compost to the soil to help it retain water.

▓ Plant carefully: some plants can shade others and terracing helps keep water from eroding the soil.

▓ Make sure any water feature in your garden, such as a fountain, recirculates the water.

▓ Install windbreaks, hedges and fences to reduce the drying effect of the wind.

▓ Create a mini-wetland in your garden to temporarily store, filter and clean run-off water from your roof and lawn and water from your bath and washing up (provided you use biodegradable washing products).

▓ Save as much water from home use as possible – the water leftover from watering your house plants, water used to rinse the dishes, bath water and so on – and use it on the garden. The average bath contains 80 litres (18 gallons) of water, so make use of it by investing in a bath water diverter, which makes sure this water does not disappear down the plug hole. It is a good idea to filter this water by tying finely meshed cloth at the end of your hose, and do not let this water touch above-ground edible fruit and foliage, especially those that are likely to be eaten raw, such as spring onions (scallions) and lettuces.

Pest control

For many people, the most worrying aspect of going green in a garden is how to cope with unwanted visitors, be they weeds, insects or animals. For the regular gardener the response is usually a highly toxic one – applying herbicides, insecticides and traps liberally throughout the garden in a war against all unwelcome predators. These chemicals, which have mostly been only available for the last 50 years, are harmful to other (beneficial) species, can leave toxic residues behind in the flowers, fruit or vegetables that are being grown and can contaminate ground-water supplies.

Clearly, there was a time when gardeners and farmers managed quite well without them, and the green gardener is living proof that this can still be the case. The green gardener seeks to minimize the need for intervention in the first place, but if it is necessary, ensures that any intervention causes the least disruption to the rest of the garden and the creatures within it as possible.

Disease and infestation

If you start off with the healthiest possible combination of soil, plant and insect life in your garden then it is less likely to fall victim to disease and infestation. Just as if you eat properly, exercise and get enough rest and relaxation, so you are less likely to succumb to illness.

In practice you need to take the following measures in establishing your garden:

■ Choose the healthiest plants available to you. If you are growing your own from seed, make sure they are well looked after at every stage of growth, that is, kept in good soil with plenty of space for root growth.

■ Keep the soil in tip-top condition by using compost, mulches, manures and so on.

■ Pick plants that will thrive in the available conditions and that are most resistant to pests and diseases.

■ Avoid overcrowding, since pests and diseases can take hold in cramped conditions.

■ Mix and match your plants so that your garden is balanced and no pest can dominate.

■ Rotate your planting, giving the soil a break and making sure that no pest or soil-borne disease can take hold in one place for years on end.

■ Get rid of the diseased part of a plant as soon as you spot it, remembering not to add it to your compost, and likewise crack down on a pest the minute you see one.

■ Proper watering can limit the spread of some diseases; trickle irrigation, which takes water directly to the soil, may be particularly helpful.

■ Use traps and barriers such as cloches, fences and enviromesh sheets to protect plants – many different varieties are available from organic gardening catalogues (*see Resources, pages 178–83*). Sticky traps also help you assess the level of infestation.

■ Encourage natural predators by planting companion species next to your crops. They attract insects that will dine out on the pests ravaging your plants.

■ Create a suitable habitat for frogs and toads, which eat slugs and snails.

■ Sow plants at times when pests and diseases are not such a problem.

■ Deter pests with repellents – some, available by mail order, use natural substances, such as a slug and snail repellent containing a yucca extract and a cat repellent containing natural essential aromatic oils.

■ Know your enemy – the more you understand about a pest the better able you will be to outfox it and you may also discover that it is part and parcel of the bigger picture in your garden. For example, the caterpillar eating your plant may turn into the butterfly you have been trying to attract to your garden with another plant nearby. A pest may be attracted to your plant only when it is a seedling, so protection may be necessary only in the early stages.

■ Be ever vigilant – the earlier you spot a problem the easier it is to tackle it.

If you have tried all of the above and you are convinced you have an infestation that is beyond reasonable levels then you may need to bring out some bigger guns, but there is still no need to reach for synthetic chemicals.

The first option is to use biological controls, usually available by mail order. These are living organisms that you introduce into your garden specifically because they feed on the pest you are having problems with, but they are safe for humans, pets and beneficial creatures. So, for example, you can buy microscopic nematodes that seek out and kill slugs, or delphastus, a relative of the ladybird, which can control severe white-fly infestations.

The main downside of these controls is that many of them require warm soil in which to survive and some are suitable for use only in the controlled and relatively compact environment of a greenhouse. They also need to be used as soon as you spot a pest problem, must be applied on the day of delivery and are sensitive to any sprays, including organic ones.

Pest control tips

- Don't forget your hands! Many insects can be removed by hand and dropped into soapy water or vegetable oil.

- Make protective cloches out of old plastic bottles – cut the tops off and sink them into the ground around your seedlings.

- Scare birds, rabbits and deer away by stringing up old CDs above your crops – the shiny surfaces will deter birds, but remember many birds are useful pest eaters and should be enticed into your garden.

- Use old dry Christmas holly around the edges of freshly sown peas to deter mice.

- Soap is worth a try – a squirt of soapy water can kill aphids.

- Slug beaters include saucers of old beer or milk in the ground, which attract slugs, which then drown. Some gardeners suggest that human hair bordering their plants dissuades slugs from an attack and crushed egg shells, coarse sand, bark chips, soot and sawdust sprinkled round plants can stop slugs in their tracks as they dislike a gritty surface. You could try piling comfrey leaves in the centre of the bed you are about to sow – slugs love comfrey, although only in spring for some reason, and will be drawn to the pile. Leave it for several days then blitz the pile and remove the slugs that have collected there. After a few more days you can remove the leaves and compost them, sow your plants and surround them with a continuous ring of comfrey leaves to keep the slugs at bay. But this will only work in dry weather.

- Create your own foul liquid of dead slug remains by plucking as many slugs out of your garden as possible (go hunting at night for the richest pickings). Leave them to decompose in a bucket of rainwater for a few weeks and then pour the contents in areas where slugs congregate – this is said to be the ultimate deterrent, but is for the non-squeamish only!

- Start plants that are particularly attractive to pests when they are young, such as cucumbers and pumpkins, indoors where they are protected.

- Garlic grown near roses is supposed to keep them clear of green fly, and a solution of bicarbonate of soda can control some fungal diseases on roses.

- Try out some of the natural insect-deterrent sprays recommended by gardeners over the years, such as those made from bracken, elder, rhubarb, nettle, seaweed and horsetail tea. You can find out how to prepare them by going to the website www.organic.mcmail.com/hints.htm.

If you are still convinced you have a problem and nothing else has worked, then the green gardener can turn to sprays and powders as a last resort, but not conventional highly toxic brands. It is better to make use of those sprays approved for use in organic agriculture, which are generally of plant origin and biodegradable. These include: derris, a liquid or powder made from a number of tropical plants, which kills aphids, spider mites, thrips, caterpillars and sawfly; pyrethrum, made from a certain type of chrysanthemum which kills aphids; and sulphur, which controls powdery mildew on fruit, flowers and vegetables.

Although effective, these and other treatments may also kill beneficial insects, damage other plants and kill fish, so they come at an environmental cost – hence their being last on our list.

Weeds

If you are intent on creating a green Eden in your backyard it is important to reappraise the humble weed, since an environmentally friendly garden will never be weed free. Many weeds are useful as lures for beneficial insects that prey on those eating your crops, others help enrich the soil and other plants by storing nitrogen in their roots, and most add to the diverse mixture of plants in your garden that make it so attractive to wildlife.

However, none of us want to see our lovingly planted beds overrun by couch grass or clover, so keeping weeds at tolerable levels is important even for the green gardener. But this does not mean that it is all right to douse the area liberally with chemical weed killers, since this would contaminate the garden, leaving it dangerous for animals, other plants and children. Herbicides also put a stop to any hopes of recycling weeds, since chemically treated plants must be destroyed.

The aim of the green gardener should be to remove weeds in a way that does not disturb any other species in the garden and to reuse them in some way. Weeds can be invaluable for starting off a compost heap, for example, especially nettles and chickweed. Many can be eaten in salads or soups, some can be drunk as teas and others have medicinal properties. You can even use weeds as feed if you keep chickens or rabbits. Cut weeds can also be dug into your soil to provide valuable nutrients, provided the roots of perennial weeds are removed and they are not in seed – this is best done in dry weather when they are less likely to recolonize your garden.

Hand weeding is obviously the first choice for many green gardeners and this can be made easier by using traditional weeding tools such as a *kirpi*, a specially shaped hoeing blade that is widely used in India and available from mail-order catalogues (*see Resources, pages 178–83*). Care should be taken to avoid disturbing the root systems of your plants, so hoeing should always be a surface activity only. Unfortunately, for long-established perennial weeds with long deep tap roots, such as buttercups, or an invasive creeping root system, like bind weed, hoeing doesn't help and heavy spadework is needed.

Mulching is another green way of controlling weed growth – by smothering them, preventing light and oxygen reaching the weeds. The best of all mulches are those that break down over time, enriching the soil as they do so. Examples include leaf mould, grass clippings, straw and bark chips. However, you will need to top up these mulches as they decay and persistent weeds may still find a way through them. Other more weed-resistant mulch options include flax matting, black plastic (go for recycled if possible), carpet, recycled glass chippings, newspaper or cardboard. These are often covered in a layer of loose mulch to improve their appearance (*see Mulches, page 131*).

The final method available to the green gardener – a flame gun that burns back weeds – should really be used only as a last resort, since it uses paraffin or propane gas, which are pollutants. It is, however, still a greener option than chemicals and is a useful method for clearing a large garden, an allotment or paths and driveways in one hit.

What to grow

If creativity is missing in your life then get gardening. Whatever size canvas you have to work with you can create the most wonderful sights, smells, textures and tastes by working with nature. Your garden can be a wildflower-filled wilderness or a pungent herbal paradise, you can feed your family from your soil or tempt frogs, bats and hedgehogs into your very own wildlife reserve. But no matter what your aims are, it is essential that you take a few things into account before you rush off to the garden centre.

The first thing to consider is the environment in which you are hoping to create your green paradise. You should be trying to achieve a perfect balance between the conditions in your garden – the soil type, the amount of sunshine, wind and rain it receives – and your aims for the garden. By so doing you should have a garden that requires minimum intervention of any kind, be it heavy watering or pest control. A green gardener does not attempt to grow plants that need a lot of water in a dry, wind-swept garden or in a large, heavy container on a balcony, for example.

To assess the capabilities of your garden, observe it at different times of the day: notice where the sun reaches at certain points in the day, where the heaviest frosts are, where the drainage is at its poorest and where the wind hits.

To find out the type of soil you are dealing with, take some in your hand and rub it between your fingers. If it is sticky and rolls into a ball it is clay soil; if it is crumbly and dry and looks grey it is chalky; if is gritty and will not form into a ball it is sandy soil; and if it is smooth and silky it is silt. It is also useful to determine the acid/alkaline balance of your soil by using a pH testing kit, available from garden centres. Some plants prefer one soil over another; for example, roses dislike sandy soils, and rhododendrons and azaleas love an acidic soil. Also, if you are in an urban environment with a garden close to a busy road, you may want to get your soil tested for lead content by the local environmental department. Should contamination be high and you want to grow edibles, then don't despair – container gardening is a good option, or you can build some raised beds with clean topsoil.

Once you know the capabilities of your garden, you must then consider how much time and effort you are willing to put into your garden and how much space you have in which to achieve your aims. If you have limited time then growing fruit and vegetables may not be the thing for you, but tending to a few herbs in a window box and growing perennials and self-sowing annuals in your beds should be perfectly possible, and just as pleasing to the local wildlife.

Don't listen to those who say green gardening is more labour intensive than any other type of gardening. If you have a perfect balance of nature in your garden then you may actually find you have more time than conventional gardeners, as the frogs are eating your slugs and the mulch is smothering your weeds.

Having only a small space in which to garden is also not as limiting as many believe it to be. There are a wide variety of miniature fruit and vegetable plants that can be grown in containers, herbs take up very little space and a natural sanctuary can be made out of even the smallest, concrete-filled backyard, flat roof or balcony.

However, for the green gardener there are other considerations when it comes to choosing what to grow. Obviously, growing your own organic herbs, fruit and vegetables is a great way to use your garden as you will be saving money, getting food you can trust and reducing the polluting effects of transporting the food you would otherwise buy to the local retailer. But even just growing wildflowers, installing a water feature or planting a tree will help your local environment and make a difference to the planet as a whole.

The things to avoid are high-maintenance exotic plants that are not suited to your climate, have been transported for miles to reach your garden centre, and are not attractive to local wildlife. It is also best to avoid buying large, established plants, as again they will have taken more energy to transport to you and may have been chemically treated. Ideally, you should grow from seed and the seeds should be organic or untreated, since conventional seeds are often given a chemical coating to combat fungus or disease.

Once your garden is established, you can harvest seeds from your plants and plant them again. Tomatoes, marrows, pumpkins, melons, aubergines (eggplant) and green peppers, for example, all have seeds that are easy to collect and can be sown again. Flower seeds, too, can be harvested by tying a paper bag over the seed head as it is ripening and shaking the seeds out when the head is dry. Seeds should be separated out from any dead plant material, dried and stored in labelled packets in a cool, airy drawer, before sowing the following year.

When buying plants, look beyond the standard varieties of fruits and vegetables used by commercial farmers. Instead, opt for tastier, traditional varieties that are no longer commonly grown and do your bit towards maintaining genetic diversity in our environment. Since these varieties were established before the advent of chemical fertilizers and pesticides they should also thrive in the organic conditions in your garden.

Beware of plants harvested from the wild. Stealing bulbs from the wild not only destroys the delicate eco-structure of the habitats from which they are taken, but the bulbs could easily be diseased. But it is important that we continue to plant wild species of plants, provided they come from reputable sources. These species are disappearing from their natural habitats at an alarming rate, so it is important to do our bit towards biodiversity. (Flora & Fauna International's *The Good Bulb Guide* lists companies that have pledged to never knowingly sell wild bulbs or who will clearly label all wild collected bulbs as 'From Wild Source' – *(see Resources, pages 178–83.)*

Containers

If you have a flat roof, balcony, small backyard or just a few window ledges, then container gardening is for you. No matter how small the space available, there is nearly always a container that will fit and an abundant choice of plants to grow in them. We are not just talking pelargoniums and pansies – herbs, dwarf vegetables and some fruits can all be grown in this way and often more easily than in beds, since soil conditions and pest control are far easier to manage in a small defined area.

Lack of shade and wind are possible problems on balconies, roofs and ledges, so it is best to choose low-growing plants and/or plants that will thrive in the sun, such as Mediterranean herbs, vines, tomatoes, shallots and peppers. Wooden trellises can also act as windbreaks.

Another consideration in these areas is the weight of your container – growing a miniature fruit tree may prove too much for your balcony to bear. But you can still cultivate some herbs in a small pot.

green tips for container gardening

- Avoid buying new, plastic containers and try to make your own using old car tyres, a tree stump, an old sink, a chimney pot, ceramic bowls, a toilet cistern or an old wheelbarrow. Be sure to drill holes in the bottom for drainage.

- You can 'age' containers by coating them in yogurt to promote the growth of lichen.

- Look for organic growing bags instead of the conventional ones. These should contain organic materials, peat from sustainable sources only (if at all), and are reputed to require less feeding and watering. Or try making your own using a sealed strong plastic bag filled with home-made compost, using composted bark instead of peat.

- Growing bags can be recycled. You can use them for potting bulbs or growing hardy annual flowers once your tomatoes and cucumbers have had their go. Or use the contents as mulch, add it to the soil on seedbeds or in seed trays, or add it to your compost heap.

- Avoid using sphagnum moss as a liner in your hanging baskets (*see page 126*). Try lining them in recycled wool, coconut fibre or hemp (burlap) fibre instead of moss. These are often biodegradable, from sustainable sources, and hold water well, so reducing the need for watering.

- Be adventurous. Try baby tomatoes; herbs such as sage, chives, parsley and thyme; or strawberries in your hanging baskets. Fig trees, peach trees, dwarf apple trees and grapevines can all be grown in large tubs or pots, while lettuces, oriental greens, chard, spinach and trailing cucumber can thrive on ledges.

- Remember to use your home-made compost in containers. It will enrich the soil and help it retain moisture – a particular problem with container gardening.

- Use a container to make a water feature – attracting useful garden helpers such as frogs and toads and providing valuable water for birds and insects (*see pages 144–5*).

Herbs

Herbs are pretty much the ideal plant – they smell wonderful, taste fantastic, look great, and are a living medicine chest. On top of all this, they are pretty easy to grow, can be grown in the smallest of spaces and are a hit with bees, butterflies, hover flies and other garden helpers.

Growing your own herbs is worthwhile for those concerned about the environment. Store-bought herbs may look healthy but they are often the product of environmentally damaging and toxic growing practices. Dried herbs may have been irradiated or fumigated and fresh herbs may have been bombarded with herbicides and insecticides, with a top dressing of etherol – a ripening agent.

With the demand for year-round herbs increasing, they are now often grown in energy-guzzling glasshouses, using chemically enhanced, soil-free growing media, or flown in from sunnier climes. They may be sold in individual pots, which look natural and long lasting but which all too often disappoint, with the herb fading fast, or in plastic packs gas-flushed with nitrogen and carbon dioxide to extend their shelf life.

Nothing can compare with the simple pleasure of reaching out of your window and grabbing a handful of fresh mint to throw into your bowl of steaming buttered new potatoes or some basil leaves to scatter on freshly cooked pasta. And by indulging yourself like this you will be saving energy, reducing waste and benefiting your health.

Some **herb growing** tips

- Most herbs suit containers of all types – from bay trees in large tubs to creeping thyme in a hanging basket – but they nearly all require good drainage and some sunshine.

- Growing from seed is the best method – look for the increasing variety of certified organic seeds now available.

- Try growing culinary varieties such as basil, parsley, chives and rosemary in a window box, and fragrant varieties, such as peppermint, lemon verbena or sweet myrtle, in boxes on the indoor ledges to scent your house.

- Some herbs are best suited to growing in their own pots rather than being mixed into a window box, since the more rampant ones, such as mint and tarragon, can swamp the others.

- If you use a lot of one particular herb, such as basil, then grow several close together and pick from a different one each time – that way each plant will have time to recover.

- Herbs can also be grown in beds and borders, acting as ground cover around larger plants, and with plenty of space to spread.

- Many herbs are good companion plants, benefiting the growth of nearby plants. For example, garlic and chives deter green fly from roses, nasturtium does the same for woolly aphids on apple trees and French marigold deters white fly from tomatoes and repels eel worm.

- Other herbs are useful in the fight against pests. For example, the liquid produced from steeping camomile flowers in boiling water for ten minutes is said to have insecticidal properties.

- Apart from many culinary uses, herbs are also very handy in other areas of our lives and make valuable green alternatives to many conventional products. They can deter insects and household pests, aid house cleaning and decorating, be used in beauty preparations, and help make an effective first-aid kit (*see pages 74–5*).

Beds and borders

Provided you have a backyard of even the smallest dimensions, then there is every chance you can use it to grow flowers, fruits, vegetables and herbs in a bed or border. You can create raised beds in a concrete yard, cut out an interestingly-shaped bed in the middle of your lawn or dig some borders around the edge of your lawn.

For truly green gardeners, the main aim with their beds and borders will be growing their own fruit and vegetables, but even these keen gardeners will find that plants grown purely for their flowers and foliage are essential to create a balance in the garden and attract a variety of useful bugs and birds.

Vegetables

Containers will not really allow you to grow serious amounts of vegetables, especially root crops, so if you have some beds and borders available make use of them by growing some vegetables. With the addition of some compost, weeding and watering, you should be able to cultivate most vegetables, so the first step is to decide what you want to grow.

This decision should first and foremost be based on what you like to eat, since there is little point in growing hundreds of radishes if you don't actually like them. Bear in mind also that some of the easiest vegetables to grow include: beetroot, broad (fava) beans, ruby chard, courgettes (zucchini), lettuces, leeks, onions or shallots, potatoes and, yes, radishes.

Most vegetables can now be grown from organic seeds, either sown directly in your bed or started out in pots or trays indoors. Biodegradable pots made from coir and other fibres are best for both the plant and the environment, since they can be planted directly into the soil, where they will break down, without disturbing the plant's roots . Alternatively, make your own pots from newspaper, which act in the same way (avoid paper with coloured inks and glossy pages) – you can buy kits to do this. Trays, too, can be made from biodegradable paper or recycled plastic, or use empty egg boxes and yogurt pots.

Square foot gardening

If you are keen to be as self-sufficient as possible – but have only a small space to play with, you could try using the principles of 'square foot gardening' – a gardening method that originated in the USA in the 1980s. The idea is to start with a 1.2 m (4 ft) square raised bed and divide it into 0.3 m (16 x 1 ft) squares using string or sticks. You can then plant each square with a different crop.

Don't overplant (use just a pinch of seeds in each space) or crowd your seedlings – allowing enough space between each plant should still give you a total of 256 plants. It is also important to rotate your crops and to stagger planting and harvest times, and ideally to garden in a bed that has sun on it for six to eight hours each day to give your plants the best chance of thriving.

Once seedlings appear or are planted out in your beds or borders, protect them from the elements and any predators by covering them with a cloche. Again, look for those made from recycled plastic or make your own from old plastic bottles. Beware of the sun though; seedlings can die pretty quickly if left under a plastic cloche in the hot sun all day.

Remember to mark what you planted where and to use the basics of green gardening – adding compost to the soil, chemical-free pest control and crop rotation – and you should soon have a harvest to be proud of. But remember, start small and have fun – you may not be self-sufficient in one year, but you will be well on your way to having enough delicious produce for a good dinner party.

Fruits

Plucking fresh fruits from your garden is not only the preserve of those lucky enough to live in sunny climates and you don't have to limit your fruit-growing ambitions to a few apple trees and some strawberry beds. A wide variety of fruits can be grown by a patient green gardener, as long as the basics are there – a fertile soil, in as sunny and protected a spot as possible.

You could try apples, cherries, plums and pears or raspberries and of course strawberries. Organic varieties of blackcurrants, redcurrants, whitecurrants and gooseberries are also available.

It is easy to see why green gardeners would want to grow their own fruits. Many fruits in our stores have come under chemical bombardment from conventional growers both pre- and post-harvest, some have their skins waxed and most of them are picked under-ripe in order to aid transportation. It is also getting harder and harder to find many truly tasty varieties of fruits. Although there are thousands of recorded varieties of apple, for example, only a limited number are used for the bulk of commercial production. Many commercial growers have decided to phase out some of the more interesting but less predictable varieties in favour of the hardier, thick-skinned, but less juicy fruits that will travel well.

So most people will need little persuasion of the benefits of planting a fruit tree in their garden. Apart from avoiding all these nasty elements, it is also very cost effective. Most soft fruit plants will continue to produce fruit for 20 years, apple trees can keep going for 50 years and cherry trees even longer.

Lawns

A velvety carpet of close-cropped lush grass, free of brown spots and weeds, is high on the list of priorities for many a home gardener. It makes a great soft surface on which children can play safely and an inviting spot for an afternoon snooze in the summer. But maintaining an immaculate lawn can be exceptionally damaging to the environment. For example, a sprinkler can use about 650 litres (145 gallons) of water in an hour, a petrol-driven lawnmower, when used for an hour, causes as much pollution as driving a large car for 50 miles, and chemical fertilizers and herbicides contaminate water supplies and are even trodden into the home.

The first thing a good green gardener should do is put aside any preconceived notions of what constitutes a perfect lawn. Learning to live with some dandelions and buttercups in your lawn, allowing it to go brown during dry summers and letting it grow just a little bit longer than normal are all good green things to do.

The following tips should also prove useful:

Seeding
The cheapest and greenest lawn will be one grown from seed. There are a wide variety of seed blends available for lawns, some suited for shady conditions under trees and others for grazing animals, for example. Choose one to suit your needs, such as a hard-wearing mixture containing perennial rye grass, which will be easier to maintain.

Watering
You do not need to water your lawn – too much water can weaken it by encouraging roots to seek the surface rather than dig deep for water supplies. And grass is a remarkably good survivor of drought – brown patches will soon go green again when rain arrives. Spiking the lawn with a fork or with spiked boots will help it to absorb dew and rainfall.

Mowing
Allow the grass to grow to at least 4 cm (1½ in) before cutting it and don't cut it too short – about 3 cm (1 in) is ideal – close cropping weakens the grass and this will reduce unnecessary mowing. The greenest mower is a hand-pushed model, giving you a good workout as a bonus. Petrol mowers pollute the air with emissions and, like electric mowers, waste energy. Leave the mowings to lie on the lawn where they replenish the soil, unless they are very long or it is cold and damp, in which case add them to your compost heap (see box, page 127).

Feeding
Use only organic fertilizers or natural fertilizers like calcified seaweed, if absolutely necessary. In preference, you can sprinkle sifted compost on the lawn in mid-spring, ideally after rain. Brushing worm castings on the lawn on a dry day and raking the lawn in spring and autumn are also good ways to help the condition of the lawn.

Weeding

If weeds are starting to take over, hand weeding is the answer. Use a kitchen knife to dig out dandelions, plantain and dock, removing as much of the roots as possible. However, if the grass is flourishing it should overcome weeds so moss and persistent weed problems are probably a sign that there are other problems, such as water logging, too much shade or high acidity.

The ultimate green lawn is one that has been allowed to go wild. (*For more on creating a wildflower lawn or meadow, see page 143.*) Another green option is to have a herb lawn using low-growing varieties of camomile or thyme. Popular in medieval gardens, herb lawns release fantastic fragrances as you walk on them and they do not need mowing, but they are not hard-wearing enough for ball games!

Trees

If you have the space then no green garden should be without some trees. They provide a home to wildlife, help clean the air, provide shelter from the wind and sun for you and your garden and they can reduce your heating and cooling costs if sited near enough to the home.

Obviously you should choose your tree and its site carefully – a large, deep-rooting tree planted too close to a garden wall or house could spell disaster some years down the line.

Generally it is best to select a native species – it is more likely to support a variety of insect species and to harbour birds. Be careful though not to choose a species that is already overplanted in your area, as this will not aid natural diversity and could add to the conditions necessary to allow a single pest to dominate, such as was the case with Dutch elm disease in the USA a few years ago.

The ideal time of year to plant most trees is either at the end of summer or at the end of winter, when the ground is not too cold and the weather not too hot. Mulching around the base of the tree and providing protection around the trunk from rabbits and lawnmowers are also good ideas.

Creating a wildlife haven

A green gardener does not have to be obsessed with the size of his or her marrows. You can do as much for your environment by providing a sanctuary for local wildlife.

In fact, given the rate at which our meadows, forests and hedgerows are disappearing, doing your bit to help redress the balance is just about as environmentally friendly as you can get. The first thing you must do is set out your aims – do you just want to see a few birds at your bird table or are you planning something a little more ambitious, such as recreating a mini-wetland in your backyard? There are plenty of minor changes you can make to your garden that will encourage more birds, bees and butterflies to pay a visit, so no matter how much time and effort you want to put into it, you will reap rewards almost immediately.

Next on your list should be an assessment of how you garden in general. Planting the most wildlife-friendly plants and trees will count for nothing if you continue to use toxic chemicals in your garden, such as slug pellets and weed killers. You also need to make sure you are maximizing the conditions for wildlife with what you have in your garden already. Are you leaving seed heads on dead flowers, as they can provide valuable food for birds? Or are you keeping such a 'tidy ship' that there is precious little in the way of food or shelter for any wildlife in your garden?

Once you have made sure that your gardening practices are as wildlife friendly as possible then it is time to consider ways in which you can go further, such as those outlined below:

Attracting birds

Birds are at the sharp end of industrial farming practices – in the UK alone, tree sparrows, grey partridges, corn bunting, bullfinch, skylarks and spotted flycatchers have all declined by between 70 and 89 per cent in recent years. But it is not just commercial growers who have contributed to their decline. Gardeners, too, with their fondness for slug pellets and the like, have done their bit to decimate bird populations. So green gardening is your chance to reverse this sad decline.

Beyond following good green gardening principles, there are several other measures you can take to help our feathered friends. Providing food and water for them is the first priority. Obviously you can put up a bird table or a squirrel-proof bird feeder in your garden (well away from prowling cats), but, best of all, you can make sure there is plenty for birds to eat naturally in your garden. As well as ensuring a variety of fruits and seeds are available all year, you can encourage earthworms to the surface by spreading leaves on your beds. Provide water in the form of a pond (prevent it from icing over completely in winter by placing a rubber ball in it) or in a water dish left out for the purpose.

You can also help provide birds with suitable nesting sites – many have been lost with the removal of trees in towns and the loss of hedgerows generally. Many birds like dense and bushy plants such as pyracantha, trees obviously are home to many others and if all else fails, you can buy or make a nesting box and attach it to a tree or on a high wall. Make sure wooden boxes are made from sustainably produced wood (*see page 40*), or opt for 'nests' made from seagrass, fern or coir, available through some mail-order catalogues (*see Resources, pages 178–83*).

Finally, if you own a cat that likes to hunt birds, make sure it has a bell on its collar to warn any unsuspecting bird of its presence.

Bringing in butterflies

In almost every country worldwide butterfly species are diminishing as a direct result of the destruction of their favourite habitats. Obviously all butterflies were once caterpillars and it is hard to convince anyone of the joy of these insects when their prize plants have just been decimated by the little furry creatures. But, if possible, a level of caterpillar activity should be tolerated in our gardens if we are to preserve our butterfly population.

Adult butterflies require food in liquid form, like nectar from flowers and the juices of extra-ripe fruit, so plant nectar-rich flowers, such as buddleia and fruits in your garden. They also need water, so if you do not have a pond or water feature, put out a shallow dish of water or leave some in the hollow of a rock in your garden.

Providing a basking site, where butterflies can warm up from the chill of an early morning, will also help them. You can do this by adding a light-coloured rock or garden sculpture to your garden which will absorb the sun's heat and to which butterflies will be attracted .

Encouraging bees

Bees are vital to the environmental food chain, pollinating many plants and producing delicious and healthy honey as a bonus. About 30 per cent of our overall diet is estimated to come as a result of a pollinating visit by a bee to flowering fruit trees or vegetable plant, so you can see how important they are. And by encouraging bees to come into your garden you may end up increasing the quality and quantity of your own fruit and vegetables.

Bees love nectar and are drawn to white, blue and yellow-flowering plants. But newer plant varieties are threatening their survival, especially that of the long-tongued bumblebees. They need access to deep flowers with an abundant supply of nectar throughout the spring, summer and autumn months in order to survive. But many hybrids of traditional flowers often have no nectar, no spurs on which the nectar collects or they are in a form which helps honeybees get to the nectar that only bumblebees could reach in the past. Plus some exotic nectar-rich plants in our gardens are of little value to our bees as they are adapted to other pollinators like humming birds, with their specially designed long beaks (*see page 143*).

To attract bees plant traditional cottage garden plant varieties. Bumblebees like common and musk mallows, woundworts, purple loosestrife, meadow clary and knapweed in particular. Other bee favourites include: aubretia, polyanthus, yellow alyssum, borage, hyssop, honeysuckle, red clover, larkspur, snapdragon, nasturtium, lemon balm, sage, ageratum, lavender, thyme, buddleia, Michaelmas daisies and sedum.

You can also help provide shelter for bees in your garden by drilling holes in a block of untreated wood and hanging it under the eaves of your house or garden shed, protected from direct sun and rain.

Attracting frogs and toads

Toads and frogs can be a real asset to a green gardener, munching their way through a good many slugs and snails. Obviously a pond of some sort is a first requirement (*see pages 144–5*), especially one with gently sloping sides, but they also hibernate out of water, under rocks or logs, so leaving the garden a little untidy should help.

Drawing in bats

A bat can eat half its own weight in insects in a single night, so they are pretty useful creatures to have around. They feed on night-flying insects such as mosquitoes, moths and beetles, and a single brown bat can catch up to 600 mosquitoes in an hour. To encourage these night prowlers to stay on your patch and do their good work you should put up a smallish untreated wooden box at least 4 m (15 ft) high in a position that gets the sun most of the day. A pond would also help.

Humming birds

If you are lucky enough to live in an area that receives these delightful summer visitors, you should do what you can to encourage them into your garden. Like bees (*see page 142*) humming birds thrive on nectar, so plant a variety of good nectar-rich sources, such as bee balm, trumpet vine, any of the many varieties of honeysuckle, annual nasturtium, morning glory and delphiniums.

Creating a wildflower meadow

The astonishing devastation of meadowland all over the countryside has led to the extinction and near extinction of many species of birds, insects and plants. So if you have access to a piece of land, however small, one of the most ecologically friendly things you could do with it is transform it into a wildflower meadow.

If you have a lawn already, you can create your meadow by inserting pot-grown wildflowers or small nursery-grown wildflower seedlings as plugs directly into the turf. The good news is that a wildflower meadow will need mowing only a couple of times a year, but you will need to clear the grass cuttings to prevent them from suffocating new growth.

You can also create a new meadow from scratch using wildflower mixtures or wild flower and grass mixtures – you can even buy mixes aimed at particular wildlife such as a 'Bats in the Garden Mix' or 'Wild Bird Mix'. Make sure the soil is not too rich and that it is clear of weeds, then mix the seeds with dry silver sand to aid thin and even sowing.

As well as a beautiful meadow that sways gently in the summer breeze, you will attract a wide range of wildlife – from butterflies to dormice – and the birds will really appreciate it.

---

wildlife **tips**

Build a pond or provide clean, fresh water every few days in a saucer or hollow of a rock.

Plant native plants.

Choose plants that flower and bear fruit at different times of the year.

Leave some 'mess' in your garden such as dead, dying and hollow trees, and fallen fruit.

Do not use chemical pesticides and herbicides.

Ponds in the garden

Few people feel their garden is complete without a water feature and it is not just because it is of value to the flora and fauna. Water is innately soothing and the sound of running water could be all that you need to shake off the tensions of the day and relax.

There are two options available to you if you are keen to introduce a pond into your garden: you can either dig a big hole and line it or use a container such as a glazed pot or wooden barrel. If you are using a liner then try to find one made from recycled plastic.

Pond tips

- Build the soil up slightly around the pond to make sure water drains away from it and not into it. (But make sure that any drainage from the pond is away from your house.)

- There will be less maintenance if your pond is not under trees. Most aquatic plants grow better in full sun and you will reduce the problem of leaves collecting in the pond (covering the pond with a net in the autumn will also help).

- Let the pond sit for a few days before adding fish and plants. This allows chlorine to evaporate from the water.

- Consider a mix of emergent, submergent and floating species of plant in your pond.

- In tiny ponds floating species of plants such as duckweed (*Lemna minor*), water lettuce (*Pistia stratiotes*) and water hyacinth (*Eichhornia crassipes*) may be adequate to maintain clear water.

- Avoid electricity-gobbling special effects such as fountains, waterfalls and so on, although you can now buy or make solar fountains, which will work on sunny days and bright cloudy days (*see Resources, pages 178–83 for suppliers*).

- Don't waste electricity heating your pond in winter – fish will survive provided the pond does not freeze over and gases can escape. Placing a rubber ball in the water should make sure the pond does not freeze over completely.

● A 'balanced' pond will have algae at acceptable levels but scavengers, such as snails, will help clean up wastes from the bottom of the pond. Avoid chemical controls: if you have a real problem then try eco-friendly products such as pond pads, which use barley straw as a natural agent for controlling algae in ponds.

● Locate the pond where it is least likely to attract unattended children and always be very vigilant!

● Most people surround their ponds with rockeries in order to make them look more natural and provide places for frogs to hibernate. Try to use local rocks, thus avoiding the environmental costs of transportation. It would be even better to use second-hand rocks, that is, those being removed from a building site anyway, rather than from a quarry.

● At all costs avoid using the limestone rocks that are found in many garden centres. Limestone pavements are rare geological formations formed during the Ice Age, which are home to several rare species of plant and butterflies. Demand for limestone from gardeners has led to the destruction of the UK's limestone pavements to such an extent that there are only 3,000 hectares (7,500 acres) left – only 3 per cent have escaped damage.

● The well-known British organic gardener Geoff Hamilton came up with a way of making your own 'limestone' rocks. Begin by digging a hole as a mould for the rock, lining it with strong polythene, and mixing two parts coir with two parts sharp sand and one part fresh cement. Add enough water to make a stiff consistency. Put some of the mixture in the hole, spreading it up the sides to make it hollow. Leave it for a few days to set, remove from the hole, peel away the polythene and leave the 'rock' to dry.

In the home

Green gardening in the home follows the same principles as outdoor gardening. The aim is to avoid using pesticides, to make the best use of natural resources such as water and light, to recycle where possible and to make sure that anything purchased is as environmentally friendly as possible – both in its production and distribution.

Apart from using natural pest control, one of the main ways in which you can make a difference immediately is to avoid peat-based potting composts for your house plants (*see page 126 for more on why this is important*). It is possible to make your own potting compost or to buy peat-free compost suitable for house plants.

Worm compost (*see box, page 130*) can be used for planting house plants and a liquid feed made up of compost and water in equal measures can provide a boost to ailing house plants.

Apart from improving the look of your room, house plants can provide a variety of functions, such as reducing pollution by filtering the air – particularly useful in your home office (*see pages 84–93*).

You can also grow food at home by planting indoor window boxes of herbs, starting garden vegetable seedlings off indoors or growing sprouting seeds. Home-grown sprouting seeds are a great way to garden indoors; they are fun for children, easy to grow and incredibly nutritious, plus they will save you money on store-bought sprouts.

To harvest your own regular supply of delicious sprouting seeds all you need is a sieve, a glass jar, some muslin (cheesecloth) and some filtered water. Start by soaking the dried beans or seeds – the choice includes mung beans, alfafa seeds, lentils, chickpeas, adzuki beans and pumpkin seeds, – overnight. Rinse and drain them in a sieve, then transfer them to a glass jar and cover it with a square of muslin held in place with an elastic band or string before putting it in a warm, dark place such as an airing cupboard.

All you then have to do is to fill the jar with water and tip upside down to drain through the muslin before putting them back into the covered jar. Repeat this process twice a day until the sprouts are nearly ready to eat (it should take three to five days). Just prior to eating, the sprouts should be put on a windowsill for a couple of hours. Then wash and eat them as soon as possible.

You could also try growing wheatgrass on trays. You will need a mixture of organic compost and top soil spread on a tray and moistened. Then sprinkle with seed, which should have been soaked and left to germinate for 12 hours, and lay another tray on top to keep in moisture. After three days lift the top tray off, water and place the sprouts in sunlight. Four days later you should have a crop of wheat grass that can make a power-packed juice (*for Recipes see page 166*).

Green house plant tips

The minerals in cold tea are said to help flagging pot plants, so mix some in with your water.

The water produced from leaving egg shells soaking for several days is also said to revive indoor plants.

A few drops of almond oil on a damp cloth can help clean the leaves on shiny-leaved plants, such as mother-in-law's tongue.

Make your own plant pots from old yogurt and ice cream pots. Remember to put drainage holes in the bottom and use the lids as saucers underneath.

To maintain steady watering, even if you are away, place one end of a length of thick wool in a saucer of water and the other in the plant pot. The water will steadily drip from one to the other.

Save water from your bath and washing up to use on your indoor plants. Also remember to use the water left over in the kettle or the waste water produced when installing a new water filter.

ⓘ Try ivy, a peace lily, spider plant or rubber plant if you want to enjoy nature in your home at the same time as removing pollution from the atmosphere. They all help to cleanse the air by absorbing potentially harmful VOCs.

garden
accessories

Gardens are about more than just plants. Some people choose to grow very little in their gardens, using them more as an extra room for outdoor entertaining, but that does not mean that they are necessarily ignoring the impact their garden has on the environment.

Not all kinds of patios, fencing and garden furniture are created equal when it comes to the environment – some are definitely greener than others. But it is still early days in terms of how much information you can find on the environmental impact and sustainability of garden products. Work is being done by some ecological organizations to devise organic standards that can be applied in this area, but in the meantime the best advice is to question your local garden centre, do-it-yourself chain or manufacturer to find out where the product comes from, how it is produced and how much energy has been used in order for it to reach you. They might not have the answers readily available, but without public pressure they might never bother to find out.

Patios and terraces

There is life beyond a lawn, and it used to be crazy paving, but these days people are opting for more natural-looking patio surfaces in their gardens than concrete. Avoiding concrete is a very good idea – it blocks natural drainage, absorbs heat and smothers all living things on which it is poured. But even with alternative surfaces there are still some important points to consider.

Decking was the garden design hit of the 1990s, but just because it is wooden does not mean it is necessarily green. The wood could be from poorly managed forests or have been treated with toxic chemicals (*see box, page 41*), so get as much information as possible before you buy. Instead of buying new, you could try using reclaimed wood to give a unique look to your patio. Old railway sleepers are also useful for bed edging.

You can also buy second-hand for your patio if you use bricks or paving – reclaimed bricks and paving are available from some builder's merchants (*see Resources, pages 178–83*). If you are buying new paving stones, look for local stone to save on the polluting cost of transportation.

Whatever your choice of surface, remember the principles of green gardening and learn to live with a few 'imperfections', such as moss. Do not use chemicals to blitz all plant life growing between the cracks in your paving. If things are really getting out of control, try the traditional tried-and-tested method of weeding by hand.

Fences, walls and hedges

No matter how small or large your garden, it is likely to be bordered by fencing, wall or hedge.

The ideal green boundary is a hedge – a living fence. Hedges have become rare commodities in today's countryside, with large commercial farms having ripped out many to make way for larger fields and to allow farm vehicles access.

Hedges are hugely valuable as a home to birds, animals and insects, as well as providing a safe habitat for wildflowers and other plants. But on a practical gardening level, they also act as far more effective windbreaks than fences. Wind tends to bounce up and over when it hits a solid boundary such as a fence, and swirling on the leeward side often damages plants. This can also create the conditions that lead to fences being blown down. Hedges on the other hand filter and slow wind down and every 30 cm (1 ft) of hedge height offers 3 m (10 ft) of shelter.

So you will be helping both the conditions in your garden and the environment as a whole by keeping any existing hedges and planting others if you have a suitable space. It need not be at the edge of your property – hedges can also be used to segregate different areas in the garden, such as a lawn from a vegetable patch.

If you are not convinced of the merits of hedges over fences then choose your fencing carefully (*see Woody Issues, pages 151–2*). If you prefer walls then make sure they are built using reclaimed bricks or stone if at all possible, or, failing that, select a stone that is local to your area. If you are painting or staining fences or walls then remember to choose natural organic products that do not use petrochemicals (*see page 41*).

Finally, use the walls and fences as vertical canvases on which to continue your garden by fixing trellises on them and growing climbing plants such as vines, clematis, honeysuckle or wisteria. Western red cedar wood is commonly used to make trellises, but the Canadian forests from which the wood comes have not been well managed so avoid this wood unless it has the Forest Stewardship Council (FSC) mark (*see page 40*).

Helpful **hedge tips**

- As with all planting in your garden, keep it local – there are locally distinctive hedgerow types so find out which ones predominate in your area before deciding which to grow.

- Consider which hedges attract the most wildlife – oak, blackthorn (sloe) and hawthorn, for example – and help further by planting wildflowers and grasses at the foot of the hedge.

- Remember you don't have to plant just one variety – you could mix the all-green varieties of holly or privet with variegated species. Hedges can also provide colour in the garden – try planting flowering shrubs such as spiraea, barberry or escallonia in informal hedges.

- Low-growing hedges can be used for ornamental effect between borders, and can also appeal to other senses – try aromatic varieties such as lavender and rosemary.

- Avoid the infamous fast-growing Leyland cypress, which monopolizes soil nutrients over a wide distance and can reach a height of 135 m (150 ft). Opt for hawthorn, yew and beech if you want a quick-growing hedge.

- Don't be overzealous with the trimmer (use garden shears instead) and avoid shaping the hedge into an upright rectangle, as this can lead to top-heavy growth with gaps below. Training the hedge into an 'A' shape (when seen from the side) makes sure the lower levels get as much light as the top and gives a much stronger and healthier structure that makes a better wind- and weatherbreak.

- If your hedge has become thin and gappy, it can be partially revived by the seemingly drastic technique of cutting it almost right down to the ground (with a sloping cut). New growth will usually appear by the next spring, which, with new planting to fill any large gaps, will give a reasonable hedgerow within three to four years.

Garden furniture

There is no point having a gorgeous green garden if you do not spend any relaxing time in it – which is where garden furniture comes in. If you have comfortable seats in which to flop and listen to the bees buzzing on a hot summer's day then you will appreciate your garden all the more. But before you rush off to get your picnic table and sun loungers, take time to consider what materials have been used to make them.

If you are buying hardwood tables and chairs for example, then be sure of the timber's origins, especially if they are made from teak, iroko or nyatoh – again look out for the FSC mark (*see page 40*).

If plastic furniture appeals to you, check the recycled content. There are now many suppliers of recycled plastic furniture (*see Resources, pages 178–83*).

Cast-iron furniture is also popular in gardens, but it is important to check what paint has been used to coat it. Is it lead-free? Does it contain solvents? And also, how far has the furniture travelled from manufacturer to retailer?

For the ultimate green seat, however, consider using turf as furniture. The Henry Doubleday Research Association will be able to provide advice on how to create a turf table and stools using an old cable drum and chicken wire as it has done in one of its gardens (*see Resources, pages 178–83*).

Woody issues

When choosing wood to use in your garden, be it for decking, trellises, fences, furniture or a shed, there are some key issues to be aware of.

The first is the kind of wood being used and how it has been produced. Garden furniture in particular has been made using wood from some of the most vulnerable forests in the world, the tropical rainforests; wood from poorly managed western red cedar forests in Canada is also commonly found in garden products. So it is important to find out if the wood has come from a sustainable source.

Just asking your retailer or manufacturer may not be the answer. A recent survey by Friends of the Earth and Global Witness showed that most retailers and suppliers do not know where the hardwood garden furniture they sell comes from – and still fewer know about the social and environmental impact of these products. The most reliable way of checking out the wood you buy is to look for products that carry the Forest Stewardship Council (FSC) mark (*see page 40*). This is an independent guarantee that the forest or woodland of origin is managed according to agreed social and environmental principles and criteria. These include the concept that forest management 'shall conserve biological diversity and its associated values, water resources, soils, and unique and fragile ecosystems and landscapes, and, by so doing, maintain the ecological functions and the integrity of the forest'.

Plenty of retailers make green claims for their wood furniture but the FSC scheme is the only credible certification for wood products.

The second major issue of concern when it comes to wood in your garden is the use of wood preservatives, such as creosote. Used to prevent rot and decay by bacterial and fungal agents, preservatives are commonly used on fence posts, compost boxes, bed edging, fence panels and sheds.

The most dangerous preservative for the environment is creosote, which leaches into the soil, gives off vapours for seven years and is harmful to people and animals. CCA-treated timber – sometimes called 'tanalized' timber or 'pressure-treated' timber – can also pose a risk to the environment since it uses incredibly toxic chemicals such as copper arsenate. These chemicals are meant to stay in the wood once dry but American researchers have found traces of arsenic in the soil and on the hands of children who have been playing on equipment made from this timber. There may be a danger to you if you fail to use gloves when handling the wood and a mask when sawing it, and certainly this wood should never be burned.

There are other preservatives available, such as those based on boron and acetypetacs zinc and copper, which are all said to have a low toxicity to plants, humans and animals. There are also an increasing number of plant-based preservatives on the market, although these will not necessarily have been endorsed by organic gardening groups. But even these preservatives should be used only if essential. It is better for you and the environment if you avoid the need for any preservatives by taking the following steps:

- Set posts in concrete or use metal 'shoes' for fence posts as the main area of decay is likely to be where the wood meets the soil and air.

- Oil wood that is in contact with the soil – linseed oil is easy to apply and allows the wood to breathe, avoiding trapped moisture.

- Choose the right wood for the job – without preservatives, oak, sweet chestnut and western red cedar will last 20 years in contact with the soil, and untreated pine and larch will last five and ten years respectively. Heart wood and well-seasoned wood is more resistant to decay.

◼ Consider whether you need to use preservatives at all – most wood will not decay for years anyway and does it matter if wood used on bed edges and compost boxes eventually decays?

◼ Most wood sold for outdoor use in garden centres and large do-it-yourself stores will have already been treated so if you want to avoid them opt for wood sold for indoor use or visit your local sawmill and ask for untreated wood.

◼ If you want a green easy life, avoid wood altogether and choose 'wood alternative' instead. Made from recycled plastics, this synthetic wood is now used to make fence posts, panels, trellises, bed-edging boards and boards used in garden benches. With no need for preservatives, stains or paints, this option could be the easiest and greenest going and should be available from a large do-it-yourself store or garden centre.

The happy gardener

It is no good creating a green garden paradise if your mosquito bites are so bad you dare not enter it. And slapping chemical insect repellent all over yourself is not the answer, considering the lengths you have gone to avoid chemicals in the rest of your garden. So have the following natural products handy before you go out into the garden to make sure you are as happy in it as all those insects.

Citronella oil
This essential oil repels mosquitoes, but smells pleasantly lemony to humans. It can be applied directly to the skin if diluted in a carrier oil, can be added to a vaporizer, or is often found added to outdoor candles. Lavender oil can also be used in this way, or you could try washing the skin in a pennyroyal or elderflower infusion.

Tea tree oil
A fantastic all-rounder for any gardener, this essential oil is antibacterial, antiviral and antifungal. It can soothe an insect bite, sting, cut or graze and prevent it becoming infected.

The **green barbecue**

● As soon as the evenings get lighter and warmer the urge to cook and eat outdoors gets stronger and by the middle of summer the barbecue season will be in full swing. They are a great way to get you and your friends out in the garden, but are barbecues environmentally friendly?

● The first consideration is the kind of barbecue you plan to use. Probably the best type is home-built, using old bricks or an old tin drum, but if you have to buy one then check that any wood used as shelves and knobs is from a sustainably managed source.

● When it comes to what you burn in the barbecue, most people opt for charcoal, which has an uncertain environmental record. Ideally, charcoal should be produced from old wood that is a by-product of good forestry, that is, the thinnings. But there have been concerns that in some countries trees are being felled for the sole purpose of making charcoal. There are also worries that some countries are destroying environmentally sensitive mangrove forests in tropical coastal areas in order to produce charcoal.

● Given the question marks over the sustainable nature of charcoal, production overseas and the amount of polluting air miles notched up to bring in this kind of charcoal, it would be best to buy your charcoal locally, where it is likely to have come from managed coppiced woodland.

Aloe vera

This plant has a huge number of uses, but it is good for gardeners since it soothes sunburn and can also help heal cuts. Have a go at growing the plant yourself – it thrives in hot, sunny conditions so you may have more luck on an indoor window ledge – or buy an aloe vera preparation.

Homeopathic remedies

Keeping a homeopathic first-aid kit can be helpful to a gardener. Try pyrethrum tincture for bee stings, arnica or ledum tinctures for wasp stings, and a mixture of hypericum and calendula tinctures for gnat bites. For skin that has come into contact with poison ivy, bathe it with milk and take anacardium 6c every 15 minutes. Ask a registered homeopath for more information on specific remedies.

Sun protection

No one should need reminding of the dangers of prolonged exposure to direct sunlight and gardeners are especially at risk. Always cover up as much as possible (even if working in the shade), wear a hat that shades the back of your neck, and wear sunscreen. Choose a sunscreen with a sun protection factor (SPF) of at least 15, which protects against UVA and UVB rays, and look out for those that contain certified organic ingredients or that are available through health-food stores, as they are likely to have fewer petrochemicals in them. You could also try taking 30 mg of beta carotene daily during the summer as this has been shown to give greater protection against the dangers of radiation on the skin.

The atmospheric garden

All five senses can be stimulated in a garden – you can relax as you watch and listen to bees buzzing around heavily scented honeysuckle, while lying on soft grass, munching a home-grown apple. Paying attention to the sensory effects of your garden will bring rich rewards, so try some of the following:

Water

For many people, the key to relaxation is water – be it the sound of crashing waves or a long hot soak in the bath – so bring water into your garden with a pond. It does not have to be a big lake; you can start small by making a mini water feature in a container on your patio. (*See Pond Tips, pages 144–5.*)

Light

A garden at night is a special place, often unrecognizable from its daytime guise. Many different animals and insects come out in the evening and the cool air is often filled with the scents of different flowers that have opened during the day. Lighting your garden by night will help you make the most of it – allowing you to see it an entirely different way and making it a warm and welcoming place for evening entertaining.

But this does not mean you should call in the electrician immediately. Give the latest in solar-powered lighting a try – solar globe lights will give up to 20 hours of light when fully charged, switch on automatically at dusk, and best of all can even be used floating in your pond. Or consider soft lighting from candles and oil burners. Large garden flares can last for many hours and many candles have the added bonus of deterring insects with the addition of citronella oil. Look, too, for recycled glass lanterns or put tea lights in old glasses and position these around your garden. Don't just concentrate on your patio – the rest of your garden can look wonderful with lights dotted around, too.

Scent

Choosing your plants carefully can help make your garden more than just a visual experience. Plant according to scent, especially in areas where you are likely to brush past plants, such as raised beds abutting a path. Herbs grown near a kitchen or by your outdoor dinning table will arouse the taste buds with their scent and a summer's day will be that much sweeter with the smell of jasmine, sweet William and phlox filling the air. Look out too for plants that release their scent in the evening, such as tobacco plants.

Sound

Encouraging wildlife into your garden will provide you with the perfect soundtrack to relax to – birds, bees, frogs and grasshoppers all contribute to a soothing garden symphony. But you can add your own sounds with running water in your pond and wind chimes made out of old wood. Just sit back, close your eyes and unwind.

green food
and drink

If you wish to live a truly green life you cannot afford to ignore what you eat. Much of the planet is used to grow food, be it wheat on the American prairies, rice from the fields of China or bananas from a Caribbean island. So many countries give over most of their land to food production that the type of agriculture that is practised is vital for biodiversity and environmental conservation. By opting for 'green' food you could be making a difference to the ecology of many countries – your decision has a global impact.

Conventional farming practices do not have a good record when it comes to protecting the environment and they are costing us all dear as a consequence. But the good news is that it is relatively simple to make a green choice when it comes to food – go organic. Whether you grow your own or buy it in, you will know that organic food has been produced in a way that nurtures rather than exploits the environment. And by buying only certified organic produce you know that there is a legal system ensuring that producers' green credentials are as good as they say they are.

The organic difference

The aim of organic farming is to work with nature to create the healthiest conditions in which to grow food, without the need for artificial inputs such as fertilizers, pesticides, antibiotics or growth-promoting hormones. The emphasis in organic farming is about achieving a natural balance with the environment in which a farm exists and to be as self-sustaining as possible.

The following are the key differences between organic and conventional farming:

Soil health

To maximize the chances of producing healthy crops organic farmers pay a great deal of attention to the health of their soil. Techniques for soil improvement include crop and animal rotation, planting soil-enriching plants or green manures and adding manure and home-made compost. By doing this, organic farmers avoid the need for artificial nitrate fertilizers and they make sure the soil can support a rich variety of life. This is important, since it has been estimated that it takes 500 years to form 2.5 cm (1 in) of topsoil; keeping it in good condition and preventing its erosion is therefore vital for the environment.

Conventional farming on the other hand often makes heavy use of artificial fertilizers – around 80 million tonnes are used globally each year – two-thirds of which leach away from the land and end up contaminating our water supplies with excess nitrogen. Water companies are having to introducing more and more treatment programmes costing millions to tackle this contamination.

Self-sustaining

Organic farmers aim to be self-sustaining. For example, they keep livestock alongside crops, thereby providing valuable manure for the land and organic animal feed. They rotate crops and pastures, preventing disease and soil imbalances. Growing plants known to attract pest-eating insects beside a valuable crop – companion planting – is another way in which they work with nature.

Conventional farmers are more likely to buy in their animal feed, ship out their manure and look outside the farm for solutions to pest problems and soil fertility, ignoring the answers in their own backyard. Overall, organic farms are likely to use far less energy and non-renewable resources (such as diesel fuel) than conventional farms.

Conservation

Organic standards demand that farmers conserve natural wildlife habitats such as grassland, hay meadows and moorland. They also ensure that old farm buildings are protected, existing ponds are maintained, and old hedgerows and stone walls are looked after. In addition to conserving habitats, organic farmers are encouraged to contribute further to the environment by planting native trees, creating ponds, and nurturing wildflowers and grasses in wide borders between cultivated fields.

Conventional farming has, in recent times, meant intensive farming, whereby the larger the scale of a farm the cheaper it has been to produce the crop. However, the cost to the environment of this kind of farming has been heavy. For example, in the last 50 years, half the UK's natural woodlands and 40 per cent of its hedgerows have been destroyed as farmers expand their cultivated land.

The loss of wildlife as a result of this habitat destruction has been enormous – huge numbers of species of birds, bees, butterflies, wildflowers and insects are disappearing fast because of this kind of agriculture.

Avoiding synthetic chemicals

One of the biggest differences between conventional and organic farming systems is the former's reliance on synthetic chemicals – either pre- or post-harvest. There is no place in organic farming for synthetic chemical pesticides. Instead, organic farmers concentrate on improving soil health, planting disease-resistant varieties, inspecting their crops frequently, rotating crops, and encouraging natural predators with companion planting and by creating ponds, hedgerows and so on.

Occasionally, even organic farmers have such a severe pest problem that they turn to insecticidal sprays, but these must be approved by organic certifiers and are based on natural compounds, which biodegrade quickly.

Mainstream farming has, in contrast, come to depend on highly toxic synthetic pesticides. The result of all this spraying has not been a decrease in the loss of crops to insects; in fact the global loss has almost doubled in the last 50 years as insects, diseases and weeds have developed more and more resistance to these products.

These pesticides have in fact also contributed to the disappearance of many farmland birds as the bugs they feed on are wiped out or poison the birds that eat them. Wildflowers have also been devastated by mass spraying of land, as have the insects and butterflies that feed on them. Land and water pollution is another by-product of this.

Of major concern is the fact that many countries with the most fragile and threatened eco-structures are becoming the biggest users of these pesticides and they are also often the least careful in terms of safe usage and disposal of these chemicals.

Post-harvest chemicals are also popular with conventional growers since they extend food shelf life. For example, methyl bromide is applied to strawberries and to sterilize grain after harvesting. Other foods likely to have been sprayed in this way are bananas, citrus fruits, grapes, apples, pears and cherries – even potatoes can be sprayed with a toxic fungicide to inhibit sprouting.

Apart from their possible impact on human health, some of these chemicals are highly damaging to the environment. Methyl bromide is thought to be 60 times more damaging to the ozone layer than the more commonly known CFCs (*see page 59*), and 50–90 per cent of the substance enters the atmosphere when sprayed on crops.

Biodiversity
Encouraging natural biodiversity is an inherent aim of organic farming, not only in the greater environment in which the farm exists, but also in terms of the kind of crops and livestock that are being farmed. Organic farmers often grow unusual varieties of fruits and vegetables that are fast disappearing from our countryside, and they are also more likely to rear traditional breeds of livestock, since these will be best suited to the local conditions.

Variety has all but disappeared from conventional farming, with farmers relying on just a few types of seed and animal, bred specifically to meet their needs – yield and size – and not that of consumers – which is taste. In India, for example, there used to be over 30,000 different varieties of rice, but just ten varieties are expected to cover 75 per cent of the rice-producing land in the next ten years. And in France, the Golden Delicious apple accounts for nearly 75 per cent of all apples grown. In the UK there are 2,300 known varieties of apple but just two – the Cox and the Bramley – now dominate; and of 550 different sorts of pear, three varieties are generally available. Virtually half of Britain's pear orchards and nearly two-thirds of its apple orchards have been destroyed since 1970. These orchards were wildlife havens for many plants and bats, hares, badgers, owls and woodpeckers.

On the livestock front, the world is losing at least two breeds of animal every week. One thousand different breeds of domestic animal have become extinct during the past century and one-third of surviving breeds are endangered, according to the United Nations Food and Agriculture Agency (FAO). They blame this on the success of breeders in the developed world in exporting animals that have been bred to produce more and better meat or milk. The poultry and pig industries are highlighted as being reliant on only a handful of specialized breeds.

The impact on the environment of monoculture or 'genetic erosion' is severe. We are endangering thousands of other species that rely on these plants and animals, losing plants that may well prove of medicinal use in years to come and creating an environment in which disease and pests run rife.

Genetic modification
The only way to be sure your food has not been genetically modified (GM) – whereby a gene or genes from one species is inserted into another – is to buy organic food. Worldwide organic standards prevent genetic modification or the use of GM ingredients for many reasons, including the unknown impact of this technology on the environment.

The use of GM seed encourages farmers to depend on a single seed supplier and reduces the chances of a variety of seeds being sown, thereby further threatening natural biodiversity. Even English Nature, the UK government's own wildlife advisor, has called for a moratorium on the growing of these crops. But despite the fact that research concerning the impact of genetic modification on the environment and human health is still pretty thin on the ground, GM crops are already being cultivated and eaten in many places around the world. In the USA, in particular, conventional farmers have greeted genetic modification with enthusiasm and many thousands of acres of land have been dedicated to the cultivation of GM soya and maize. This has led to the widespread introduction of GM ingredients in food production – up to 90 per cent of processed food may already contain GM material.

Local and seasonal

Although not actually written into the legal standards that govern organic food, the majority of organic growers support local food initiatives, which encourage consumers to buy their food locally and seasonally. The organic community supports local food initiatives such as farmers markets, where farmers sell their own produce usually in monthly gatherings held in local towns and cities; box schemes, whereby mostly organic fruit and vegetables that have just been harvested are delivered to your door for a fixed fee; and small independent stores such as healthfood stores or organic fruit and vegetable stores.

As these are often run by the farmers themselves they reinforce the link between grower and consumer that has been lost over the years in developed countries and which many believe has led to the mistrust and divisions between town and country. Such consumers may come to change their habits – learning to cook seasonal recipes with ingredients they may not have seen since their grandmother passed away, and mastering the art of making the most of a glut of certain crops, such as tomatoes and fruits.

Buying local produce also avoids the costs of pollution associated with conventional food production and distribution. Conventional farmers and retailers appear to pay little heed to the environmental cost of shipping crops around the world and growing strawberries in mid-winter. As a result, air transport – now the fastest-growing source of carbon dioxide emissions – is used for an increasing number of food imports. Further pollution is generated when the food is then brought to a central depot before being trucked out to the individual supermarkets, and then driven home by a customer.

Also, food that has travelled long distances tends to require more packaging in order to protect it on its journey, resulting in the waste of huge amounts of plastic, cardboard and glass.

Some specific
environmental
concerns:

● Crops that have been genetically modified to resist insects kill not just the target insect but also beneficial insects. Pollen from GM plants can kill endangered butterflies such as the monarch, for example.

● Planting herbicide-resistant crops could encourages the use of larger quantities of herbicide, so all plant growth other than the crop is removed. This in turn wipes out seed-eating and insect-eating wild birds, such as skylarks and blackbirds, and small mammals, such as dormice.

● Insects can become resistant to the insecticide produced by GM plants and some GM plants may crossbreed with wild species to produce 'superweeds', which could out-compete and disrupt the natural biodiversity of an area (this may also happen with animals, such as GM salmon). As a consequence, the use of GM technology may not reduce the need for toxic chemicals in farming but increases it, as the search goes on for ever-more effective weapons against pests.

● GM plants can contaminate non-GM plants and honey.

Proof of the **pudding**

Research into the benefits of organic farming on the environment is still at an early stage, but findings so far have been compelling. Nine studies looking at the impact on biodiversity of organic farming compared with conventional farming systems came up with the following results:

- Wild plants: there were five times as many wild plants in arable fields, 57 per cent more species, and several rare and declining wild arable species were found only on the organic farms.

- Crop pests: there was a significant decrease in aphid numbers and no change in the numbers of pest butterflies.

- Invertebrates: there were 1.6 times as many of the arthropods that comprise bird food; three times as many non-pest butterflies in the crop areas; one to five times as many spider numbers and one to two times as many spider species.

- Birds: there were 25 per cent more birds at the field edge, 44 per cent more in-field birds in autumn/winter; there were 2.2 times as many breeding skylarks and higher skylark breeding rates.

- Land use and crops: the field boundaries had more trees, larger hedges and no spray drift; the crops were sparser, with no herbicides, allowing more weeds; there was also more grassland and a greater variety of crop types.

Other benefits

You can feel virtuous about more than just the environment if you eat organic food. It has many other benefits too:

More jobs created

By using traditional farming techniques, such as hand weeding, organic farms offer more employment opportunities to hard-pressed rural communities. In Germany, for example, organic farms employ 10–20 per cent more people than conventional farms. Overall labour requirements tend to be 10-30 per cent higher; in addition, many organic farms provide new business opportunities nearby, such as box schemes.

Better for health

By eating organic your chances of avoiding any synthetic chemical residues in your food are higher. These chemicals are increasingly being linked with damage to the nervous system, birth defects, cancer, dropping fertility levels, and other human ailments. Most governments do set minimum acceptable levels allowed in food but few take into account the effect of eating a variety of these residues – the 'cocktail effect' – or adjust these levels when considering children's intake.

In 1999, a UK government report found that there has been a significant increase in the quantity of fresh fruit and vegetables containing pesticide residues, up from 33 per cent to 43 per cent of samples. And most of these residues do not wash off easily since many are designed to withstand rain, and some are designed to actually enter the plant, ruling out peeling as a way of getting rid of them.

Pesticides do not just threaten your health; they are also incredibly dangerous for farm workers worldwide. It has been reported that 40,000 people are killed every year due to pesticide exposure and the World Health Organization found that up to 30 per cent of Latin American farm workers it tested showed signs of exposure to organophosphates, chemicals linked with serious health damage.

Organic crops are also believed to be healthier in terms of their chemical structure. Recent research in Germany, Denmark and Switzerland has found that organic produce has higher nutrient levels when compared with conventional produce.

If you eat organic you are also less likely to be eating food that contains antibiotic residues, since organic farmers are not allowed to routinely give their animals antibiotics as a preventive medical measure or in the form of growth promoters. The use of antibiotics has increased by 1,500 per cent in the past 30 years, and 65 per cent of all antibiotics are used in conventional farming. It is widely believed that this overuse of antibiotics in farming has led to worrying levels of antibiotic-resistance in humans, leaving us with fewer weapons against infection, and the rise of drug-resistant superbugs such as MRSA.

Lastly, organic food can help reduce the problems associated with food safety such as bovine spongiform encephalopathy (BSE). There has not been a case in any herd in full organic management prior to 1985. Given that organic standards do not permit the use of animal-based products in feed, the BSE crisis in Europe, with its huge cost to the taxpayer, could probably have been avoided altogether if organic farming had been the norm.

The risk of food poisoning should also be lower if you eat organic, especially organic meat. This is because factory farming often keeps animals in such cramped and stressful conditions that disease is more likely.

Improved animal welfare

Strict animal welfare conditions are included in organic standards, such as the requirement that animals have free access to fields or outdoor areas; that they have ample natural bedding, such as straw; and plenty of space in indoor areas such that they are able to express their natural behaviour patterns. So you will never find battery hens in organic farming.

All organically reared animals must be fed natural organic feedstuff, and graze on organic pastures such as herb- and clover-rich grass. They are not pumped full of antibiotics and growth promoters – instead, through a mixture of good husbandry and natural and homeopathic remedies, animals are healthier and require less medication.

Some certifying bodies also specify the maximum time any animal can spend travelling to an abattoir – the Soil Association in the UK, for example, requires that this is no more than eight hours – and they encourage the use of local abattoirs.

Tastier

While this is purely subjective, organic food is often the tastiest option. This is because organic farmers often grow traditional, uncommon varieties of fruit and vegetables that have been selected for their taste rather than their suitability for transportation or yield. Also, if you buy your organic produce from a local source, such as at a farmers' market, it is likely to be fresher, which always makes for a better taste. And since organic fresh produce is not sprayed with post-harvest chemicals to prevent decay, you will not be fooled into buying an apple that has been hanging around for some time in the belief that it was picked that morning.

Frequently asked questions

How can I tell whether something is organic?

Organic is a legal definition when applied to food, so for a food to be labelled or sold as organic it must have been produced according to national organic farming and processing standards, and this is true worldwide. In the case of processed foods, such as biscuits (cookies). UK standards state that at least 95 per cent of all ingredients must be certified organic. The other 5 per cent can be non-organic only if approved by the certifier – this occurs only if there is difficulty finding an organic version of the ingredient and may be only a temporary measure.

What stops producers calling their produce organic anyway?

Certifiers in every country carry out regular inspections to ensure that organic standards are being met and will give products that meet these standards a mark or number as a guarantee of authenticity. If you want to be sure that the food you are buying is organic then look out for either of these on a label or, if buying unpackaged products, ask the retailer for proof.

Are all organic foods healthy?

Yes and no. Organic foods are less likely to contain chemical and antibiotic residues (*see pages 158–9*), and they are not allowed to contain hydrogenated fats, artificial additives, flavourings or preservatives, so in this respect they are healthier. However, they are not 'health foods'. You can buy organic ice cream, biscuits and chocolate, for example, none of which should be eaten to excess if you are concerned about your health. But organic foods are definitely healthy for the environment.

With so much organic food coming from overseas, how green can it be?

Organic imports feature heavily in many countries around the world, and there are clearly environmental costs to transporting food in this way. However, the environmental benefits of organic farming are so great that anyone serious about green living should buy organic. In addition, the more people that buy organic the more likely it is that farmers will convert their farms to organic production and that governments will help by subsidizing these farmers during the conversion process (up to three years).

Do buy as much of your produce locally as you can and eat seasonally. The organic community encourages both.

What about workers – do they fare better?

The term 'organic' does not automatically mean that a product is fairly traded as well. There is a separate mark to look out for – the Fair Trade mark – if you want to be absolutely certain that workers are paid a fair wage, work in safe and humane conditions and are given training. But at present this is given only to coffees, teas, bananas, cocoa, orange juice, chocolate and honey and exists in only 18 countries worldwide.

Organic agriculture is rarely at odds with the principles of Fair Trade, since by avoiding the use of synthetic chemicals, for example, workers are already being given a healthier working environment. And organic producers have traditionally had a strong ethical basis which has seen them provide long-term contracts at fixed fair prices to suppliers, along the same lines as those that exist in fair trading.

So it is likely that, if you are buying organic, workers will benefit. However, with larger, less ethically conscious companies getting in on the organic act, this may not always be the case, so keep a look out for goods that are both organic and Fair Trade.

Why does it seem that there is not enough organic produce to go round?

There genuinely isn't enough to go round. Consumer demand for organic food is rising but farmers are not converting to organic production quickly enough to keep up with this demand. Even for those farmers who are converting it takes a minimum of two to three years to achieve organic status, so there is a time lag between demand and supply.

More needs to be done by governments to make conversion an attractive proposition to farmers, since farm incomes drop dramatically while they are in the process of converting. Subsidies are crucial and make sense if governments are as keen to help the environment as they say they are.

To maximize your chances of getting what you want, shop in specialist stores if you are lucky enough to have one near you, or consider mail order – you can buy organic meat and fish directly from farmers, for example.

Why is organic food more expensive?

The price of organic food is coming down, but it is true to say that it does cost a bit more than conventional produce. This is mostly because it costs more to produce – manual labour is required for weeding and spreading compost, fewer animals are squashed into one shed and better-quality feed is given to these animals, for example. It is also costly to get your food certified as organic and to keep testing it to ensure that it is free from genetically modified organisms (GMOs) – pollution from GM crops has already occurred.

However, the price of your weekly shop is not the entire cost to you and your family. The true cost of the food you eat should reflect the amount you pay in tax and water bills, since it falls to governments and utilities to clean up the environment, to tackle food scares and to subsidize the threatened rural communities that often result from conventional agriculture. Taking the environmental, social and health costs of conventional food into account makes organic food a bit of a bargain.

Why does organic fresh produce often look worse than conventional produce?

If you mean a carrot that is not perfectly straight or an apple that does not gleam, then it is probably because organic produce is not manipulated in order to look good. In the organic world, food is judged as much on content as looks, so apples are not routinely waxed, for example.

Requiring your produce to conform to supermodel good looks comes at a cost. Supermarkets apply such strict rules regarding physical attributes that tonnes of produce fail to make the grade each year and is left to rot. For example, in 1996 more than 2,000 tonnes of eating apples were officially destroyed in the UK for this reason and the unofficial figure is said to be far higher.

But organic produce is not such a poor relation – organic farmers have made huge leaps in

developing new natural ways of preventing the disease and pest problems which often ruin the appearance of fresh produce.

Are organic farmers just anti-progress?

No. Organic farmers do not hand weed just because it harks back to the good old days. It is done because it is the best way to remove nuisance plants without damaging crops, other beneficial plants and the soil, while also helping the early detection of pest problems and providing much needed local employment.

Neither do organic farmers reject all science. In fact they draw heavily on the latest research into farm management as they seek new ways of achieving good results without falling back on conventional methods, such as pesticides.

What organic farmers do reject is failed science – pesticides, for example. Despite increasing use around the world, pest populations and crop losses have continued to rise. They also avoid what they consider to be unproven high-risk science, such as the genetic modification of crops.

Food and drink

To be truly green your store cupboard, fridge and freezer will be full of organic food and drinks – from organic baked beans to organic smoked salmon – but realistically this is going to take time to achieve.

As with all things green, the key message is that every little bit helps, so even if you swap just a few of your weekly food items for organic versions you will be helping, and hopefully you will have started a trend that will grow each time you shop.

Below are a list of key items that should be top of your organic hit list. Start with them and you will serve your environment and family well.

Fruit and vegetables

Eaten raw and often unpeeled, fruit and vegetables grown with the use of pesticides and subject to post-harvest treatment pose a particular threat to our health from chemical residues. For example, an independent working party in the UK has found one in three pieces of fruit and vegetables tested at random contained such residues and almost 2 per cent of the samples tested had higher levels than those permitted by law. The highest in terms of detectable residues were: celery – 72 per cent; lettuces – 56 per cent; and apples – 47 per cent.

Apples can be sprayed with pesticides up to 35 times before they reach your local supermarket and the average pear is sprayed more than 13 times. Given that children, with their less developed immune systems, drink 16 times more apple juice than the average adult, then you can see the impact non-organic apples could be having on your family.

In addition, with so many of our fruits and vegetables coming from overseas where different rules apply as to the use of pesticides and other chemicals, it is hard to know what has been used.

Fruit and vegetables are sometimes the subject of other environmentally-wasteful agricultural practices, such as being picked when they are under-ripe to aid transportation, and then being ripened in chambers pumped full of ethylene gas. Some are grown in heated, lit glasshouses so they can be grown year round and of course they are

increasingly appearing on the list of the geneticists, looking to modify fruit in particular to make it less susceptible to disease and to ripen slowly.

The lack of choice in varieties is another problem (*see Biodiversity, page 156*). Organic farmers are more likely to pick traditional varieties since they often offer better resistance to disease or are juicier than the mainstream ones. So supporting local organic fruit growers is essential.

Dairy produce

Organic milk, cheese, yogurt and butter – all originate from cows who graze on organic pastures, who will not have been routinely given antibiotics, and whose welfare is high on the list of priorities for the farmer. The benefit for you is that it is less likely to contain unwanted pesticide or antibiotic residues. The UK government found traces of lindane – one of the most dangerous substances in the world and which has been linked with breast cancer among many diseases in over 40 per cent of non-organic milk, cheese and butter samples in 1996. Lindane is commonly sprayed on sugar beet, a key part of conventional cattle feed.

By choosing organic dairy produce you will also be assured that the genetically modified hormone, BST or rBGH, has not been used on the dairy herd. The hormone is injected into one-third of American dairy cows to increase milk production, but it causes a five-fold increase in a protein that has been linked with breast cancer.

Chocolate

The cocoa plant is one of the most heavily sprayed crops in the world and intensive cocoa production is the cause of much soil erosion and deforestation in tropical countries. By going organic, you will be supporting a safer working environment for plantation workers and getting a healthier product, since organic chocolate contains up to twice the amount of cocoa solids as conventional brands, and no hydrogenated fats, refined white sugar or artificial flavourings.

Baby food

A child's immune system does not fully develop until about the age of 5, so bombarding them with pesticide-drenched food does not give children the best start in life. They are also far more likely to be eating food that contains residues – milk, fruit and vegetables – and are thus five times more likely to be consuming residues than an adult. And most governments' safety limits on pesticide residues are based on levels considered safe for adults.

Meat and fish

It is better for the animals as well as you if you opt for organic meat. Organic livestock are kept in more humane conditions, fed GM-free feed and not dosed with antibiotics.

Organic fish, too, are better cared for. Farmed fish such as trout and salmon are not kept in over-crowded tanks and not fed artificial colourings to turn their flesh pink; no routine medication is allowed and the fish are killed as humanely as possible. Organic standards also do not allow genetically modified fish – GM salmon are being trialled in conventional fisheries.

The environmental hazards of conventional fish farming, such as pollution of surrounding waters, are also avoided. Such pollution is mainly due to the use of chemical pesticides to control infestations such as sea lice, and other chemicals used to clean cages and prevent weed build-up. Fish waste and excess feed can also build up beneath cages, reducing oxygen levels in water and leading to dangerous algae blooms. Intensively farmed fish are also fed fish meal in pellets, often derived from threatened species of fish – these pellets are now being blamed for contaminating salmon with toxic chemicals, since they concentrate the trace amounts present in the fish from polluted oceans.

Many species of ocean fish are clearly endangered because of overfishing and the toxic effects of pesticides and other pollutants that run into the sea or are dumped there deliberately.

Processed foods made with soya and maize (corn)

In reality this is most processed foods since soya and maize (corn) are on the ingredients list of up to 90 per cent of manufactured foods. They are not always in forms you would immediately recognize either; for example, they are commonly used in anti-caking agents, colourings, emulsifiers, flavourings and food supplements.

The main reason you should opt for organic is the GM issue. Both GM soya and maize have been enthusiastically planted by American farmers and they meet much of the Western world's demand. Limited labelling is in place in some countries, so if you are lucky you should be able to tell whether GM ingredients feature in your food. However, the surest way to avoid them, and the health and environmental risks that may come with them is to eat organic.

You will also avoid many processing aids altogether, since organic standards restrict the number that can be used and requires as much transparency as possible on labelling with regard to ingredients and processing methods.

Tea and coffee

Tea and coffee plantations have suffered a similar fate to cocoa plantations. Drenched in pesticides, they have become larger and larger, with an increase in the resulting deforestation and soil erosion. But it is not just conventional tea that has environmental consequences; herbal teas may also have a poor environmental record, since herbs are commonly grown in glasshouses, in soil-free substrates, with heavy use of chemicals before and after harvest.

Wine and beer

You may not realize how far from its traditional image modern winemaking has come. Once again, the chemicals are out in force in most vineyards and there is little by way of other vegetation left for the local wildlife. Chemicals also feature in the winemaking process, with high levels of sulphur often finding their way into the finished product – these have been linked with allergies and headaches. Here, too, the geneticists are busy – genetically modified vines are on their way.

Organic wines are, needless to say, produced in an entirely more environmentally-friendly manner, with grasses and wildflowers cropping up beneath the vines. Lower levels of sulphur are specified in organic standards and chemicals are less likely in all stages of winemaking.

It is worth seeking out organic beers as well – conventional beers are produced using hops that are likely to have been sprayed with over 15 different pesticides around 12 times a year.

Where can I **buy** organic **food and drink**?

● These days, you can find organic products in almost every store almost everywhere; not only are all the big supermarkets devoting ever larger amounts of shelf space to organic food and drink, but even local convenience stores stock some organic products. But, if you cannot get what you want from the shops then you will certainly be able to from the Internet or a local box scheme.

● When choosing where to buy your organic food you should run through a green checklist. This might include the following questions:

● How much fuel do you use to get to your retailer of choice and how much energy has been used to get the food on the shelves of that retailer? For example, when assessed on the environmental cost of their food distribution practices, supermarkets do not fare particularly well. Food is flown in from all corners of the globe and carrots grown by your local farmer will probably have travelled to and from a national distribution centre before reaching your local supermarket.

● Consider your retailer's green credentials in other areas, too, such as the use of packaging, efforts to recycle, support for organic agriculture, and so on.

● Beyond the environmental questions, there is matter of choice. It is perfectly possible to eat a totally organic diet, but can you get all you need from your chosen store? Supermarkets might suddenly have quite a few organic products on their shelves, but the range will not be as large as in a specialist organic store. Small, local organic producers making specialist varieties of food, such as cheese, cannot produce enough to the tight deadlines and strict specifications stipulated by supermarkets, so such local organic products are a rarity in these stores, even in the areas in which the producers are based.

● Alternative sources of organic food are healthfood stores, farmers' markets, local box schemes and mail-order services, including those on the Internet (*see Resources, pages 178–83*). The numbers of each are rising all the time, so you may not have realized that a farmers' market has opened near you.

● The advantage of most of these outlets is that they are generally a lot closer to the original source of the food they sell, so they are more likely to sell food that you can trust. In the case of farmers' markets, local healthfood stores and box schemes, you will also be supporting much-threatened local retailers.

Top tips for green eating

● **Grow your own.** There are no transportation costs for your food to reach you, no waste packaging, no polluting and dangerous pesticides, and, if grown using your own compost, then it is the ultimate form of recycling.

● **Buy local.** Support outlets as close as possible to where your food is grown or made, such as farm shops, farmers' markets, box schemes, local grocers and healthfood stores. Your food will have travelled fewer miles to reach you, costing less in terms of pollution, and you will know you are getting food you can trust. In addition, they are likely to be small businesses in need of your support.

● **Buy certified organic produce.** This way you know your food has been produced with the utmost care and attention being paid to its environmental impact and you will be sure that it has met stringent legal standards.

● **Buy unusual varieties.** You will be encouraging biodiversity and signalling to retailers and growers that there is a market for more than just Granny Smiths and Golden Delicious, for example.

● **Buy loose.** Avoid all the packaging that comes with your food by buying it loose – and not just fruits and vegetables. Look for bulk bins of rice, beans and pulses, dried herbs and spices, nuts and grains, most commonly found in healthfood stores. If you cannot find it loose then choose a brand with as little packaging as possible, preferably one that uses recycled and biodegradable packaging materials.

● **Wise up on labels.** Learn to spot ingredients that are likely to have been genetically modified, look for organic certifying marks or numbers, and look for country of origin and local producer information. Avoid generic, mass-produced, poorly labelled, non-organic products.

● **Buy and eat seasonally.** By doing so you will be sending a message to retailers and growers that it is not necessary to fly strawberries around the world in winter and you will be discouraging the use of energy-guzzling hothouses to grow summer fruits in winter.

● **Keep processing to a minimum.** Look for food as close to its natural state as possible, without the addition of colourings, preservatives, flavour enhancers, bulking agents and so on, which has not been through many stages of manufacture. And at home, eat as much raw food and do as much home cooking as possible rather than buying pre-prepared and cooked food. (*For more on the greenest methods of cooking, see pages 60–1*).

● **Eat low on the food chain.** It takes less input and energy to produce grains, fruit and vegetables than it does meat and fish, and of the meats it takes less grain and water to produce pork or chicken than it does beef, for example. By mainly eating a meat-free diet you are opting for the most energy-efficient diet.

● **Support your local and national organic and green organizations.** They are working to guarantee you a supply of good-quality food produced in a sustainable way. They will keep you updated on availability, campaigns and threats to your right to choose.

recipes

Eating seasonally needn't be a challenge because our bodies are naturally attuned this way and will guide you toward warm orange squashes in the autumn and crisp, crunchy salad leaves during the summer months. All you have to do is follow your instincts and explore local produce.

To help you on your way, we have compiled a selection of seasonal recipes. You will need a few basics in your storecupboard (pantry) and these should be organic, as should all the ingredients in your cooking. Use medium (US: large) eggs throughout from organically reared hens and all recipes serve four unless otherwise stated. We suggest you invest in the best-quality organic extra virgin olive oil you can afford, organic dried herbs (for when your fresh supply from the garden runs out) and spices, organic garlic purée, butter and flour.

If you care about your health and are concerned about animal welfare and the environment you will make sure all your meat and fish is organic, or, in the case of ocean fish, caught in a sustainable manner. So we have included some recipes using meat and fish available in organic form. Elsewhere, we have tried to use ingredients that you should be able to purchase in organic form, although occasionally you might need to source some of these through a specialist organic mail-order service (*see Resources, pages 178–83*), because not all food stores stock a wide range of organic produce.

What would be best of all, however, is if you are able to obtain many of these ingredients direct from your garden or window boxes. Hopefully, these recipes will not only inspire you to get cooking, but to get gardening, too.

lunches & dinners

SMOKED SALMON SANDWICHES

1 bunch chives, finely chopped

200 ml (7 fl oz) *crème fraîche* (or sour cream)

bread of choice

500 g (1 lb) *organic smoked salmon*

Lemon Oil (*see page 173*)

herb salad of spinach, rocket (arugula), sorrel, lamb's lettuce (mâche), dandelion or salad burnet

a handful of parsley

edible flowers, such as violas or marigold petals

sea salt and freshly ground *black pepper*

In a bowl, mix the chives together with the crème fraîche (or sour cream) and a good amount of black pepper. Warm the bread and cut or break it into chunks. Spread a layer of crème fraîche (or sour cream) on the bread before adding some salmon. Finish with a drizzle of lemon oil and salt and pepper to taste.

Serve with a leafy herb salad. Combine the leaves in a bowl with the parsley, season and decorate with flowers. Again, drizzle with lemon oil.

SPINACH 'TARTS'

500 g (1 lb/2 cups) fresh *ricotta*

5 tbsp *sour cream*

1 egg, lightly beaten

a pinch of *nutmeg*

500 g (1lb) *baby spinach* leaves

1 tbsp *water*

50 g (2 oz/½ cup) *Parmesan cheese*, finely grated (shredded)

2 tbsp *pine kernels*, chopped and toasted

1 tbsp chopped *dill*

freshly ground *black pepper*

Preheat the oven to 160°C/325°F/Gas 3. In a bowl, smooth the ricotta with a fork, then combine with the sour cream, egg, nutmeg and black pepper. Wilt the spinach in a pan with the water for 1 minute; drain and chop finely. Stir the spinach, Parmesan, pine kernels and dill into the ricotta mixture. Spoon into greased individual 10-cm (4-in) tart tins (pans) and bake for 25–30 minutes until firm and golden. Leave to stand for 1–2 minutes, then remove from the tins and transfer to a cake rack for 5–10 minutes before serving.

MOROCCAN BURGERS

500 g (1lb) minced (ground) *organic lamb*

1 large *courgette* (zucchini), grated

1 clove *garlic*, peeled and crushed

a handful of fresh *mixed herbs,* such as rosemary, mint and parsley

a handful of chopped *fresh mint (reserve a few sprigs to garnish*

a little *olive oil*

8 *pitta breads,* to serve

sea salt and freshly ground *black pepper*

Yogurt dressing

150 ml (¼ pint/⅔ cup) live natural (plain) *yogurt*

1 clove *garlic,* peeled and crushed

1 tsp clear *honey*

sea salt and freshly ground *black pepper*

Tahini dressing

2 tbsp *tahini*

1 tbsp *olive oil*

2 tbsp *lemon juice*

1 tsp *clear honey*

a splash of *tamari sauce*

sea salt and freshly ground *black pepper*

Place all the ingredients for the dressing of your choice in a bowl. Season and whisk together with a fork. Garnish with mint. Cover and chill.

Combine all the burger ingredients in a bowl. With lightly floured hands, divide the mixture into eight portions and shape into burgers. Brush with a little olive oil and barbecue or grill (broil) for 6–7 minutes on each side. Serve in pitta bread with fresh Yogurt or Tahini Dressing.

Serves 8

BEEF AND GINGER STIR-FRY

1 tsp *salt*

500g (1 lb) *organic rump* (sirloin) *steak,* shredded

2 tbsp *sesame oil*

2 cloves *garlic,* peeled and chopped

1 large piece of *ginger* (gingerroot), shredded

4 tbsp *soy sauce*

2 tbsp dry *sherry*

4 *spring onions* (scallions), trimmed and shredded

fresh noodles, to serve

Sprinkle the salt over the beef. Heat the oil in a wok and fry the garlic until golden. Add the beef and ginger (gingerroot) and stir-fry for 2 minutes. Stir in the soy sauce and sherry; cook for another minute. Add the spring onions (scallions), then place in a dish. Serve immediately with noodles.

HALOUMI KEBABS

500 g (1 lb) *haloumi cheese,* drained and broken into chunks

1 *red and 1 yellow* (bell) *pepper,* seeded and cut into chunks

1 *courgette* (zucchini), halved and cut into chunks

1 *red onion,* chopped into wedges

1 tbsp fresh *oregano,* finely chopped

extra virgin olive oil

Thread the cheese chunks, interspersed with the vegetables, onto damp wooden skewers. Sprinkle with oregano and drizzle with oil. Grill (broil) or barbecue until the cheese is just melting and the vegetables are pleasantly charred.

SPICED ROASTED CHICKEN AND GARLIC WITH COUSCOUS

juice of 2 *lemons*

2 tsp ground *cumin*

2 tsp ground *coriander*

2 tsp *paprika*

2 tsp ground *turmeric*

1 *organic chicken*

1 head of *garlic*

225 g (8 oz/1⅓ cups) *couscous*

425 ml (¾ pint/2 cups) *vegetable stock*

1 bunch *coriander* (cilantro), chopped

1 bunch *parsley*, chopped

1 bunch *chives*, chopped

sea salt and freshly ground *black pepper*

In a bowl, mix together the lemon juice, cumin, ground coriander, paprika and turmeric. Rub the marinade beneath the chicken skin. Cover and leave in the refrigerator to marinate overnight.

The next day, preheat the oven to 180°C/350°F/ Gas 4. Place the chicken in an oiled roasting tin (pan). Break the cloves away from the garlic head and scatter around the chicken. Roast the chicken for 20 minutes per 500 g (1 lb) plus 25 minutes, or until the juices run clear when you pierce the thigh, turning every now and then. When thoroughly roasted and golden, leave to rest in a warm place for 15 minutes.

Meanwhile, place the couscous in a large, shallow bowl and pour over the stock. Leave to stand for 15 minutes, then break up with a fork. Stir in the herbs and season with salt and pepper. Serve with the chicken and garlic.

vegetables

SPICY POTATOES

550 g (1 lb 2 oz) *potatoes*, peeled and chopped

½ tsp ground *turmeric*

½ tsp red *chilli* powder (cayenne pepper)

2 tbsp *olive oil*

1 tsp *cumin seeds*

200 ml (7 fl oz) *Greek yogurt* (thick plain yogurt)

100 ml (3½ fl oz/7 tbsp) *milk*

½ tsp *salt*

1 tbsp freshly chopped *coriander* (cilantro) leaves

Place the potatoes in a pan of boiling salted water and leave to simmer until tender. Drain and combine with the turmeric and chilli powder (cayenne pepper) in a bowl. Heat the oil in a pan. Sprinkle in the cumin seeds and cook for 1 minute or until they start to pop. Add the potatoes and cook for 10 minutes until golden. Stir in the yogurt, milk and salt. Reduce the heat and cook for 5 more minutes. Stir in the fresh coriander (cilantro) at the last minute and serve immediately.

CHILLIED CHARD

olive oil for frying
4 shallots, peeled and chopped
2 cloves garlic, peeled and chopped
1 red chilli (chili), seeded and chopped
1 kg (2 lb) red or green chard
a pinch of ground nutmeg
2 tbsp breadcrumbs
1 tbsp grated Parmesan
sea salt and freshly ground black pepper

Preheat the oven to 180°350°F/Gas 4. Heat some olive oil in a pan and soften the shallots and garlic. Add the chilli (chili). Peel, chop and wash the chard stalks. Cook in boiling water for 5–8 minutes until tender. Drain and add to the shallots; season with nutmeg and salt and pepper. Cook for 5 minutes. Wilt the chard in the mixture, then transfer to a greased baking dish. Sprinkle with breadcrumbs and cheese. Bake for 10 minutes or until golden.

BRAISED FENNEL

1 tbsp olive oil
1 bulb of fennel, quartered
2 cloves garlic, peeled
and crushed
6 tomatoes, skinned (see below)
sea salt and freshly ground black pepper

Heat the olive oil in a heavy-based pan and add the fennel quarters face down. Cover with a tight-fitting lid and sweat the fennel over a gentle heat for 25 minutes, turning occasionally. Add the crushed garlic and simmer for 5 minutes. Score the tomatoes with a sharp knife, immerse in boiling water for 1 minute and then in cold water for 30 seconds. Transfer to paper towels and peel. Add the tomato flesh to the pan, replace the lid and simmer gently for 40 minutes. If the sauce becomes too watery, remove the lid for the last 5 minutes. Season to taste and serve hot.

PEAS PLEASE!

500 g (1 lb/3 cups) fresh peas
(shelled weight)
225 g (8 oz) French (thin green) beans
25 g (1 oz/2 tbsp) butter
1 bunch spring onions
(scallions), sliced
225 g (8 oz/1½ cups) courgettes
(zucchini), cut into wedges
200 ml (7 fl oz/scant 2 cups)
crème fraîche (or sour cream)
3 tbsp chopped mint
1 tsp sugar
sea salt and freshly ground black pepper

Boil the peas and beans in a pan of boiling salted water for 5 minutes, then drain. Melt the butter in a pan and sauté the spring onions (scallions) and courgettes (zucchini) for 3 minutes. Stir in the crème fraîche (or sour cream) and slowly bring to a boil, then simmer for 2 minutes. Mix in the peas beans, mint and sugar and season to taste.

Serves 4–6

AUBERGINE (EGGPLANT) STUFFED PEPPERS

4 large *red* (bell) *peppers*

1 large *aubergine* (eggplant)

7 tbsp *olive oil*

400 g (14 oz) *tomatoes,*
skinned and finely chopped
(*see Braised Fennel, page 170*)

3 cloves *garlic,*
peeled and finely chopped

3 tbsp finely chopped *parsley*

75 g (3 oz/1½ cups) fresh white
breadcrumbs

50 g (2 oz/½ cup) *Parmesan,*
freshly grated (shredded)

a pinch of ground *nutmeg*

sea salt and freshly ground *black pepper*

Preheat the oven to 200°C/400°F/Gas 6. Halve the peppers and aubergine (eggplant) lengthwise. Scoop the seeds out of the peppers and scrape the aubergine flesh away from the skin with a knife and finely chop. Heat 2 tablespoons olive oil in a pan and fry the aubergine for 5 minutes or until soft. Remove from the heat and allow to cool.

In a bowl, mix together the tomatoes, garlic, parsley, breadcrumbs, Parmesan and nutmeg with the aubergine and frying oil. Season and spoon the mixture into the peppers and place in an oiled baking dish with 2 tablespoons olive oil. Drizzle the remaining oil on top. Bake for 40 minutes. Serve hot or cold.

You can also fill the peppers with cubed haloumi cheese, cherry tomatoes and basil, or experiment with other combinations of vegetables.

salads

ARTICHOKE VINAIGRETTE

500 g (1 lb) *Jerusalem artichokes*
(sunchokes)

1 tbsp *lemon juice*

4 tbsp *olive oil*

2 tbsp *white wine vinegar*

1 tsp *wholegrain mustard*

a handful of chopped *parsley*

1 tbsp *pumpkin seeds,*
plus extra for garnishing

Grate (shred) the artichokes coarsely into a mixing bowl. Add the remaining ingredients. Toss together to combine and leave for 1 hour. Garnish with extra pumpkin seeds and serve as a side dish.

WINTER SALAD

2 large *leeks,* trimmed

1 small *red* (bell) *pepper*

a handful of *walnuts,* chopped

a handful of toasted *pine kernels*

grated zest and juice of 1 *lemon*

90 ml (3½ fl oz/7 tbsp) *mayonnaise*

1 bunch fresh *tarragon,* finely chopped

sea salt and freshly ground *black pepper*

Shred the leeks very finely and then blanch them in boiling water for 2 minutes; drain, plunge into cold water, drain again and cool. Slice and seed the red (bell) pepper; transfer to a salad bowl, together with the leeks, walnuts and pine kernels. Mix the lemon with the mayonnaise and tarragon. Season to taste and toss with the salad.

Serves 4–6

SOY-LENTIL SALAD

250 g (8 oz/1½ cups) Puy or other grain *lentils*
1 *red onion*, sliced
1 *red* (bell) *pepper,* seeded and diced
1 bunch flat-leaf *parsley,* chopped
sea salt and freshly ground *black pepper*

Dressing:

100 ml (3½ fl oz/7 tbsp)
extra virgin olive oil
3 tbsp *cider vinegar*
2 tsp tamari *soy sauce*
2 tsp *Dijon mustard*
2 *garlic* cloves, peeled and crushed

Whisk the dressing ingredients together in a bowl and set aside. Place the lentils in a pan. Cover with water. Bring to a boil and boil for 5 minutes, then simmer for 20 minutes until just tender. Add to the dressing. Stir in the dressing and allow to cool, stirring occasionally. When cold, stir in the onion, pepper and parsley, then season to taste.

Serves 8

SPRING CABBAGE SALAD

250 g (8 oz/3 cups)
spring cabbage, shredded
3 tbsp *soy sauce*
1 tbsp *lemon juice*
175 ml (6 fl oz/¾ cup) toasted *sesame oil*
1 clove *garlic,* peeled and crushed
3 *sticks celery*
4 *spring onions* (scallions), chopped
1 *red* (bell) *pepper,* seeded and diced

Place the cabbage in a bowl with the soy sauce, lemon juice, oil and garlic. Toss together thoroughly and leave for 1 hour. Add the remaining ingredients and toss again. Serve immediately

WINDOW-BOX SALAD

500 g (1 lb) *baby courgettes* (zucchini)
500 g (1 lb) fresh *asparagus,* trimmed
500 g (1 lb) *sugar-snap peas*
200 g (7 oz) *baby spinach* leaves
a handful of *parsley* leaves
a handful of *chervil,* chopped
a handful of chopped
coriander (cilantro) leaves
3 tbsp *capers*
a handful of *sesame seeds or*
1 dsp *pine kernels,* toasted
2 tbsp *olive oil*
2 tbsp *lemon juice*
sea salt and freshly ground *black pepper*

Slice the courgettes (zucchini) in half lengthways. Blanch the asparagus, courgettes and sugar-snap peas in boiling water for 1 minute, then set aside. Rinse and tear up the spinach leaves, then place in a large bowl. Add the blanched vegetables, the capers and your choice of fresh garden herbs – parsley, chervil and coriander (cilantro) are good options. Sprinkle with toasted sesame seeds, or pine kernels if you prefer, for a lovely nutty flavour.

The vinaigrette is very simple to make, just like the salad. Just whisk together the olive oil, the lemon juice and salt and pepper. Pour over the salad leaves and serve immediately.

herb oils

Make the most of your herb garden or herbs growing in your window box by preserving their flavour in oils and vinegars. Here, we use rosemary, but you can also try thyme, basil, tarragon and bay for a traditional herb-flavoured oil. Drizzle the oils on salads, or use them as a dipping oil with warm ciabbatta – you can even add them to your bath.

ROSEMARY OIL

6–7 thick sprigs of *rosemary*
250 ml (8 fl oz/1 cup) *extra virgin olive oil*
1 tsp *white wine vinegar* (optional)

Add five or six sprigs of rosemary to a sterilized lidded jar, together with the oil and vinegar, if using. Seal and leave on a sunny window sill for two to three weeks, shaking the bottle occasionally. Strain and transfer it to a clean bottle with the remaining rosemary sprigs. Seal tightly and refrigerate. Will keep for up to two weeks once open.

Fills a 250 ml (8 fl oz/1 cup) jar

LEMON OIL

juice and grated zest of 2 small *lemons*
200 ml (7 fl oz/scant 1 cup)
extra virgin olive oil

Pour the lemon juice into a bowl, together with the olive oil. Sprinkle over the lemon zest, cover and leave to stand for two days. Strain through a fine sieve (strainer) and store in a sterilized jar or bottle with a tight-fitting lid in the refrigerator. Will keep for up to two weeks once open. Serve at room temperature and remember to shake before use.

Fills a 200 ml (7 fl oz/scant 1 cup jar)

HERB BREAD

a little melted butter
1 tbsp fresh *yeast*
300 ml (½ pint/1¼ cups) *water,*
at room temperature
450 g (15 oz/3 cups)
wholemeal (wholewheat) *flour*
1½ tsp *salt*
50 g (2 oz/4 tbsp) *butter*
3 large handfuls of finely chopped *herbs*
– try basil, parsley or thyme
saltwater glaze

Soak six small terracotta flowerpots (9 cm/3½ in in diameter) in cold water overnight. Leave to dry, then brush with melted butter. Preheat the oven to 200°C/400°F/Gas 6. Meanwhile, mix the yeast with the water in a bowl. Add the flour and salt to another bowl. Rub in the butter and stir in the herbs. Make a well in the middle and pour in the yeast liquid; mix together well. Place the dough on a floured surface and knead for 10 minutes until smooth. Transfer to an oiled bowl, cover and leave in a warm place for about 1 hour until double in size. Knead again for 2–3 minutes.

Divide the dough into six and shape into rounds. Place inside the pots. Brush with salt water and bake for 6–10 minutes, then reduce the heat to 180°C/350°F/Gas 4 and bake for 20 minutes. Turn the bread out of the pots and bake for a further 5 minutes to crispen the edges. Serve warm.

Serves 6

soup

Soup is delicious all year round, but it really comes into its own in the winter when there is nothing more inviting than a steaming bowl of hearty vegetables. It is a great way of ensuring that you get the most out of your garden produce, because nothing needs to be thrown away and the options for variations are pretty much endless.

ALL-SEASON SOUP

225 g (8 oz/1⅓ cups) *chickpeas* (garbanzo beans), soaked overnight and drained

2 tbsp *olive oil*

2 *leeks*, trimmed and sliced

2 *carrots*, trimmed and sliced

2 sticks *celery*, sliced

1.15 l (2½ pints/5¼ cups) *vegetable stock*

2 *potatoes*, peeled and diced

500 g (1 lb/3½ cups) fresh, chopped *tomatoes* (blanched and skinned if you prefer)

2 *garlic cloves*, peeled and chopped

1 small green *cabbage*, thinly shredded

225 g (8 oz/4 cups) *spinach*, chopped

sea salt and freshly ground *black pepper*

Place the chickpeas (garbanzo beans) in a large pan of cold water and bring to a boil, then simmer for 45 minutes; drain well. Heat the oil in another large pan and add the leeks, carrots and celery. Fry gently for 10 minutes and then add the stock, chickpeas, potatoes, tomatoes and garlic. Cover and gently simmer for 30 minutes. Add the cabbage, spinach and seasoning. Cover and simmer for 15 minutes. Serve with fresh, crusty bread or Herb Bread (*see page 173*).

QUICK BEAN SOUP

If you don't want to use organic baked beans, replace them with canned borlotti beans.

olive oil for frying

1 large *onion*, chopped

1 large *potato*, diced

1 stick *celery*, chopped

1 *green* (bell) *pepper*, chopped and seeded

1 *red* (bell) *pepper* chopped and seeded

1 l (1¾ pints/4½ cups) *passata* (strained puréed tomatoes)

1 x 400 g (13 oz) can organic *baked beans*

1 bunch of fresh *oregano*, chopped

sea salt and freshly ground *black pepper*

Heat the olive oil in a large pan and fry the onion, potato and celery for 5 minutes. Add the pepper and cook for 2 more minutes. Pour in the passata, season and stir well. Allow to simmer for 20 minutes, then stir in the baked beans and oregano; heat through and serve.

Note: If you can't find passata in your supermarket, look for jars of it at an Italian deli.

desserts

SUMMER FRUIT CREPES

Crêpes
125 g (4 oz/¾ cup) *plain* (all-purpose) *flour*
a pinch of *salt*
1 *egg*, lightly beaten
300 ml (½ pint/1¼ cups) *milk*
1 tbsp *vegetable oil*
double (heavy) *cream* or
crème fraîche (or double/heavy cream),
to serve

Fruit filling
900 g (2 lb) mixed soft *summer fruits*
– raspberries, strawberries, blueberries
6 tbsp *water*
4 tbsp *caster* (superfine) *sugar*

To make the crêpe batter, sift the flour and salt into a large bowl. Make a well in the middle and pour in the egg. Whisk, then gradually beat in the milk, drawing in the flour from the sides to make a smooth batter. Cover and leave to stand for 20 minutes. Heat the oil in a heavy-based frying pan (skillet). Pour in enough batter to thinly coat the pan. Fry over a high heat until golden brown. Toss and cook for 1 further minute until golden on both sides.

Repeat and stack the crêpes on top of each other with greaseproof (waxed) paper between each one.

Wash and hull the fruit. Place it in a large pan with the water and sugar. Cover and cook gently until the juices flow and the sugar has dissolved. Cool slightly, then use to fill each crêpe. Fold and serve with crème fraîche or double (heavy) cream.

Serves 8

EASY RHUBARB DELIGHT

450 g (15 oz/3½ cups) *rhubarb*,
trimmed and sliced
50 g (2 oz/4 tbsp) raw *brown sugar*
(demerara or Barbados)
50 g (2 oz/4 tbsp) *butter*
250 ml (8 fl oz/generous 1 cup)
double (heavy) *cream*

Place the rhubarb, sugar and butter in a pan over a gentle heat until the butter melts. Simmer gently until the rhubarb softens and remove the pan from the heat. Leave to cool, then cover and chill in the refrigerator until cold. Whip the cream in a large bowl until it stiffens, then fold in the rhubarb. Pour into individual bowls, refrigerate and serve chilled.

Serves 4–6

CINNAMON PLUM PUDDING

1 tbsp *butter*
½ tsp ground *cinnamon*
450 g (15 oz) *plums,* halved and pitted
2 medium (US large) *egg yolks*
50 g (2 oz/¼ cup) *caster* (superfine) *sugar*
150 ml (¼ pint/⅔ cup) dry white *wine*
seeds from 1 *vanilla pod* (bean)
4 tbsp *single* (light) *cream*

In a small bowl, mix the butter with the cinnamon. Place the plums, skin side down, in a single layer in a shallow baking dish. Dot with butter and grill (broil) for 8–10 minutes, turning halfway through. Whisk the egg yolks, sugar and wine together in a heatproof bowl, then place the bowl over a pan of simmering water (make sure the base doesn't touch the pan); whisk again until thick and frothy. Add the vanilla seeds and cream; whisk again for 1 minute. Spoon the mixture over the plums and grill (broil) for 3–4 minutes until the topping becomes a golden colour.

preserves

With spare fruit often in abundance in early autumn, it is a great time to perfect the art of making jams and other preserves, just as our grandmothers did before us. Preserves must be stored in sterilized jars and sealed when cold to prevent mould from growing on the surface. Try the following recipes and then experiment with other fruits.

PICKLED PEARS WITH GINGER

1.8 kg (3½ lb) firm *pears*

a squeeze of *lemon juice*

1 *cinnamon stick*

25 g (1 oz) piece fresh root *ginger* (gingerroot), peeled and sliced

3–4 whole *cloves*

600 ml (1 pint/2½ cups) white wine *vinegar*

800 g (1 lb 10 oz/4 cups) *sugar*

Peel, halve and core the pears before immersing them in a pan of water with the lemon juice. Simmer for about 1 hour or until just tender. Place the remaining ingredients in a large heavy-based saucepan or preserving pan. Heat gently until the sugar is dissolved, stirring occasionally. Bring to a boil and then simmer for 5 minutes. Use a slotted spoon to lift the pears out of the water and place in the spiced vinegar syrup. Simmer for 15 minutes. Remove the pears from the syrup and pack into sterilized jars with tight-fitting lids. Boil the syrup for 5 minutes to thicken, stirring occasionally, before pouring over the pears to completely cover them. Cool in the jars, then cover with greaseproof (waxed) paper. Seal with an elastic band and a lid and store in a cool, dark place during the winter months. Once open, refrigerate and use ???

Makes about 1.5 kg (3 lb)

APPLE JAM

Early autumn is always good for jam-making. This recipe is especially suitable for using up a glut of cooking apples.

1.5 kg (3 lb) cooking *apples*

1 l (1¾ pints/4½ cups) *water*

1.5 kg (3 lb) pale raw (demerara) brown *sugar*

½ tsp ground *cinnamon*

½ tsp ground *cloves*

Chop the apples (do not peel or remove the cores). Transfer to a large pan, cover with water and simmer until they form a pulp, about 15 minutes. Sieve (strain) and weigh the pulp before returning to the pan. Add 350 g (12 oz/1¾ cups) sugar for every 450 g (15 oz/2 cups) apple pulp and stir in the spices. Heat gently, stirring occasionally, until the sugar is dissolved, then boil until the jam reaches setting point, about 15 minutes. To test the jam, drop a spoonful onto a chilled saucer and leave to cool. If the jam wrinkles on the surface when prodded with your fingertip, it is ready. Pour into sterilized jars and leave to cool. Seal with greaseproof (waxed) paper and a tight-fitting lid when cold.

juices and crushes

Juicing, blending and crushing vegetables into nutritious drinks is a great way to ensure that you get all your daily vitamins and minerals in one go. This, of course, doesn't mean that you can skip fresh fruit and vegetables throughout the day, but a vitamin-packed drink is a good idea if you've got a hectic schedule without much time for cooking. Try experimenting with different ingredients until you find your favourite combinations.

CHILLI CRUSH

1 kg (2 lb) *carrots*, trimmed

500 g (1 lb) *tomatoes*

3 sticks of *celery*, trimmed

a dash of *Tabasco* (hot-pepper) sauce

a dash of *Worcestershire* sauce

juice of 1 *lemon*

1 small green *chilli* (chili), seeded

sea salt and freshly ground *black pepper*

Put the carrots, tomatoes and celery through a juicer – if you don't have one, use a blender to whiz them up with 250 ml (8 fl oz/1 cup) chilled water, then push through a strainer. Add the salt, pepper and Tabasco and Worcestershire sauces, the lemon juice and the chili. This fresh, fiery drink makes a good start to the day – serve it chilled.

AVOCADO SMOOTHIE

For a variation, try adding chopped coriander (cilantro) instead of dill as a garnish.

1 bunch of fresh *dill*

1 bunch of fresh *chives*

1 *avocado*

400 ml (14 fl oz/1¾ cups) natural (plain) *yogurt*

juice of 1 lemon

ground *cardamom*

sea salt and freshly ground *black pepper*

Wash the herbs and chop them finely, then set aside. Slice the avocados in half lengthways and remove the stone (seed). Use a spoon to scrape the flesh away from the skins and purée with the herbs and yogurt. Season with lemon juice, salt, pepper and cardamom. Pour into tall glasses and garnish each drink with 1 teaspoon of chopped herbs. Serve chilled.

Makes 2 glasses

Resources

Chapter 1

Association for the Conservation of Energy
Westgate House
Prebend Street
London
N1 8PT
Tel: 0207 359 8000
Fax: 0207 359 0863
Promotes energy conservation.

BioRegional Development Group
The Ecology Centre
Honeywood Walk
Carshalton
Surrey
SM5 3NX
Tel: 020 8773 2322
Fax: 020 8773 2878
E-mail: info@bioregional.com
www.bioregional.com
Promotes sustainable land use and biodiversity.

Brighton and Hove Wood Recycling Project
7–8 Regent Street
Brighton
East Sussex
BN1 1UL.
Tel: 01273 570 500
Fax: 01273 570 600
E-mail: info@woodrecycling.org.uk
www.woodrecycling.org.uk
Project to recover and reuse waste timber.

Centre for Alternative Technology (CAT)
The Centre for Alternative Technology
Machynlleth
Powys
SY20 9AZ
Tel: 01654 702400
Fax: 01654 702782
E-mail: info@cat.org.uk
www.cat.org.uk
An environmental centre and charity which promotes the use of renewable energy.

Clothworks
PO Box 16109
London
SE23 3WA
Tel: 0181 299 1619
Fax: 0181 299 6997
E-mail: info@clothworks.co.uk
www.albedo.co.uk
An online catalogue for natural textiles.

Construction Resources
16 Great Guildford Street
London
SE1 0HS
Tel: 020 7450 2211
Fax: 020 7450 2212
E-mail: info@construct.com
www.ecoconstruct.com
Environmentally friendly building materials supplier.

Ecological Design Association
The British School
Slad Road
Stroud
Gloucestershire
GL5 1QW
Tel: 01453 765575
Fax: 01453 759211
Ecologically-minded design.

EcoTech Charitable Trust
EcoTech Centre
Swaffham
Norfolk
PE37 7HT
Tel: 01760 726100
E-mail: info@ecotech.rmplc.co.uk
An educational charity which aims to educate about the need for sustainable living.

Environmental Construction Products
26 Millmoor Road
Meltham
Huddersfield
West Yorkshire
HD7 3JY
Tel: 01484 854898
Fax: 01484 854899
Environental building products.

Friends of the Earth
26–28 Underwood Street
London
N1 7JQ
Tel: 020 7490 1555
Fax: 020 7490 0881
www.foe.org.uk
Environmental pressure group.

Greenpeace UK
Canonbury Villas
London N1 2PN
Tel: 0207 865 8100
Fax: 0207 865 8200
E-mail: info@uk.greenpeace.org
www.greenpeace.org.uk
Environmental pressure group.

International Association for Energy-Efficient Lighting
IAEEL, c/o Borg & Co
Sveav. 98, 4th floor
S-11350 Stockholm
Tel: 08 673 11 30
Fax: 08 673 04 44
E-mail: nils@borgco.se
www.iaeel.org
A global contact network and an information resource for high-quality, energy-efficient lighting.

Magpie Greenbox
Saunders Park Depot
Lewes Road
Brighton
East Sussex
BN2 4AY
Tel: 01273 688022
Fax: 01273 622415
E-mail: magpie@solutions.co.uk
A domestic waste collection and recycling scheme.

National Recycling Forum
Ground Floor Europa House
13–17 Ironmonger Row
London
EC1V 3QG
Tel: 020 7253 6266
Fax: 020 7253 5962
www.nrf.org.uk
An independent not-for-profit organization promoting the principles of waste reduction, reuse and recycling.

Waste Watch
Ground Floor Europa House
13–17 Ironmonger Row
London
EC1V 3QG
www.wastewatch.org.uk
Government-backed waste reduction & recycling organization.

Chapter 2

Alphabeds
92 Tottenham Court Road
London
W1T 4TL
Tel: 0207 636 6840
Fax: 0207
E-mail: enquiries@alphabeds.co.uk
www.alphabeds.co.uk
Manufacturers of wooden bedframes and mattresses specializing in all-natural materials.

Echo Designs
Unit F25
Parkhall Road Trading Estate
40 Martell Road
London
SE21 8EN
Tel: 020 8766 8766
Fax: 020 8766 8704
E-mail: hub@echodesigns.co.uk
www.echodesigns.co.uk
A furniture design and interiors co-operative specializing in natural materials.

Ethical Consumer
Unit 21
41 Old Birley Street
Manchester M15 5RF
Tel: 0161 226 2929
Fax: 0161 226 6277
www.ethicalconsumer.org
The UK's only consumer organization looking at the social and environmental records of companies behind brand names.

Freeplay

Freeplay Energy Europe
Cirencester Business Park,
Love Lane
Cirencester
Gloucestershire
GL7 1XD UK
Tel: 01285 659 559
Fax: 01285 659 550
E-mail: info@freeplay.co.uk
www.freeplay.net
A range of products including radios and torches driven by wind-up technology and solar energy.

Gaiam Inc.

360 Interlocken Boulevard
Suite 300
Broomfield, CO 80021
Tel: 0303 464 3600
Fax: 0303 464 3700
A provider of information and goods for sustainable and healthy lifestyles.

The Green Culture

PO Box 1684
Laguna Beach, CA 92652
Tel: 01 800 233 8438
Fax: 01 800 480 8270
www. greenculture.com
Online directory of eco products and services.

Greenfibres

Freepost Lon 7805
Totnes
Devon
TQ9 5ZZ
Tel: 01803 868001
Fax: 01803 868002
A natural and organic clothing company.

The Green Shop

Bisley
Stroud
Gloucestershire
GL6 7BX
Tel/Fax: 01452 770629
E-mail: general@greenshop.co.uk
www.greenshop.co.uk
Green mail-order shopping service.

The Healthy House

Cold Harbour
Ruscombe
Stroud
Gloucestershire
GL6 6DA
Tel: 01453 752216
Fax: 01453 753533
E-mail: info@healthy-house.co.uk
www.healthy-house.co.uk
An online and mail-order catalogue of green products for people who want to reduce pollutants in the home.

Hemp Food Industries Association

PO Box 204
Barnet
Hertfordshire
EN5 1EP
Tel: 07050 600 418
Fax: 07050 600 419
www.hemp.co.uk
Hemp information and consultancy organization.

Keepers!

PO Box 12648
Portland, OR 97212
Tel: 01 800 799 4523
www.gladrags.com
Makers of GladRags reusable sanitary protection.

The Natural Collection

Eco House
Monmouth Place
Bath
BA1 2DQ
Tel: 0870 331 33 33
Fax: 01225 469673
www.naturalcollection.com
An online and mail-order shop for everything from compost bins to battery rechargers.

Textiles From Nature

84 Stoke Newington Church Street
London
N16 0AP
Tel: 020 7241 0990
Fax: 020 7241 1991
www.textilesfromnature.com
Organic clothing, textiles, carpets and paints.

Wildfield Studios
PO Box 355
Branford, CT 06405
Tel: 203 335 8570
Fax: 203 483 7838
**One-of-a-kind environmentally friendly home
furnishings, handmade from 200-year-old barnwood
and recycled nails.**

Chapter 3

Community Composting Network (CCN)
67 Alexandra Road
Sheffield
Yorkshire
S2 3EE
Tel: 0114 258 0483
Fax: 0114 255 1400
E-mail: Heeleyfarm@gn.apc.org
www.othas.org.uk
**A network of community composting projects and
composting organizations in the UK.**

HDRA – The Organic Organization
Ryton Organic Gardens
Ryton-on-Dunsmore
Coventry CV8 3LG
Tel: 01203 305517
Fax: 01203 639229
E-mail: enquiry@hdra.org.uk
www.hdra.org.uk
**The UK's largest organic membership organization, which
promotes organic food, farming and gardening. Particularly
useful for all aspiring organic gardeners as it has its own
publications, including step-by-step leaflets, and organic
gardens that can be visited for inspiration.**

**The National Council for the Conservation of
Plants and Gardens**
The National Office
The Stable Court Yard
Wisley Gardens
Wisley
Woking
Surrey GU23 6QP
Tel: 01483 211465
www.nccpg.org.uk
**UK conservation group which has set up the National Plant
Collections Scheme to save traditional UK garden plants.**

National Wildlife Federation
11100 Wildlife Center Drive
Reston, VA 20190-5362
Tel: 703 438 6000
www.nwf.org
**The largest member-supported conservation
group in the USA.**

Natural Surroundings
Centre for Wildlife Gardening and Conservation
Bayfield Estate
Holt
Norfolk
NR25 7JN
Tel: 01263 711091
E-mail: loosley@farmersweekly.net
**The largest wildlife gardening centre in the UK, which holds
regular events highlighting the importance of widlife and
is open for school visits.**

The Organic Gardening Catalogue
Riverdene Business Park
Molesey Road
Hersham
Surrey
KT12 4RG
Tel: 01932 253666
Fax: 01832 252707
E-mail: chaseorg@aol.com
**The official gardening mail-order catalogue of
the HDRA – invaluable for sourcing organic seeds,
pest-control aids and organic gardening books that
may be hard to find locally.**

Plantlife
21 Elizabeth Street
London
SW1W 9RP
Tel: 020 7808 0100
Fax: 020 7730 8377
E-mail: enquiries@plantlife.org.uk
www.plantlife.org.uk
**The UK's only national membership charity dedicated
exclusively to conserving all forms of plant life in its
natural habitat.**

Food

Fairtrade Foundation
Suite 204
16 Baldwin's Gardens
London
EC1N 7RJ
Tel: 020 7405 5942
Fax: 020 7405 5943
www.fairtrade.org.uk
Promotes fair trade in the UK – has a mark which is displayed on goods which have met strict fair trade conditions.

National Farmers' Market Association
South Vaults
Green Park Station
Green Park Road
Bath
BA1 1JB
www.farmersmarkets.net
Can provide a full list of farmers' markets in the UK.

The Organic Alliance
400 Selby Avenue
Suite T
St Paul, MN 55102
www.organic.org
American charity dedicated to encouraging an ecologically and socially responsible agriculture.

The Organic Consumers Association
6101 Cliff Estate Rd
Little Marais, MN 55614
Tel: 218 226 4164
Fax: 218 226 4157
American public interest organization for organic food.

Organic Trade Association
PO Box 547
Greenfield, MA 01302
Tel: 413 774 7511
Fax: 413 774 6432
E-mail: info@ota.com
www.ota.com
Represents the organic trade in the USA, Canada and Mexico. A good starting point for finding organic retailers and producers near you.

Pesticides Trust
Eurolink Centre
49 Effra Road
London
SW2 1BZ
Tel: 020 7274 8895
Fax: 020 724 9084
E-mail: Pesttrust@gn.apc.org
www.gn.apc.org/pesticidestrust
An action group who are working to eliminate the hazards of pesticides.

Soil Association
Bristol House
40–56 Victoria Street
Bristol
BS1 6BY
Tel: 0117 929 0661
Fax: 0117 925 2504
E-mail: Info@soilassociation.org
www.soilassociation.org
A UK membership charity that campaigns for organic food and farming. It also operates Local Food Links to promote links between local food producers and consumers, plus it operates a separate company which is the leading UK certifier of organic produce.

Willing Workers on Organic Farms (WWOOF)
PO Box 2675
Lewes
BN7 1RB UK
www.pennine.org.uk/wwoof.htm
WWOOF can put you in touch with organic farmers who are willing to accept helpers in return for accommodation.

General

The Green Directory
PO Box 5903
Basildon
Essex SS12 2YY
Tel: 01268 468 000
Fax: 01268 451 111
www.thegreendirectory.co.uk
UK guide to green products and services, published as a book and also on the Internet.

Forest Stewardship Council (FSC)
Unit D
Old Station Building
Llanidloes
Powys
SY18 6EB
Tel: 01686 413916
Fax: 01686 412176
E-mail: Fsc-uk@fsc-uk.demon.co.uk
www.fsc-uk.demon.co.uk
**Certifies timber producers based on environmental
and social standards. The FSC mark should be displayed
on timber that has met these standards.**

Real Nappy Association
PO Box 3704
London
SE26 4RX
Tel: 020 8299 4519
www.realnappy.com
**Membership organization providing information on
cloth nappies.**

Women's Environmental Network
PO Box 30626
London
E1 1TZ
Tel: 020 7481 9004
Fax: 020 7481 9144
E-mail: Wenuk@gn.apc.org
www.gn.apc.org/wen
**Charity which focuses on environmental issues that
particularly affect women, i.e. sanitary protection.**

Websites

www.ecodirectory.com
**Eco Directory – directory of natural foods, green products
and eco-friendly services.**

http://eco-web.com/
**Green Pages – a global directory for environmental products
and services.**

www.ethical-junction.org
A one-stop shop for all websites that have an ethical basis.

www.greenliving.org
**A general American site on green living, including tips,
book lists, and links elsewhere.**

www.nhm.ac.uk/fff
**The Postcode Plants Database generates lists of native
plants and wildlife for any specified postal district in the UK.**

www.nrcs.usda.gov
**The Natural Resources Conservation Service – an American
Federal agency that aims to work in partnership with the
American people to conserve and sustain natural resources.
Publishes tipsheets through its Backyard Conservation project.**

www.nwlink.com/~van/greenlnk.html
**Green-Link – a central point of reference for websites
on the environment.**

www.primalseeds.org
**A site which aims to inform and inspire people to take the
protection of biodiversity and the creation of food security
into their own hands.**

www.thegreenhouse.co.uk
**A site that shows progress on a house in Cambridgeshire
(UK) which uses many innovative energy-saving strategies.**

Further Reading

Environmental building and interiors

Borer, Pat and Harris, Cindy
The Whole House Book
UK, Centre for Alternative Technology (CAT), 1998
USA, New Society Publishers, 2001

Bower, John
Healthy House Building for the New Millennium
USA, Healthy House,1999

Chiras, Daniel D
The Natural House
USA, Chelsea Green Publishing Company, 2000

Pearson, David
The Gaia Natural House Book
UK, Gaia Books, 2000

Pearson, David
The Natural House Catalogue: Everything You Need to
Create an Environmentally Friendly Home
USA, Fireside, 1996

Stein, Kathy
Beyond Recycling: A Reuser's Guide
USA, Clear Light, 1997

Sydenham, Mark
Friend's of the Earth Scotland's Green Home Handbook
UK, Friends of the Earth Scotland, 1996

Gardening

Anthony, Diana
Creative Sustainable Gardening
UK, CAT Publications, 2000

Bartholomew, Mel
Square Foot Gardening
USA, Rodale Press, 1981

Caplin, Adam & James
Urban Eden
UK, Kyle Cathie Limited, 2000
USA, Trafalgar Square, 2001

Cunningham, Sally Jean
Great Garden Companions:
A Companion-Planting System for a Beautiful,
Chemical-Free Vegetable Garden
USA, Rodale Press, 2000

Elphinstone, Margaret and Langley, Julia
The Green Gardener's Handbook
UK, Thorsons, 1990

Gallimore, Patricia
Organic Year: A Guide to Organic Living
UK, BBC, 2000

Hamilton, Geoff
The Organic Garden Book
UK & USA, Dorling Kindersley, 1987 & 1994

Long, Cheryl
Rodale Organic Gardening Solutions:
Over 500 Answers to Real-Life Questions
from Backyard Gardeners
USA, Rodale Press, 2000

Marshall Bradley, Fern & Ellis, Barbara W (eds)
Rodale's All-New Encyclopedia of Organic Gardening
USA, Rodale Press, 1997

Pears, Pauline & Green, Charlotte
All About Compost: Recycling Household and
Garden Waste
UK & USA, HDRA & Search Press, 1999

Pears, Pauline & Stickland, Sue
RHS Organic Gardening
UK, Mitchell Beazley, 1999

Riotte, Louise
Carrots Love Tomatoes: Secrets of Companion Planting
for Successful Gardening
USA, Storey Books, 1998

Stickland, Sue
Heritage Vegetables
UK, Gaia Press, 1998

Food

The Real Food Book
UK, Friends of the Earth, 1999

The Organic Directory
UK, Green Books, 2000

Blythman Joanna
The Food We Eat
UK, Penquin, 1998

Brown, Lynda
The Shopper's Guide to Organic Food
UK & USA, Fourth Estate, 1998 & 1999

Carson, Rachel & Gore, Albert Jr
Silent Spring
UK, Penquin, 1999
USA, Houghton Mifflin, 1994

Charlton, Carol
The Organic Café Cookbook
UK, David & Charles, 1999

Charlton, Carol
The Family Organic Cookbook
USA, Trafalgar Square, 2000

Cummins, Ronnie and Lilliston, Ben
Genetically Engineered Food: A Self-Defense
Guide for Consumers
USA, Organic Consumers Association, 2001

Dibb, Sue & Lobstein, Dr Tim
GM: A Shopper's Guide to Genetically Modified Food
UK, Virgin, 1999

Dibb, Sue
What the Label Doesn't Tell You
UK, Thorsons, 1997

Elkington, John & Hailes, Julia
The New Foods Guide
UK, Victor Gollanz, 1999

Lambert, Daphne & Maxted-Frost, Tanyia
The Organic Baby & Toddler Cookbook
UK, Green Books, 2000

Ruben, Richard
The Farmer's Market Cookbook
USA, Lyons Press, 2000

Vann, Lizzie
The Organic Baby & Toddler Cookbook
UK & USA, Dorling Kindersley, 2000 & 2001

Waldin, Monty
The Friends of the Earth Organic Wine Guide
UK, Thorsons, 1998

Ziff Cool, Jesse
Your Organic Kitchen
USA, Rodale Press, 2000

General

Antczak, Dr Stephen and Gina
Cosmetics Unmasked
UK & USA, Thorsons, 2001

Benhaim, Paul
HEMP Healthy Eating Made Possible
UK, Fusion Press, 2000

Blackmer, Alice
The Organic Pages: 1999 North American Resource Directory
USA, Ota Press, September 1999

Budd, Jo
Beyond the Bin
UK, Livewire, The Women's Press, 2000

Christensen, Karen
Eco Living
UK, 2000, Piatkus

Jenkins, Joseph C.
The Humanure Handbook
USA, Jenkins, 1999

Maxted-Frost, Tanyia
The Organic Baby Book
UK, Green Books, 1999

Whitefield, Ann & Terry
The Green Guide to Better Living
UK, Need2Know, 2000

Index

Authors' Acknowledgements

We would like to thank our family, friends and colleagues for their support during the writing of this book and, in particular, Sam for all your help and patience and Nick for your enthusiasm, for looking after Ellen and Maisie, and all those cups of tea.

Publisher's Acknowledgements

The Forest Stewardship Council trademark that appears on the front cover is copyright © 1996 Forest Stewardship Council A.C.